CAERSWS

The Cambrian Railways Village

by
Brian Poole

THE OAKWOOD PRESS

British Library Cataloguing in Publication Data
A Record for this book is available from the British Library
ISBN 978 0 85361 722 8

Typeset by Oakwood Graphics.
Repro by PKmediaworks, Cranborne, Dorset.
Printed by Gomer Press, Llandysul, Ceredigion.

Mr E. Wilson retired around 1925 and was the station master at Moat Lane Junction with many extra duties during World War I. He died in June 1940 at the age of 81. He was asked to make a presentation in 1930 to R. Jenkins and L. Hamer when they retired. The presentation took place at Moat Lane chaired by the then station master, Mr J. Evans. Many retirement gifts were walking sticks with an engraved silver handle.

Front cover: BR Standard class '4MT' 4-6-0 No. 75026 and a 'Manor' class 4-6-0 are seen at Caersws with the second portion of the down 'Cambrian Coast Express' on 15th August, 1959.   *J.J. Davis/Colour-Rail.com/380232*

Rear cover, top: 'Manor' class 4-6-0 No. 7800 *Torquay Manor* crossing the River Severn at Caersws in May 1962. Wooden trestle bridges were a specialism of the Cambrian Railways.   *J.G. Dewing/Colour-Rail.com/BRW617*

Rear cover, below: 'Manor' class 4-6-0 No. 7801 *Anthony Manor* at Moat Lane Junction with a train for the Brecon line.   *Colour-Rail.com/321419*

By the same author
The Mawddwy, Van & Kerry Branches (jointly with Lewis Cozens and R.W. Kidner), Oakwood Press, 2004.

Published by The Oakwood Press (Usk), P.O. Box 13, Usk, Mon., NP15 1YS.
E-mail: sales@oakwoodpress.co.uk
Website: www.oakwoodpress.co.uk

Contents

	Introduction	5
Chapter One	**Local Entrepreneurs and Junctions**	7
Chapter Two	**Caersws and its Environs**	
	Caersws, Llandinam, Pontdolgoch, Penstrowed	
	quarry siding and Scafell	17
Chapter Three	**Moat Lane Junction**	
	The station, sheds, refreshment rooms described with	
	memories from staff that were on site including drivers,	
	firemen and guards	49
Chapter Four	**Working to and from Moat Lane Junction**	
	Permanent way gangs and relayers gang at Newtown –	
	Trains from the east, south from Tylwch and beyond	
	and west from Talerddig and Machynlleth	107
Chapter Five	**The Bridge Department at Van Junction, Caersws**	163
Chapter Six	**Memories from the Oswestry Division**	185
Chapter Seven	**Caersws Section Staff 1964-1984, and later**	197
Chapter Eight	**Friog Rocks and the Barmouth Bridge**	209
	Postscript	222
	Conclusion	223
	Bibliography	224

Map close to zenith of the Cambrian Railways. Two lines were subsequently added. In 1911 the Dinas Mawddwy line re-opened and in 1913 the Vale of Rheidol narrow gauge line was absorbed into the company. In 1905 the Cambrian had a route mileage of 276 miles of which 97 per cent was single track and total mileage of 368 miles including sidings.

Railway Year Book, 1907

Introduction

I came to live in the Upper Severn Valley in 1967. My work was that of a lecturer in the local Further Education College within the Agricultural Department. The college had a lowland teaching farm at Vaynor or Faenor that is now a housing estate on the outskirts of Newtown. The farm was split by the railway with an overbridge and a cattle creep within the farm perimeter plus an underbridge over the trunk road and two river bridges just out of the farm border. Steam had just finished in March 1967. The double line section from Newtown to Moat Lane Junction had recently been singled. I would often help the farm staff with such duties as relief milking. In the summer, the cows would be collected from their pasture around 6.15 am. The down mail train would pass and the driver of this locomotive-hauled train was ready to give a wave and a smile. I did not realise that I had taken on an inherited role that had been part of this section of the Upper Severn Valley for 100 years. Many worked within a myriad of small farm businesses and their related support such as merchants or within the railway. Many families had members in both industries. The Vaynor farm was less than four miles up from the then recently closed Moat Lane Junction. This junction employed over 60 people until the start of service decline in the 1950s. The line curved into Caersws where there was another junction to the Van lead mines. This junction and workshops had become the main engineering sub-section from Oswestry for the maintenance and inspection of the bridges for the Cambrian Railways, then the Great Western Railway (GWR), then the British Railways (Western Region) (BR/WR) employing over 80 staff until around 1964 when it was reduced to a small team within BR London Midland Region with the main office at Crewe.

In March 2006 I began to collect information and illustrations from local sources, with the aim of recording the social and economic effect of the railway in the area so that local people would have a record of what was once a very important source of employment. There have been many popular volumes published on the Cambrian lines. Moat Lane Junction unfolds as a railway story and there are similar junctions in other parts of Britain set in countryside. Examples of villages such as Woodford Halse in Northamptonshire and Tebay in Cumbria with engine sheds, etc., spring to mind. The Bridge Department soon became a very large project. Three generations of local men starting from 1895 developed skill in every facet of both inspection and maintenance of bridges, sea walls and tunnels within the Cambrian Railways and with the extra territory added by the GWR. They also constructed replacement bridges and assisted contractors on major projects. The terrain variation is immense and includes flood plains, rolling pasture, peat bogs, uplands, watersheds, estuaries, cliffs, shorelines and salt marsh. The area receives a high rainfall so the challenge was to maintain a range of bridges and culverts throughout the system where prolonged rain would quickly turn a quiet stream into a torrent.

Place name spelling can be confusing. There are names where the English will be used such as Welshpool rather than the Welsh of Trallwng. There are names that only exist in English such as Four Crosses. There are a number where the English and Welsh is phonetically similar such as Ruabon/Rhiwabon or Kerry/Ceri. The author has made a choice. Both forms are used within the community therefore both, whether historic or current, must be correct. An example is Dyfi that just flows easier than Dovey when writing the script. The problem is eased in that most names are Welsh albeit with a variation of spelling. Such examples are Carno, Llanidloes, Harlech and even Llynclys, Pant and Llanyblodwel that are over the border in Shropshire.

The local photographs have been selected because they add to the narrative. Most are more than adequate but several have poor focus or are in poor condition. All photographs are identified to the source. Many of the source names will occur within the narrative or they have been taken from one of the local archives. The story behind many of these photographs would have been lost within the next decade due to the relentless passage of time.

I walked every section of both standard gauge and tramways when researching the revision of the Mawdwy, Van and Kerry branches' book (published by Oakwood Press in 2004). It would be a huge challenge to walk every redundant length of the Caersws Bridge Department. However, the lines have been closely followed by car taking various side turns for bridges. Some disused sections have been walked. Examples are Poolquay to Buttington Junction, Bettisfield to Peat Sidings plus the narrow gauge peat railway, Marteg to Rhayader, Moat Lane to Morfodion, the Llanymynech loop, Tregaron to Trawscoed plus others. Extra journeys have been made on current train services between Shrewsbury and Aberystwyth and Dyfi Junction to Pwllheli. Additional visits have been made to the heritage lines including a ride on some.

The bridge section is an immense topic. Bridges are important and many are crossed by the public with great frequency. Some that were once quiet occupation lanes have become important pedestrian routes with the urban expansion of Newtown and Aberystwyth. Even lonely bridges have a local story and history recalled by a villager or a retired member of a family farm. An example is 'grandad' driving his new Standard Fordson off the side bridge into the ditch in 1940 or the amorous bull with concussion because he forgot he was under a cattle creep with his lady friend.

The local railway families have gone to much effort to help. They are thrilled that their dad or grandad's seemingly mundane duties are of value in seeking to record this history.

So let the story unfold. It has been a privilege and a joy to research and gather in the information. The material far exceeds that necessary for this volume so editing has been necessary. However, every item discussed and every visit has been appreciated and there is a tinge of regret that everything cannot be used.

Brian Poole
Newtown
2012

Chapter One

Local Entrepreneurs and Junctions

The railway system came late to Mid-Wales. There were numerous schemes of which some were only at the concept stage while others got as far as a Parliamentary Act and a desultory start. The nearest system in the early 1850s was the Shrewsbury to Chester line with a branch from Gobowen to Oswestry. These lines became part of the standard gauge section of the Great Western Railway. Both the GWR and the London & North Western Railway (LNWR) had rival interests in extending the railways so both may have slowed progress in an effort to prevent the rival company getting the spoils. The Montgomeryshire Canal was not completed to Newtown until around 1820. The canal was important for a short period in the late 1850s when much railway material came into the wharf at Aberbechan and the canal basin terminus at Newtown. The company became the Shropshire Union Railway & Canal Co. and the canal company must have sensed future economic problems of the upper branch because it was within the sponsors for the Parliamentary Act 1846 for a Newtown (Montgomeryshire) to Crewe (Cheshire) railway. The railway company was to purchase the western branch of the canal. Portions of the canal were to be stopped up and the canal bed sections east and west (of Welshpool) were to be used for the railway. The repeal of the Corn Laws in the early 1840s led to a rapid reduction of lime trade in and grain out. The route of this line would follow much of the future lines of both the Oswestry & Newtown, and the Oswestry, Ellesmere and Whitchurch lines. There was a packet or fly boat for a very short period between Rednal on the Shrewsbury to Chester railway and Newtown. This was in the late 1840s and was soon discontinued due to wash damage to the canal bank and lack of custom. The one major deviation was between Welshpool and Abermule where the future line proceeded south of the Severn via Forden and Montgomery leaving the important village of Berriew outside the railway system. The opposition can be seen within the Canal Conversion Act that stated that no station was to be constructed near Glansevern Hall or within 100 yards of the Rectory bridge in Berriew. The canal company became part of the LNWR followed by the London, Midland & Scottish Railway (LMS) until closure and abandonment in the 1930s/1940s.

Aborted schemes were often on routes to actual or potential ports to Ireland. The Bishops Castle Railway reversed at Lydham Heath and never reached a junction near Montgomery. Many of these lines were a potential route from Worcester to the Welsh coast especially centred on Porth Dinllaen on the Llŷn north of Pwllheli. The Shropshire Mineral Railway and the so called 'Potts' line ceased at Nantmawr on the Llanymynech loop. Shrewsbury to Llanymynech became part of a light railway with life extended by the War Department in the 1940s. The Manchester & Milford line was built from Penpontbren Junction near Llanidloes to Llangurig and this section was only ever used by contractors' locomotives. The routes of these lines faced the major problems of either the Cambrian or the Berwyn Mountains and of travelling across from valley to valley rather than following the river valleys. If these had been built, they could have given the Caersws maintenance team some very long tunnels and some spectacular masonry arch viaducts. There was one route that would have crossed the River Severn between the higher salients of land so Newtown could have been been dominated by a railway bridge not unlike the bridge that straddles Stockport between Crewe and Manchester.

Right: Albert Gilbert was commissioned to make a statue of David Davies for Barry Docks. A replica was funded by public subscription and unveiled at Llandinam in June 1893. Davies is shown in workday clothes unfolding a plan of Barry Docks.

Author

Below: This photograph was taken showing Llandinam station in June 1873 for Edward (son) Davies's coming of age. The road bridge approaches on the right was the first ever contract given by Thomas Penson to Davies in 1846. The new building across the valley is Broneirion, the house built for David Davies and his family. The carriages have been placed in the siding for the day. These were four special trains with his colliers and their families from the Rhondda.

Ted Morgan, Caersws and the Cambrian Railways Museum, Oswestry

The railway systems started to move with the Llanidloes & Newtown Act of 1853 although construction did not start for several years. Much of the impetus for these railways came from local investment. There were both perceived and real difficulties in getting contractors to build them so this gave the opportunity for four local men to develop their skills as contractors, engineers and architects.

David Davies of Llandinam

The best known of these men, both locally and nationally, would be David Davies of Llandinam. Davies started life on a hard upland farm within the parish of Llandinam on the hills that sweep round to Moat Lane. He helped his father both on the farm and in the saw-pit. The family moved to a far better holding on the edge of the flood plain. Davies carried out some earthworks on the bank of the Severn to reduce flooding on some of the pasture. This work impressed Thomas Penson, the Montgomeryshire surveyor, who was building bridges and improving roads. The result was that Penson asked Davies if he would build the embankment and approaches for the Llandinam bridge. This was the first contract for Davies. Penson would pass much local work to Davies. He built the Smithfield (cattle market) at Oswestry; with Savin he built the approaches to the bridge over the Banwy near Llangadfan in 1851, some 50 years before another contractor crossed the river with a railway bridge for the light railway near Cyfronydd.

Davies took his chance when there was reluctance for an outside contractor to take on duties for the building of the Llanidloes to Newtown Railway. He was to enter into partnership with Thomas Savin. This partnership was both fruitful and stormy. Contracts followed with the Vale of Clwyd, the Newtown & Machynlleth, the Mid-Wales Railway and to take over and complete the Oswestry to Newtown line. Davies and Savin were very different personalities and they were to fall out and go their separate ways. Savin had grandiose schemes so the more cautious Davies would urge caution.

Davies was to complete several more contracts such as the Pembroke & Tenby line and also the Manchester & Milford line from Pencader Junction to Aberystwyth. He sensed that the period of major railway construction in rural Wales would soon come to a conclusion. It is of interest to note that he always attempted to have a number of 'his own' Llanidloes to Caersws men within his gangs. This is important because it almost certainly led to the commencement of the skill base that would not be formalized until around 1900 centred at Caersws. In 1864 he took on a lease of coal in the Upper Rhondda Valley. This high value steam coal market boomed so Davies was rapidly on his way to becoming a major Victorian entrepreneur and politician. He secured the passage of the Barry Dock and Railway Bill. His colliery business became the Ocean Coal Company. Both he and his future generations would become major patrons of culture in Mid-Wales as well as landowners and businessmen/ women. His grandson was a Director of the Cambrian Railways and did much to get the closed Dinas Mawddwy line to be rebuilt as a light railway. Two granddaughters became astute purchasers of art at Gregynog Hall north of Newtown and these works are now the core permanent exhibition at the National Museum, Cardiff.

An early picture of the trestle bridge over the Severn at Caersws. The partnership of Davies & Savin had now been dissolved. This was the first major construction as the Newtown & Machynlleth Railway moved from Moat Lane Junction in the early 1860s. Rice Hopkins had carried out the first survey. Sadly Rice Hopkins was to die so Piercy took on his duties and Davies built the bridge. *Powys County Council, the Powysland Museum, Welshpool*

Thomas Savin: the Llwyn-y-maen, Oswestry man who was David Davies' first partner and a contractor on other parts of the line.
Newtown Library

Benjamin Piercy: the Trefeglwys man who was the Engineer of many of the Cambrian lines.
Newtown Library

Thomas Savin of Oswestry

Thomas Savin was the foreigner across the border from Llwyn-y-maen near Oswestry. Davies and Savin first met when the Oswestry Smithfield was under construction. Savin was in partnership with a draper's business in the town. Savin was a man of charisma with boundless energy but also a risk taker. The combination of the flamboyant Savin and the austere Davies may have been of value to get their contract business under way. Davies had built the first section of the Llanidloes to Newtown from Llanidloes to Morfodion bridge over the Severn. He also received the contract for the second section but events started to slow down. The Engineer was replaced by Ben Piercy to ensure the final section from Penstrowed to Newtown was completed . He then invited Davies and Savin to make a joint arrangement to complete the work. The contracts on the Oswestry & Newtown were experiencing difficulty so the two contractors were invited to take on the work and completed it. They then moved to assist with both the Mid-Wales Railway and the Newtown to Machynlleth line. Sharp differences within every aspect of policy was now manifold between the two men and there was no alternative but to split the partnership. Davies completed the Newtown to Machynlleth line while Savin took on the construction of the Welsh Coast line (Aberystwyth to Pwllheli). Davies made the forecast that the speculation on hotels along the coast was reckless. This turned into reality in 1866 when Savin failed with financial disaster at the stage when the Barmouth bridge was under construction. It gave the newly-formed Cambrian Railways many problems to re-finance.

Savin played no further part in local railway construction but he must be remembered for his vision and innovation. He had surveyed various routes including a narrow gauge trans-Berwyn route from Welshpool to Ffestiniog and also a further consideration of Llanymynech to Bala again needing a tunnel under the Berwyns in the early 1860s. All such schemes foundered once the coast route from Chester to Holyhead had established itself and could cope with the packet traffic. There is a mention of Savin around 1881 with the concept of a tramway to assist with the construction of the Vyrnwy dam. It was this route that was to be used for the waterpipe on the first stage of the journey to Liverpool. Savin & Co. traded at Llanymynech and this company became the Porthywaen Lime Co. This quarry generated much traffic on the Crickheath Tramway and the canal followed by much coal in and lime out on the standard gauge branch that became part of the later Llanygynog Light Railway. It is thought that the Savin in the quarry business was related or may be the same Savin. There are a number of local books written in Welsh recalling village life. This is from *Llangynog Gynt* by J.D. Lloyd and translates as follows: 'A man with the name of Savin worked at the quarry and he had a *fire horse/ceffyl tan* or traction engine to carry slate to Borth-y-waun' (or the English form of Porthywaen).

Benjamin Piercy of Trefeglwys

Davies & Savin started as contractors and became skilled with the construction techniques necessary for the railway. The engineer who designed many of the Mid-Wales railway lines was Benjamin Piercy. Robert Piercy of Chirk was a skilled surveyor with much work connected with enclosures, construction of public roads and valuations within the Poor Laws and Tithes Acts. It was convenient for him to reside in Trefeglwys in the 1820s. Two of his sons, both born in Trefeglwys, played important roles in the changes of the Victorian era. Robert junior became an engineer in the large iron works at Ruabon. He was responsible for underground surveys and much of the tramways necessary within the iron and coal complex. He also spent much time in India including some railway construction.

The younger brother, Benjamin, was born in 1827. He was a junior staff member within the company run by Mickleburgh that assisted with progressing the Parliamentary Acts and the surveys for the Shrewsbury & Chester Railway. He started his own practice in 1852 with the major duty to survey the Shrewsbury to Newtown line through the Rea Valley. This line was only built as far as Minsterley. The line would have joined the current system at Forden/Montgomery isolating Welshpool. The main line became the joint GWR/LNWR line to Buttington Junction later leaving Minsterley as a branch line.

Piercy then took on duties for most of what was to become the Cambrian Railways. The decision to cut at Talerddig, rather than tunnel, plus the use of spoil and cut stone for the line down to Cemmaes Road would be an example of his design. Piercy surveyed and decided where the numerous bridges across the Vyrnwy, the Severn, the Wye and the estuary bridges were to be placed. Station sites, sidings, engine sheds, etc., were within his remit. One of Piercy's concepts was to build a bridge from Ynyslas to Aberdovey over the estuary. The bridge was designed and work began seeking a foundation using long rods within the shifting sands. The decision was soon made to take the long bend so the Dovey was crossed close to the highest reach of the tide and Dovey Junction station in the midst of saline marsh would follow. Piercy and Savin worked pressing north with the Welsh Coast route. The high tides and storms made necessary the tunnels in Aberdovey and various sea walls. The Friog rocks were an obstacle and still remains a challenging section to maintain. The Mawddach Estuary tests were a success so the Barmouth bridge was built. Piercy was noted at this stage for his advice to set up the Cambrian Railways and remain independent of either the GWR or the LNWR. His advice was also taken when the semi-autonomous Mid-Wales Railway merged with the Cambrian in 1888.

His office was based at Welshpool and then in London. Work was taken on in Sardinia. He altered a very expensive system with a redesigned route that was less ambitious and ensured construction completion of the island system. He carried out further work on the Italian mainland with the line to Golfo di Aranci from Rome to enhance the port. This involved much drainage of marshland. He did many surveys of some of the metre gauge lines. He was created a Commadatore of the Crown of Italy. He constructed the 160 miles of the Tours-Les Sables d'Olonne in France. He also was involved with projects in Assam and across the border in Burma.

His home base became Marchwiel Hall near Wrexham. This would be close to the Wrexham & Ellesmere line that would later be within the remit of the bridge department of Caersws. He helped to promote the line but died in 1888 when construction was deferred. He had purchased a section of the line which passed to the control of his trustees so his business acumen continued after his death.

It is unlikely that Davies, who was nine years older, would have met Piercy when they only lived about three miles apart as boys in Llandinam and Trefeglwys. However, there is an oral record that Davies accompanied Piercy once to Sardinia to proffer extra advice. Piercy was also involved with railways in the Wrexham/Mold area in his final years. This railway was closely involved with the Great Central Railway. The story of both Davies and Piercy, both children within a then isolated part of rural Wales, is an astonishing saga. Davies and his family that followed remained close to the culture and economy of his home patch and he is therefore the better known of these two men locally to the present day.

Stephen Williams of Churchstoke

Williams is the least known of the four local men. He was born near Mellington in 1837 and was educated at Bishops Castle and articled to a land agent with an extensive practice in Staffordshire. His first professional duty commenced in 1858 when he joined the staff of the railway engineer, Benjamin Piercy, when their office was based at Welshpool. Williams was with the Piercy enterprise within the period when the Llanidloes & Newtown Railway was experiencing difficulty so Piercy with Davies & Savin agreed to complete the line. Piercy had little interest in the details of architecture and delegated station design to the then very young Williams. It is likely that the final exterior and internals of Llanidloes were done by Williams. It is known that Williams assisted Piercy with either the total design or additions to such large stations as Oswestry, Ellesemere and Welshpool. He was influenced by a French architectural style and this can be seen within the Welshpool design. Such stations as Llynclys, Kerry and Llanfyllin have many common features and could be called the Oswestry & Newtown Railway style. Williams moved to Rhayader in March 1861 to survey the route from Llanidloes to Talyllyn. Williams had ambitions for his own business and also expressed concern with the professional ethics and gamble of the share issue as part of the payments. He was especially concerned that Savin was sailing close to the edge. He therefore started to broaden his portfolio of skills but continued some railway work in Mid-Wales including the New Radnor extension, the Kington and Eardisley lines. His final railway duty was to survey the Elan Valley branch and the initial conveyance of land necessary to build the dams in 1894. He became the County Surveyor for Radnor. He was responsible for the design of many public buildings in the county. He also took on duties of new Victorian or major restoration of existing churches in both Brecknock and Radnor counties. He died in 1899. He is remembered for his public works and churches in Radnorshire. However, his early career with Piercy has also given us some very valued railway architecture. There is some confusion within local papers on dates as there were two Stephen Williams who were both noted antiquarians. Williams designed a number of road bridges for Radnor County Council. These were functional and economic so the design did not anticipate modern traffic. There is a plaque on the modern Brynwern bridge on the Wye south of Newbridge to remember the first bridge erected in 1885 with Williams' name. A detailed recall of Williams and his architecture, railway, secular and church, is within *Volume CXLIX Archaeologia Cambrensis.*

The railway companies and the creation of the Caersws railway village

The Llanidloes & Newtown Railway was the line without a head or a tail. The then isolated line had its first Parliamentary Act submitted in 1853 with intermediate stations planned at Dolwen, Llandinam, Maesmawr, Penstrowed and Ysgafell. The line was to terminate in Newtown at the canal basin. The Newtown station was just west of the Dolfor Road bridge about 300 yards from the present site. Maesmawr

Right: Stephen Williams is shown as the distinguished retired architect. In 1889, he published papers on the excavations of the Cistercian Abbey at Strata Florida. His introduction is as follows: 'Twenty six years in the early years of my professional career, I was engaged in making surveys of many lines which at that period were spreading their network all over Wales. I was at work upon a line from Rhayader to Aberystwyth and passed the immediate vicinity of Strata Florida. I was much interested in what was seen of the ruins'.

Powys County Council,
The Radnorshire Museum, Llandrindod

Below: Welshpool station may be the most baroque of Williams' designs. This photograph dates from the late 1970s. The van with the BR insignia is for the Red Star Parcel service. The view between 1931 and 1965 would have shown a small bus often waiting as road replacement for the Welshpool-Llanfair rail service. An additional larger bus would also have been on this forecourt after 1965 for the Welshpool-Oswestry replacement service.

Powys County Council,
the Powysland Museum, Welshpool

became Moat Lane for Caersws and the site was beside the lane to Mochdre and is now known as Old Moat Lane. The first Engineer was Rice Hopkins (later replaced by Piercy) and his route had four bridges over the Severn (Morfodion, Llandinam, Doughty and Ysgafell). He kept the route well east of the flood plain of the Carno, Severn and Cerist/Trannon rivers where the rivers meandered into the Severn with a history of much flooding. The line was straight in the Moat Lane area. The line was finally opened in 1859 and operated with full services until December 1962 and closed to goods to Llanidloes in October 1967.

The Newtown & Machynlleth Railway was incorporated in 1857. The company was to have running powers between Newtown and the necessary junction which became the site for Moat Lane Junction with the very severe curve to head to Caersws. The line was completed in January 1863 within the time limit. The contractors were to be Davies & Savin but the partnership split so Davies built this company's line and Savin proceeded with the Machynlleth to Aberystwyth section. Details of the Moat Lane complex construction are not known within this community but it is likely that turntables and engine sheds were in operation by 1869. This line was very different in nature because it did not follow the gentle routes of the valleys but had to climb out of the Severn Valley and cross the watershed at Talerddig at 693 ft before descending down the feeder valleys to the Dovey valley. All engines stopped to take on water at Moat Lane before, or after, tackling this gradient until the final steam days in early 1967. The company built both Caersws and Pontdolgoch stations.

The Mid-Wales Railway extended the line south of Llanidloes. There was an Act for Llanidloes to Newbridge in 1859 and Newbridge to Talyllyn in 1860. Because the Manchester & Milford's Act covered the same route as the Mid-Wales between Llanidloes and Penpontbren there was a dispute as to who should build it. As a compromise the Llanidloes & Newtown did so and the Mid-Wales' own line started from Penpontbren. The Mid-Wales route ran on to Talyllyn Junction and then had running rights on the Brecon & Merthyr Railway into Brecon. Financial problems were continuous but the operation kept moving forward and the line opened in late 1864. Operation was beset with difficulties. The Cambrian took over working in 1888, so much change took place at Moat Lane Junction. The long waits for any connection at Moat Lane had been notorious between the Mid-Wales Railway and the Cambrian. The Cambrian set a pattern of operation that pertained until closure of the line. Moat Lane station became the exchange terminus for most passenger trains coming in from the south with the exception of several Llanidloes to Whitchurch services while virtually no train heading to or from the coast or to Newtown started its journey at Moat Lane. (There was thought to be an emergency service west immediately after the Abermule accident in 1921.)

The companies such as the Llanidloes & Newtown and the Newtown & Machynlleth had a very short operational life as the Cambrian Railways was formed in 1864 adding both the Oswestry & Newtown and the Oswestry, Ellesmere and Whitchurch companies. The Aberystwyth & Welsh Coast Railway was already in place but the company was not absorbed into the Cambrian for a further year because of legal difficulties. The Dovey Junction to Pwllheli section immediately gave the Cambrian much financial difficulty to secure the loans necessary to continue construction. Pwllheli was reached in 1869. The main structure was now in place, plus some branch lines and further additions such as the Wrexham & Ellesmere Railway, plus the light railways that would give Caersws Bridge Department the maintenance and inspection duties from 1900 onwards. The late

Victorian period was financially buoyant. This led to much expansion of both goods and passenger traffic throughout Britain. Tourist traffic increased so maybe Savin's idea of hotels along the Cambrian Coast was only 25 years too early. The Cambrian met this demand by using more powerful locomotives, longer trains and greater frequency and this increased the number of work duties required at Moat Lane. There would have been more through traffic if the Manchester & Milford original route via Penpontbren Jn had been successful.

There is very little trace of these short-lived companies in the area. The 1860 Llanidloes & Newtown Railway timetable shows four services daily between Newtown and Llanidloes with Dolwen, Llandinam and Moat Lane as stops. The Oswestry & Newtown Railway terminates at Welshpool with certain omnibus connections. The 1864 timetable covers a very sparse service between Whitchurch and Aberystwyth with morning and afternoon trains from Oswestry to Llanidloes and followed by an Aberystwyth service starting at Newtown or through Oswestry to Aberystwyth trains with a Llanidloes connection at Moat Lane. The station is now called Moat Lane Junction and Scafell station has been added, 2¾ miles to the east. Waiting time at Moat Lane was only a few minutes for Llanidloes connections except if one wished to travel to or from Aberystwyth to Llanidloes. An example was that a train heading to Aberystwyth arrived at Moat Lane at 10.16 am and departed east at 10.26 with the Llanidloes train arriving at 10.20. One would have to wait until 12.28 to travel to Llanidloes.

The Van Railway junction in the centre of Caersws was not within the original planned lines to forge a continuous system. It was an opportunist branch built to serve the Van lead mines. The contractor was David Davies. The Railways Construction Facilities Act of 1864 gave companies the chance to speed up the installation of sidings and short branches to factories, quarries, mines, etc., so no Parliamentary Act was required. The line of six miles opened to mineral traffic in 1871. The growth of the mine was spectacular with both lead extraction and an inflated share price. A Board of Trade Certificate gave the right to have a passenger service which operated only from 1873 to 1879. The price of lead fell and access to good lodes had been exploited so the whole enterprise was uneconomic. There was goods traffic only two or three times per week and the line closed in 1893. The line was re-opened by the Cambrian in 1896. The use of the line was determined by the Caersws station master. The engine servicing was moved to Moat Lane. The redundant Van station, the engine shed and the loop was 'recycled' by the company to become the local bridge department and developed to become the bridge headquarters for the company by the time of World War I.

These various events from 1853 until 1900 transferred 'Greater' Caersws from a community with no railway employment to the considerable number necessary to operate at both Moat Lane and the bridge department plus others such as station staff, lengthmen, signalmen and crossing keepers. The scene is now set for a detailed study of Caersws, the Cambrian Railways village.

Chapter Two

Caersws and its Environs

The Caersws area has been an important nodal transport system almost certainly dating from the iron age. The Upper Severn Valley starts to narrow and both the Severn and the major tributaries of the Carno and Trannon/Cerist lead to watersheds into the Wye and Dyfi valleys. The earliest site must be Cefn Carnedd iron age hill fort. The earthworks are still visible. There is a double defensive bank looking down over the Severn with a good view of the railways from Penstrowed to Pontdolgoch, Moat Lane Junction to Llandinam and much of the Van line. It must have been a major centre of power and authority.

The Roman period led to Caersws becoming a crossroad with a major line of communication to Wroxeter (Caerguricon) near Shrewsbury onwards to Watling Street leading to Londinium. The river has three names. The Romance/Latin *fluvius* is Sabrina, the Saxon is the River Severn and the Brythonic/Welsh is the Afon Hafren. The derivation of each is subject to conjecture. Sabrina may date from medieval myths written by Geoffrey of Monmouth while the other two appear in written records around 1000 AD. Sabrina is also the river goddess. She was part of the masque drama, Comus, written by Milton in 1637 and first performed at Ludlow to celebrate the 'colonial' appointment of the Lord President of Wales. Milton may have visited the Caersws area and have been inspired by the Severn to write the Sabrina fair (complexion not market) within this masque. Dolforwyn (the meadow of the maid) near Abermule refers to the Sabrian myth. Hafren is used for place and company names throughout the Upper Severn Valley including as far east as Shrewsbury.

The literally correct spelling of Caersws should be Caer-sŵs but this would be rarely used. The word Caer would immediately suggest a Roman settlement. There is Carmarthen (Caerfyrddin), Caerleon and Caernarfon and others in Wales. Montgomeryshire has Caereinion and Y Gaer near Forden. The 'Caer' English equivalent is Chester. Many Chesters have a Welsh equivalent with such examples as Chester (Gaer) plus the Latin Deva, Worcester (Caerwrangon), Gloucester (Caerloyw) and Carlisle (Caerliwelydd). Note the Brythonic Car has been retained as Cumbria is the same as Cymru (Wales) and this is still seen within some place names. Traces of the Cumbrian language were still used for counting sheep in the last century. The Caer must not be confused with cae (field) or cau (shut).

So the meaning of Caer is clear unlike the Sŵs. It may refer to a Roman person or may be a corruption of the stone used to build the fort. The Sws could be an important local Roman leader or his lady friend. One railway worker when he heard that Sws may have been a concubine was horrified as he thought a Woodbine was all that was needed at the end of a shift! (Wills Woodbine was a common cheaper cigarette commonly smoked within any mess room up to the 1950s.) There is a reference to Caer-swysen within the medieval poetry of Lewys Glyn Cothi and Dafydd Llwyd. This is not known as either a fact or a myth. There is a mound called Bedd y Frehines and a road towards Deva is called Sarn Swsan. This Swsan was a warrior Queen and she may have led a battle at Rhos-ddiarbedd that is close to Moat Lane Junction. Sws in modern Welsh is a kiss but anyone would have to wait a very long time at Moat Lane Junction for such a treat in 2013.

The first small settlement at Llwyn-y-brain was rapidly superseded by the construction at Caersws around 70 AD. The roman names for Forden Gaer and

Right: Owen Jones (Moat Lane wagon & carriage examiner) stands near Caersws crossroads. The photograph was from the *Sunday Mercury* (Birmingham) recording progress of Caersws football club in the 1950s. Note the railway name of Cemmaes Road that is now signposted to Machynlleth and Dolgellau and was the route to Caernoddfa, Carno & Cefn-caer on the Dyfi estuary. Owen is standing near the Roman crossroads so a legionnaire could have stood in the same spot. Owen is on the road in from Wroxeter and Forden Gaer. The B4569 to Trefeglwys (*left*) led to the Roman lead mines around Staylittle and there may also be an uncertain junction to camps at Llangurig and Rhayader with connection to Castell Collen and Brecon Gaer. The B4568 starts towards Aberhafesp and leads in a most direct route to Caergai near Bala.   *John Jones, Builth Wells*

Below: The Roman Fort at Caersws. Rice Hopkins was engaged to survey the line and made the ground plan through what may have been a Roman Villa around 1860. Only a few antiquarians had taken interest prior to this. Piercy and Davies took on the contract. Some relics were found on the site. Further major analysis has taken place since especially in 1909 within the main fort and in 1966 on the school site when the playground was rebuilt.   *Powysland Club, Montgomeryshire Papers*

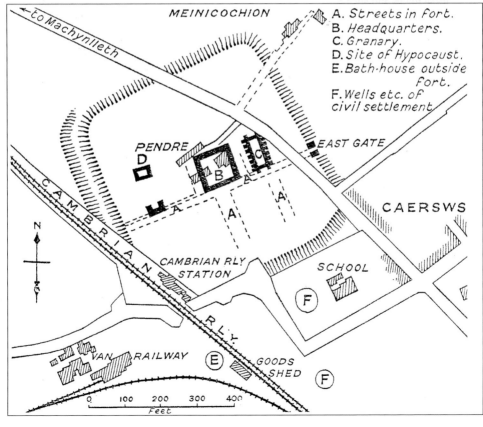

A. *Streets in fort.*
B. *Headquarters.*
C. *Granary.*
D. *Site of Hypocaust.*
E. *Bath-house outside fort.*
F. *Wells etc. of civil settlement.*

Caersws may have been Levobrinta and Mediomanum from traces of early manuscripts. Military occupation may have been for a very short period until 115 AD and the garrison (*Cohors milaria*) entirely withdrawn by 200 AD. Parts of the roads can still be traced, both locally and further afield. It was a fiveways. The main east-west route ran from Wroxeter via Forden Gaer and Caersws. A clear straight line pasture mark would appear in very severe drought at the Vaynor Farm parallel to the railway when the author worked on that farm near Newtown. The route to Pennal on the northern side of the Dyfi estuary is again subject to further research. The north-south route ran from Chester to Bala and then crossed the Berwyns to the Llanerfyl area then up over Adfa to Aberhafesp and down to Caersws. The route may have crossed into the Wye to Castell Collen near Llandrindod, Esgairperfedd near Rhayader and on to Brecon Gaer. Current research may give a better answer. This route would not be disimilar to that of the Mid-Wales Railway. There was a branch to Cae Caer, Llangurig. The Forestry Commission has opened this site and it can be clearly seen from the main road between Llangurig and Eisteddfod Curig close to where the ill fated Manchester & Milford line would have tunnelled through the Cambrian Massif. The fifth route would be close to that of the Van line. There is a trace of a Roman settlement near the lead mines of Dylife called Pen-y-crocbren. The lead was a valued resource for the Romans and there may have been a smelting site at Trefeglwys. It is likely that there was a dual culture for trading purposes with Roman influence only in the valleys along these routes and such activity rapidly vanished as the empire finished around 400 AD leaving the sites only. It is unknown history. The Caersws fort site came to prominence when the railway was built so details follow later.

The interval between Roman withdrawal and the Norman influence was dominated by Welsh Princes (or warlords!) and the Celtic church. The territory of Powys covered much of Denbighshire, Shropshire and Montgomeryshire . The original headquarters or court may have been at Pengwern sited in the Shrewsbury area or at Berth towards Ellesmere and may have moved to Mathrafal near Meifod as the Welsh rule was subjected to eviction within the eastern section of Powys. The areas on the western boundary were divided into commotes adminstered by deputies, stewards and sergeants. Caersws was within Arwystli and this was divided into two called Uwch Coed and Is Coed. The Caersws or Is Coed court was at Penprys and the site is now known as Park. The court and the Celtic church/court chapel were to disappear. The commote names still live on within the church deaneries of Arwystli, Cedewain and Ceri. The three territories were subject to dispute both political and ecclesiastical. There is one field at Penstrowed just east of Moat Lane that became within the territory of three bishops (Arwystli in Bangor, Cedewain in St Asaph and Ceri in St Davids) so there must have been some confused souls.

The history of Wales after the withdrawal of the Roman legions was different from the created power vacuum and pagan Saxon incomers in England. The Celtic church brought a vibrant Christianity. The main church within the Caersws area was St Llonio at Llandinam with cells or chapels that became churches. Examples are St Idloes at Llanidloes, St Gwrhai at Penstrowed and St Gwynog at Llanwnog and Aberhafesp. The Celtic rubrics continued long after the merged churches of Whitby synod around 664 AD. The parish structure evolved and this was important as the church was universal irrespective of which Marcher Lord or Welsh Prince had political control. There was a period where the gentry patronized the Welsh poets and the houses included Penparcprys, Maesmawr and Trewythen. The county of Montgomeryshire was formed around 1536 and this led to the establishment of seven ancient borough towns to have markets and fairs. The medieval Caersws built on the Roman *vicus* was included with

Llanidloes, Machynlleth, Newtown, Montgomery, Welshpool and Llanfyllin. This would lead to Courts as well as other rights. Caersws appeared to lapse during the reign of Charles I and started to lose the various rights and privileges. An article in 1939 records that the court leets of Caersws were deposited into the National Library. They were held to administer the affairs of the Manor of Arwystli. The main purpose was to register males and pass judgement on petty crime. It lists the period 1730 to 1804. One name available for jury service was a John Bradley, corn merchant, and his descendants' names appear for the duration of the railway history. The medieval town site gradually disappeared until reused for the third time with the housing for the railway community from 1870 onwards.

Detailed documentation commences with the enclosure of Caersws Commons around 1826. Caersws was now a few scattered houses in the parish of Llanwnog. One of the adjoining townships was Maesmawr in the parish of Llandinam and this would include the future site of Moat Lane Junction.

Changes between 1820 and 1900 transformed Caersws and the surrounding area. The roads were maintained by the parish with the help of tithes and the stone breakers of the poor law. Roads were poor and that is a polite way of saying that they were virtually useless in wet weather. Turnpikes came in in the 1820s funded by toll until the county started to take responsibility and an example would be the then massive three-arch bridge over the River Severn around 1821 that still is used today. Many previous bridges within the area were of wood and these were constantly in need of repair after being smashed by flood. Some were for pedestrian traffic only with the adjoining ford for horse/oxen carts. The site of the bridge would have a ford and such bridges could date back to the Roman period. The first turnpike headed through Aberhafesp and Llanwnog on the elevated northern side of the valley avoiding the flood plain. The new bridge led to a more direct route through Caersws to Pontdolgoch and also to the Newtown/Llanidloes turn at the now level crossing as both the wool and lead industry expanded. So Caersws started to grow again with a few decent houses, inns and three dissenting chapels ready to expand with the railways from 1863 when most of the development would be planted on what was the long-lost Roman *vicus* and the medieval borough.

The advent of schools would be important. There was a charity school at Llandinam (1839), Aberhafesp (1826) and a national school at Llanwnog (1859). These would have been closely tied to the churches. There was a poor house (tlotai) school in Caersws around 1840. Caersws school started in 1867 and would become a County Board School and would soon be the largest 'all age' school in the locality. Literacy in English quickly changed after the 1870 Acts from being maybe from 50 per cent to close to 100 per cent of younger people by 1890. This would be very important for railway recruitment. The County set up grammar schools at Newtown and Llanidloes in the 1880s and this set a tradition of scholarship, children travelling by train until 1962 (Llandinam to Llanidloes) and 1965 (Caersws/Carno to Newtown). It was not an easy period for the Welsh language. People were either English speakers from east of Caersws or Welsh speakers west and north of the village. There was not a modern concept of bilingualism. Even in 2007, many had one parent or one grandparent that spoke Welsh and a number of interviews took place in Welsh including at Frodsham and Wolverhampton when gleaning these stories. The Victorian period witnessed many large families with improved health and nutrition. Many rural communities lost population to the mining and industrial towns as well as emigration. The growth of the railways at Caersws gave many the opportunity to stay in the area. An enquiry in the late 1840s called the 'The Blue Books' are now recalled with bitterness by some. The report for the neighbouring parish of Aberhafesp stated that all classes were illiterate and ignorant of English with inferiority due to Welsh being spoken. The same result would have been given if Essex children had been tested in Welsh but imperial Britain did not think like that. It is history now and the communities have every opportunity to maintain and learn Welsh. So the railway timetables and station names are bilingual now.

Church and chapel is a complex story in every part of Wales and the Caersws area is no exception. The expanding population of Caersws led to the the building of the church of St Mary in the 1870s. The three chapels had been founded from 1800 onwards with the Wesleyan in 1800, the Baptist in 1824 and the Calvinistic Methodist in 1826, then all underwent rebuilding after 1870. The Calvinist now called Presbyterian remains a very substantial building. All are within 200 yards of each other. Many of the dissenting movements were associated with temperance. David Davies was a member of the Calvanistic Methodists and gave much financial support to the cause including support for the now Presbyterian Llandinam Chapel. He also gave much support to the temperance movement and may have had a role in temperance hotels in Llandinam, Caersws and Llanwnog. Beer, with the heating of the brewing process, may have been a safer drink than water. The problem was excess consumption. This led to a dichotomy even within families. Railway, quarry and farm work was physically hard with much dust so there was a culture of beer/cyder drinking at work and within the tavern for many men including the railway workers. The chapels in Caersws would have worshipped in English. Surrounding chapels at Llanwnog, Clatter and Trefeglwys would have worshipped in Welsh until recent years and some have faced closure.

Caersws will now be described after the railway arrived. Much will be within stories of the railway families or within the narrative accompanying the illustrations. The examples start with the retired village postmistress and introduces an example of the extended railway families in the Upper Severn Valley.

Mrs Frances Lewis was the daughter of a roadman, Frank Mills, based at Abermule. The family lived at Brook Cottage in the dingle just below Rock Mill beside the Kerry branch line. Frances would often travel the line as a passenger to Goetre Halt where Granny kept the Maip Farm. Her father was working on the road near the Court Farm on the day of the Abermule crash in January 1921 and quickly hurried to the scene. Walter and Lucy Davies were relatives. They lived at the crossing keeper's cottage at Rhydwhyman near Montgomery. Lucy looked after the gates and Walter was a specialist loader of trunk timber wherever required so his duties were called for during World War I anywhere along the main line and branches.

Maldwyn Lewis joined the Welsh Guards in 1938 as a regular. He became a prisoner of war in 1940 and was thought to be dead until a communication came from the Red Cross. He was moved all over the place working on farms in what was Prussia and is now part of Poland. He was demobbed in 1946 and immediately went to work for the Bridge Department. He was soon to marry Frances and they set up home in Caersws. His duty became that of bridge inspection working with Bert Trow. He assessed needs so that the various teams could then bring the correct materials to site on time. The work would involve lodgings so he would disappear on the early train on Monday and not return until late on Friday having travelled anywhere on the system. The Bridge Department was very busy in the late 1940s so Frances became one of the many that looked after the children and the house most weeks. The 1947 snow disrupted all plans so men were deployed on snow clearance. Maldwyn once helped to clear a route along the footpath to Moat Lane Junction to find that the drifts had filled the footpath behind them and they had to dig their way back. One week Maldwyn arranged that the young

The railway would bring in many goods at a very competitive price and this led to shops selling to the village that expanded from 1870 onwards. The cycle agent became an important feature of many larger villages from 1890 onwards and Mr T. Rowlands and his enterprise was no exception.   *Emrys Davies, Caersws*

St John's Ambulance first aid railway competitions became very important. This photograph dating from the 1920s shows the Caersws railway team. Richard Lewis, the father of Maldwyn, is seated to the viewer's right of the cup. Percy Smout stands behind Richard. Noel Manual is standing to the left of the cup. The man in uniform was the station master, Lewis Hamer. Lewis was promoted later to be station master of Aberystwyth.   *Mrs Frances Lewis, Caersws*

family stopped in a rented bungalow near Barmouth. The children thought it was great fun especially brewing tea in the gangers hut.

Maldwyn left the railway in 1956 to take on duties as the Postmaster of Caersws. Nine postmen worked from the village, two on foot around the village, three on bikes within the valley and four with a van each to Carno and the high upland farms. (The vans only came into use in the late 1940s so both bikes and ponies were used earlier on the high upland routes.) The mail was collected from Caersws station by Dic Stephens from the mail train using a four-wheeled wooden hand truck. All parcels and mailbags were dumped outside the rear door of the post office, quickly brought into the room and sorting started immediately. The reverse journey took place for the evening mail as men brought in the mail from the various post boxes. Maldwyn would cycle out during the day to deliver telegrams leaving Frances in charge of the counter. All sorting centred on Newtown from around 1970 leaving the post office with counter services only.

Maldwyn's father was a lengthman working between Tylwch and Moat Lane. Maldwyn's brother, Daniel or Danny, was a porter at Moat Lane. Their family moved to Shrewsbury after the station's closure in December 1962 so Danny worked at Shrewsbury until retirement. Sadly, Maldwyn died at the age of 72 in 1991. Frances, was aged 85 when interviewed in 2007, must now be one the last of numerous ladies that supported their husbands within the local railway industry for just over a century.

There are numerous records in the archives in Newtown Library of the interelationship between the village and the railway. The first building for a few months could often be a hut just to get customers purchasing tickets. An example from the *Montgomeryshire Express* shows that a full building was in place by September 1869. It a rather sad story. Isaac Jones and his wife had taken their first trip on a train from Penrhyndeudraeth to Aberystwyth. On return, they neglected to leave the train at Machynlleth and were taken up the Cambrian line to Caersws. They panicked and jumped out of the train when it was still in motion. Mrs Jones was dragged along the line and was found in poor state. She was taken to the waiting room and Dr Parry was called. Her left arm and leg had to be amputated and she was removed to Caersws workhouse. Her prospect of recovery was not considered favourable. Both railwaymen and passengers had to quickly learn many safety features of this new technology. A small rural, now unstaffed, waiting room and platform witnessed many moments of joy and sadness for a century.

The union workhouse equidistant between Llanidloes and Newtown area was built at Caersws. It was converted to a specialist hospital after 1945 to accommodate people with severe disability. This became known as Llys Maldwyn and generated a number of valued jobs especially for women. These ladies became very devoted in their caring role. Caersws was therefore a bustling village with many men working for the railway or farming and the ladies with a greater opportunity for work than many other villages.

The hospital closed in the 1990s with the concept of 'care in the community'. The large building has been renovated within Grade II listed status into apartments and flats. The developers have done an excellent job to ensure an historic building continues to have an economic use for the community.

Examples of life in the village from the local paper follow for the period during World War II. The Caersws Petty Sessions still took place. It was much concerned with cycling offences such as no lights, no dog licences and salmon poaching. Some of the offenders were railway staff. One case in 1940 was an alleged weighbridge fault at Llandinam station with the GWR summoned by the weights and measures inspectors. The door of the weighbridge had been left open, the weighbridge was out of balance and porter Trow was asked to explain. The weather had been appalling, the

The centre of Caersws showing the nucleus of the Victorian/Edwardian houses, the school, the church, the three chapels and the shops that served the railway village. This is the third time that this salient of land just above the flood plain has been used as it was the civilian *vicus* and then a medieval settlement. The railway would just be to the right of the picture and many local government houses were constructed in the 1920s to 1950s, just out of view on the left.   *Mrs Frances Lewis, Caersws*

The rivers are being held by the flood prevention schemes of 1970. The main Severn is joined by the Carno and the Trannon/Cerist and the water table is at the surface. Both road and rail bridges, the station and the lifted junction to the Van Railway can be discerned. The new housing development in the left lower corner is called Llys Rhufain (Roman Court).

National Monument Records of Wales (945028-44.1991)

weighbridge was checked daily and the weighbridge had been entered without authority. The porters stated that their first duty was to clean up the station and the yard including water that had flooded the weighbridge. The case was dismissed. Mrs Bessie Jones, Moat Lane refreshment room manager, was summoned for displaying a light in the roofed building during darkness. P.C. Jones was near to Moat Lane station at 10.45 pm on 28th April, 1942. The bright light was caused by a large Aladdin lamp on the table in the centre of the room. The constable inteviewed Mrs Jones who stated that she had only just come in from Caersws and had not placed blackout material in position before lighting the lamp. Effective blackout material was at hand and blackout was between 10 pm and 4 am. A fine of £1 was imposed.

There were several road mishaps including a horse bolting with a milk float. Certain items were peculiar to the war period. There was a letter from the Mayor of Birkenhead for receiving the evacuee children from Alpha Drive School with such kindness and giving the 'Rock Ferry' cheers for the people of Caersws. Various societies raised funds for war causes such as the Montgomeryshire 'Spitfire' or knitted comforts for the troops.

The railway staff took on extra duties with greater potential need for first aid so the GWR ambulance class passed out W.H. Jones (wheel examiner at Moat Lane), T. Webb (Moat Lane signalman) and E. Caffrey (acting station master at Caersws) to pass on their skills. Noel Manual of the Bridge Department was willing to arrange to show a series of films from the National Railway Association to help with the war effort.

Several social gatherings were recorded at Moat Lane Junction assuming that the refreshment room was used. Mr Thomas of Oerffrwd level crossing at Clatter retired after 49 years of service. He started with the Cambrian in 1893 on the permanent way in the platelayers gang of the Caersws, Carno, Talerddig length and was promoted to ganger between Newtown and Moat Lane. The presentation took place at Moat Lane and the gift and thanks was made by Edgar Jones, permanent way inspector.

A presentation took place for Cliff Bradley with his marriage to Miss Hilda Roberts in February 1942. The gift was from the Locomotive & Traffic Department. Mr Bradley was a shunter and had been with the railway for 15 years.

The paper, during World War II, had no advertisements of train services or current operation. The following article from April 1942 shows two railway careers. The GWR has now placed their control office at Moat Lane under dual control with the appointment of Lewis Hamer (station master at Caersws) and Mr F.R. Mills both under supervision of chief inspector J. George. Mr Hamer commenced his career over 40 years earlier as junior clerk at Caersws. He gained experience and was appointed station master at Bangor on Dee in 1915 and was then the youngest station master on the Cambrian. In 1917, he transferred to Aberystwyth to be in charge of the Rheidol line until 1922. He worked on relief station master duties until appointed as Caersws station master. It is thought that his final years were as Aberystwyth station master. Mr Mills commenced work in 1918 as telegraph clerk at Caersws. He gained experience at Pontdolgoch, Abermule and Barmouth until 1923 when he was appointed to the Control Office at Moat Lane.

Peace came in 1945 and the GWR ceased to exist when nationalization came at midnight on 31st December, 1947. British Railways had reasonable success with catching up on the backlog of maintenance caused by the war until the early 1950s. The withdrawal of petrol rationing plus the rapid growth of both car and lorry ownership soon led to cash deficit. Closure will be detailed within the Moat Lane chapter but it was a little miracle that Caersws station survived. Many towns and villages can become heavily dependent on a narrow industrial base and are therefore vulnerable to economic, political or fashion change. Caersws was no exception with over 140 railway

The official photograph of the first 'railway queen'. The GWR decided to cheer everyone up after the austerity of World War II and organized a series of railway queens within their territory. Bert Davage was the chargehand of the Moat Lane engine sheds. The token and tablet was made at the GWR Swindon works and records, 'Presented to the Moat Lane & District GWR Queen, Sept 15th, 1945, Miss Jean Davage'.

Mrs Jean Lloyd née Davage, Trewern

A special train left Caersws for Wrexham Race Course for the Welsh Amateur Cup Final on 4th May, 1963. The train stopped at Newtown to take on more supporters. The young men and young ladies had their photograph taken with the football club colours. They are, *from left to right*: Wynston Mantle, John Bates, Jennifer Bradley, Jennifer Brown, Cath Parry and Janet with the sash, Pat Evans *above* and Pat Davey *below* and finally Bethan Rowlands. Chirk won in a closely fought game. Defeat did not spoil a lovely day out.

Janet Hamer, Caersws

The Bluebird Special draws out of Caersws for Wrexham. Charlie Aldridge wrote to Paddington to get permission to use the special Bluebird headboard and the organization was done by Owen Jones, the wheel tapper at Moat Lane. Signalman Bill Corfield exchanges tokens with Archie Fleming from Machynlleth shed.

Vivian Bradley, Caersws

jobs leaching away in the early 1960s. The whole area of Mid-Wales was subject to depopulation with few opportunities for younger people. The concept of building a new town had been discussed and this led to a controversial proposal for building a linear town of 70,000 people centred on Caersws. This was rapidly modified and the Mid-Wales Development Board set out to double the size of Newtown to 11,000 and to build office and factory units throughout the towns and larger villages within the region. Seventy thousand people would have made a huge alteration to public and private transport in the area. The original new town concept at Milton Keynes had a monorail system but American consultants preferred the concept of private motoring. No doubt, the Caersws internal transport would have been influenced by the same political choice. The male redundancies were tempered by older men accepting retirement, younger men transferring to other areas of railway operation or obtaining work within construction such as the Clywedog dam and the building of new housing and factories. The textile design company of Laura Ashley was also rapidly expanding with a wide range of work at Carno until closure around 2003. The result is that the village of Caersws remains a bouyant community with a wide range of job opportunities, although many necessitate commuting by car both to and from the village.

Visitors to Montgomeryshire would think of Montgomery and Machynlleth as the important heritage towns with Welshpool, Llanidloes, Newtown and Llanfyllin also with much of value. Caersws could have been this gem if both the Roman *vicus*/fort and the medieval centre had survived.

Horses, the railway and the Upper Severn Valley

Written documentation is rare and therefore some deductions follow from oral memory. A huge length of open hill of Rhydd Hywel runs from Penstrowed to Tylwch much within the parish of Llandinam. The rector of Llandinam would place his bike on the train at Llandinam and then cycle back from Tylwch through New Chapel etc. visiting the isolated parishioners of the hill farms. The area now is the site of a large wind farm. The freeholders in the 18th and early 19th century had grazing rights that included ponies. The result was that a very hardy strain of an almost feral pony developed. The weaned foals were selected and placed in the cattle docks at Llandinam. They were loaded in cattle wagons and transported to South Wales to be trained as pit ponies. Many farmers kept brood mares. The county became well known for the quality of horses for cavalry and road transport. This business was so substantial that the horse repository was sited alongside the railway at Newtown. There are many photographs of farmers proudly standing beside a stud stallion or horses in harness or at a ploughing match but there are few at one of the railway stations.

Ron Jones recalls the GWR horses and therefore almost certainly the Cambrian. The use of horse transport from railway stations and sidings increased rapidly after 1860s. There was no huge urban complex so no large stables developed. He can certainly recall stables at Oswestry, Newtown and Aberystwyth and there may be others. The Newtown stables was close to the Dolfor bridge and there were still about four horses for both wagons and parcels at Newtown in 1946 but they were rapidly replaced by lorries. Jack Jones, the carter chargehand, became a lorry driver. The horses and wagons were owned by the railway. The smaller towns had the service contracted out to a local carrier and his wagons and van would have carried the Cambrian/GWR signwriting. Examples may have been Llanidloes, Builth, Porthmadoc, etc. Ron did not know the Caersws system but the villages had a carrier on an *ad hoc* basis to bring in and take out

Right: The Cambrian Railways goods staff at Newtown (1904) that included the carter, J. Bumford, with the horse. One of the Newtown horses was used for a very short experiment by the GWR around 1924. Planks and slates were placed between the two rails of the first bridges on the Van line. One man was required to move a full wagon with the Newtown horse from Caersws to Trewythen, Red House or Pwllglas sidings. Distance and gradient was considered too much for the poor horse (and the carter?).   *County Times*

Below: A cider press in operation at Red House, just east of Moat Lane Junction, in 1943. There was a considerable tradition of cider orchards in the county. The four-wheel waggon would be typical of what would have been taken to the local sidings to take coal back for the visit of the threshing drum and traction engine. Red House farm hosts a trotting race event every June. Trotting has a strong tradition in both Caersws and Tregaron (beside the old Manchester & Milford branch) and the meetings have very good support.   *Montgomeryshire Express*

Below right: Neville Smout sits on the horse. The load is near the now demolished Waterlow overbridge between Moat Lane and Llandinam. Dan Jones is at the front and Dic Lewis (Moat Lane to Tylwch ganger and father of Maldwyn and Dannie) stands behind. Neville dates this as 1941.   *Neville Smout, Newtown*

goods. There was no collection or delivery service from Moat Lane as it was a purely a railway exchange junction. The GWR introduced the so called 'Country' lorry in the 1920s, for example at Montgomery and Four Crosses. These worked from the towns or larger villages only. The smaller sidings therefore were mainly used for full wagons only from about 1930. This would be such items as coal, lime, bricks and stone in bulk with slag, livestock feeds in bags from vans and farm machinery on flats. Agricultural merchants traded from Caersws, Llandinam and Pontdolgoch. Farmers were advised that 10 tons of lime had arrived and they had two days to unload or face a levy called demurrage. This was always a subject of contention. There are several photographs of Montgomery station showing the heavy four-wheel wagons at the sidings and horse and trap for passengers. No horse picture has been located at Caersws station.

Station buildings and other features around Caersws

Caersws railway station including the station master's house is now Grade II listed (Cadw Ref. 54/46/277). The Newtown to Machynlleth line was completed in 1862. The station is dated as 1864 and this is coincides with the formation of the Cambrian Railways. It is a single-storey station with attached two-storey house. It has been listed as one of the few preserved rural stations from the early years of the Cambrian Railways.

The adjacent signal box (Cadw Ref. 54/46/277) was completed in 1862. It must therefore be assumed that there was a temporary station for two years. It is listed as a well-preserved example of a 'C19', one of only two preserved in Britain. It has a corrugated roof. Entrance is from the platform up steps to a lean-to hooded porch. It retains the levers and lever frame of Dutton type '1' manufactured between 1888 and 1892 when the box was modernized. It was the final remaining example where the signal box was retained for use by the crossing keeper until gate barrier automation in 2010.

Lynn Jones recalls

Lynn Jones recalls the days after he married Barbara née Rowlands when Barbara's mother moved to the keeper's cottage at Weeg to look after the gates in 1967. Dad was suffering ill health and could no longer work on a local farm. The aerial photograph (p.33) shows the well kept garden including an extra piece on the south side of the track. This was father-in-law's work. He also built some pig pens. Mum looked after the gates until automation around 1985. Lynn and Barbara would often call. The shed by the gate was used by the relief keeper if Mrs Rowland was away. The Milk Marketing Board bulk milk lorry is about to cross the gates on farm collection duties. These tankers were based at Cilcewydd depot close to the sidings and bridge complex near Welshpool.

Lynn worked for British Railways at Newtown station from 1956 to 1962. He started in the goods yard where up to 50 wagons would come in or leave on one train. A major source of business was the Phillips cycle factory with components coming in and complete bikes leaving. Wool to Bradford and livestock after sales was important. Finished goods for Woolworths and Pryce Jones came in covered wagons. Pryce Jones mail delivery items left in the parcels sections of the passenger services. Coal, animal feeds and building materials came into the correct wharf. There was an unofficial extra duty to clean the guard's van and ensure the fire was stoked for the grand sum of one Woodbine (cigarette) from Ewart Thomas who was soon to retire. Lynn regrets that he did not accept Ewart's offer to have a trip up the Kerry line in the final few weeks of operation.

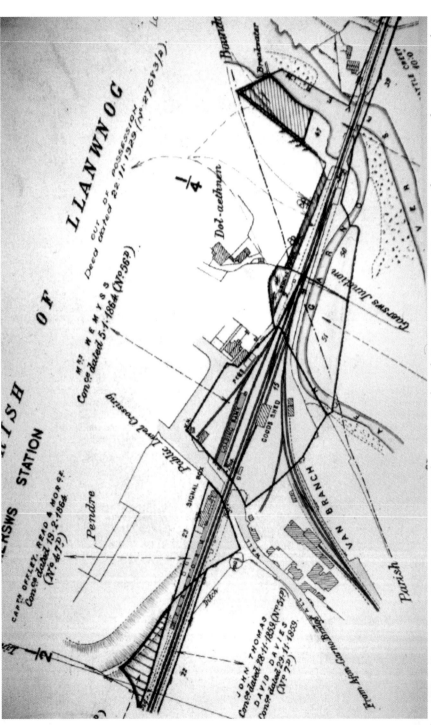

The asset transfer map from Cambrian to GWR, 1924. The second line through Caersws station is a siding only so the GWR must have converted this to a passing loop. All goods services are east of the level crossing. Coal and bulk wharves plus cattle docks were on the north side while the goods shed looped back on to the through line. The merchants store on the south siding has yet to be built. The Van branch buildings were fully utilized by the Bridge Department by this date. Parts of the Roman wall have been shaded in.

National Library of Wales

The total station complex is shown with the signal box to the fore. Note that part of the groove on the lifted loop can still be seen within the tarmac, July 1994.   *Brian Hutton, Birmingham*

Arthur Aldridge was one of six local boys, five of whom joined the railway. His father and uncle worked for the Cambrian and his grandfather was the senior driver on the Van line from 1871 onwards. This *circa* 1985 picture shows the station with part of the station master's house. The platform front is set back under the canopied slate roof. Ornate bargeboards have been retained. The gable wall shows bull-nosed rubble. This could be from from Penstrowed quarry. The interior contains the original panelled partition, the four-panelled door to the waiting room, the original benches and stop-chamfered beam.   *Arthur Aldridge/Vivian Bradley Collection*

Dennis Jones was made redundant along with many others in 1965 when Buttington to Whitchurch closed and most rural stations shut down. He returned to the railway in the late 1970s as gate crossing keeper. This would include relief at Caersws. He is stepping down from the lean-to hooded porch. *Dennis Jones, Abermule*

Left: The setting-down post for the token so that the 'Cambrian Coast Express' did not have to stop. This was obsolete from 1967 onwards. *Right:* The token is exchanged as signalman Fred Rees hands a token to the dmu driver on 13th November, 1975. This token was now Caersws to Newtown as Moat Lane West was now part of history. *(Both) Brian Hutton, Birmingham*

The up view from the platform shows the closed gates with the goods shed on same site as the Roman baths. The junction to the Van and the Bridge Department can be discerned behind the shed. Dennis Jones recalls that the lengthmen not only looked after the track and boundaries but also greased the gates hinges, bolts etc., plus greasing of signals, siding ground frames and all connection rods and wire cables and a visual inspection of the telephone (ex-telegraph) system.

David Hall, Manafon

The Weeg level crossing between Caersws and Pontdolgoch. *Lynn Jones, Newtown*

Many stations were opened for business by the pre-Cambrian companies using temporary facilities. The masonry, bricks and mortar followed several years afterwards. This is Llandinam station in 1859.   *Jeremy Pryce, Llandinam*

A postcard from the Edwardian period shows Llandinam station during its heyday with three staff including John Woosnam, the station master.   *Emrys Davies, Caersws*

Lynn was promoted to be one of the lorry drivers. One of the duties was to collect and load crated milk delivered from Central Dairies of Newtown into wagons attached to passenger trains for delivery to the coast. There were nine vehicles working from Newtown and they would also call into Caersws and Carno. Their work was to collect and deliver parcels including luggage in advance. Small drops of less than 5 cwt were delivered on behalf of the feed compounders to farms. Larger loads were delivered by the port compounder's* own vehicles. Lynn would cover relief duties from both Montgomery and Llanidloes. Any rare call at Moat Lane Junction was only ever with an internal railway item. Lynn continued his working life as a lorry driver for a company called Woodhouse. John Woodhouse purchased sleepers from the contractor lifting the Mid-Wales line in 1963. Lynn would collect these at Builth Road yard and deliver loads to local farmers who were using them to make side retaining walls for silage pits.

Crossing gates with siding, station, signal box and token exchange such as Abermule, Carno and Caersws were usually manned by men. There were several gates across some of the busier minor roads where there was a crossing keeper's cottage. These were often staffed by a lady who was often the wife of a ganger, signalman, etc., so there must have been a very favourable rent or free accommodation. Two examples were the Weeg and Old Moat Lane.

The railway in Llandinam

Llandinam covers a very large geographical area. Much of this area is high sheep walks with the additional modern land use of a large wind farm. This large parish contained the following access to railways and they are all now in the past tense. They were as follows: Moat Lane Junction, Old Moat Lane, Llandinam, Dolwen, Trewythen Sidings on the Van Line and Tylwch and Glanyrafon Halt south of Llanidloes. The only concentrated settlement was at the village of Llandinam centred around the church of St Llonio. Many local men were to find employment within the railway industry and examples follow in later chapters. The station received good passenger support including secondary schoolchildren travelling to Llanidloes. Goods facilities included a coal wharf, a public weighbridge, cattle dock and ramp, a railway workers' hut as well as the station master's house and passengers facilties. Timber and livestock would be loaded out and this would include ponies loaded into cattle trucks. The station was the local centre for groceries, lime, coal, fertiliser and building materials so the station yard would have been full with horses and wagons until the use of the lorry commenced in the inter-war period.

Pontdolgoch

Pontdolgoch is the first station after Caersws on the original Newtown & Machynlleth Railway. It served the small hamlet of Pontdolgoch with a mill and inn, Clatter with a primary school and chapel and was the nearest walk from Llanwnog. Children from Llanwnog who had a scholarship walked to Pontdolgoch with their season ticket for Newtown grammar schools rather than the longer distance to

---

* Port compounders made complete livestock feed with this area supplied from Birkenhead and Liverpool. They crushed oil seed for cooking oil and margarine and used the high protein residue to mix with imported maize, wheat and wheatings, etc., from flour milling. Companies such as Levers, Silcocks, Bibbys, etc., sold direct from local goods yards. The millers shed, on stilts, made from prefabricated concrete from Southern Region, Exmouth Junction still stands at Caersws.

Above: The railway bridge across the Severn at Llandinam was demolished soon after the line was lifted around 1969. There are numerous photographs of this bridge as focus was easy from the adjoining Penson/Davies road bridge. This bridge took much river flood punishment over the century. The replacement pier needed in the final years of operation is the third in from the west (left) bank.

David Hall, Manafon

Right: Two railway staff, Peter Poole and Ken Jones, lived in the Llandinam station house for a short period after the station closure. Peter and Ruth had lived in the flat above the refreshment room at Moat Lane Junction. Peter lived at Llandinam in 1965 for a short period when he was the final clerk at Caersws. He stands with his then two young children. The level crossing gates behind were now operated by the guard and fireman of the Clywedog cement train.

Peter Poole, Caersws

Caersws. Both Llanwnog and Clatter 'all age schools' would have educated young future railwaymen between 1870 and 1946. The area also served many isolated upland and hill farms.

Traffic started to increase in the late Victorian period. Trains could be held in the loop at Moat Lane Junction and Carno. Caersws was then served by a single through line parallel to a long siding. This siding was converted into a loop by 1900 and shortened by five chains by the GWR *circa* 1924. There was enough space dug for a loop at Pontdolgoch and a loop/siding was used to hold freight but there were problems with the gradient and wagon runaway towards Moat Lane. The down crossing loop was converted to a siding (stop blocks at the Caersws end) by 1885. The signal box became a ground frame in 1889, although a new signal box was opened on 2nd November, 1891 in connection with the installation of a new facing connection from the former down loop to the goods yard. The signal box was disused by 1923. The Newtown & Machynlleth intermediate stations have a double-storey for the station master's house while the Llanidloes & Newtown Railway stations have a single-storey. The gradient commences just after the Weeg crossing and is continuous but with variations of grade to Talerddig summit. A further loop was installed on 26th June, 1914 by the Cambrian west of Pontdolgoch and became known as the Clatter loop; the signals were disconnected out of season. The small signal box and tokens were normally only used on peak Saturdays from about 1934 onwards as more powerful locomotives could cover the distance without too much delay. There is a tale that it was to be used for a Royal Train around 1954 until the train path plan showed that it was no longer in use (the box closed on 30th March, 1952). Pontdolgoch station had one staff member and some details follow later within the narrative of Olwen Bound and Derek Llewelyn. The sidings were taken out of use in 1964 and the station closed in 1965 and is now a well looked after private residence. The station was well supported until the early 1950s.

Penstrowed quarry siding and internal tramways

This rail facility less than two miles east of Moat Lane Junction is almost forgotten. Several now elderly children of the quarry workers of 1920s and 1930s, plus archives of the Penstrowed Sub Committee, have helped to create details of what was the largest roadstone quarry owned by Montgomeryshire County Council. There was no quarry at the time of enclosures around 1815. A quarry for masonry was opened at the foot of the hill close to the turnpike and the future Llanidloes & Newtown Railway and operated in volume from about 1830 to 1890. It is now hidden midst mature trees. Thomas Penson, surveyor and road bridge builder, recommended Penstrowed stone where possible. Penson gave David Davies his first contract for the road bridge over the Severn at Llandinam. It is likely that local rail bridge abutments, etc., came from this source. Further research may produce a definite yes or no, but it is more likely to remain as maybe. What is now known as the lower quarry was opened by the Gregynog Estate around 1870 to take on supply of masonry stone as the first quarry approached exhaustion. This small quarry was purchased by the county council in 1894 with the aim of producing 1,500 tons of roadstone per annum for local class I roads. The small quarry had small cuttings into the face following the hard masonry stone seams that were easy to cleft. The council harvested all stone on the face including the shattered rock for roadstone by-passed by the masonry harvest.

The county installed an incline tramway, stone crushers, etc. Demand increased rapidly and further purchases of land was necessary as the quarry extended. The road

Pontdolgoch station around closure in 1965. The line is heading towards Carno. Note the extra platform width that was the site of the second loop/siding in the 1880s.

Elwyn V. Jones Collection, Newtown Library

This aerial photograph of Pontdolgoch dates from the late 1940s. The siding for delivery of farm products from the ports such as maize, wheat and complete livestock feeds is still in place. There was another siding for coal. Les George (of E. George & Sons) only has a young child's memory of the siding but his great-grandfather made use of this facilty in the 1880s to expand from flour milling to an agricultural merchant. The remains of the leat and mill pond are to the left of the taller building where the mill wheel was placed.   *Les George, Pontdolgoch*

The 'Cambrian Coast Express', hauled by 'Manor' class 4-6-0 No. 7818 *Granville Manor*, has just passed the curve that hides the Clatter loop and the engine is about to cross a small bridge over a side stream on a steep gorge that falls from Plasauduon. Such short streams are often dry but can quickly turn into a torrent during heavy rainfall.   *Cambrian Railway Museum, Oswestry*

The former signal box of the Clatter loop is somewhere under the ivy in May 2007. Note the upper arch of the window frame that is a frequent feature of the base of Cambrian signal boxes. This box and loop was used only for peak summer traffic and sat halfway between Moat Lane and Carno. It was staffed by one of the local signalmen, often from Moat Lane on an overtime basis. The upper part of the signal box was removed and the base re-roofed as a ganger's hut.   *Author*

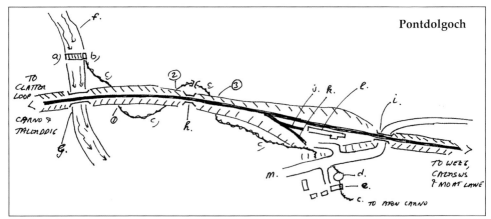

Above: The map details have been taken from the GWR asset transfer map dated 1923 held in the National Library at Aberystwyth.

Key:
a Weir
b Sluice gate
c Leat and culverts 1, 2 & 3
d Mill pond
e Corn mill and water wheel
f Afon Carno
g Weir river bridge No. 176
h Henblas cattle creep No. 175
i Aberystwyth underbridge No. 174
j Coal siding
k Provender mill siding
l Pontdolgoch station
m Main road, Machynlleth to Caersws.

Right: Mrs Freda Griffith, née Jones, on World War II service at Pontdolgoch, checks freight wagons.
Newtown Local History Group

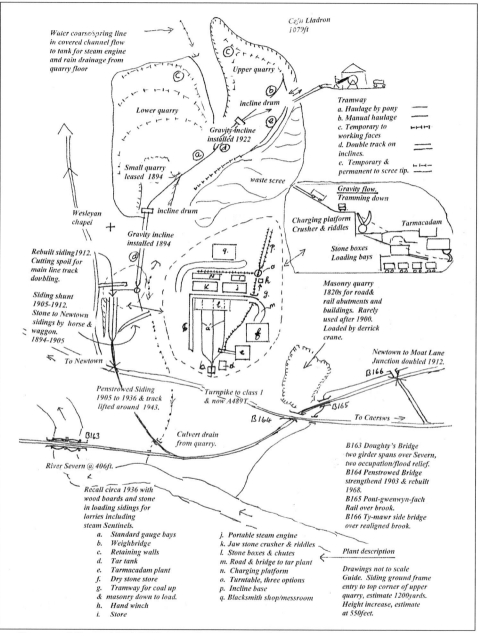

Penstrowed Quarry (1894-1950) was a classic Victorian/Edwardian design of transport and plant for a hillside quarry. This map shows the quarry as it would have been in the 1930s. Drawn by the author with guidance from the now elderly children of the quarry staff, plus drawings and narrative of the quarry at Powys Archives.

The Penstrowed quarry workforce. No details are given. No one can recall any of the young men that joined the quarry on demobilization in 1919. It must be assumed that the photograph dates before 1914. The front row, second in on the right, may be John Brown who was promoted to site manager in the 1920s. The rock face behind would be suitable for both masonry and roadstone. *Powys County Council Archives, Llandrindod Wells. M/X/182/4*

View looking down into the Upper Quarry, *circa* 1935. The head of the drum for the upper incline is in the middle left, the tramway track can be followed past a pile of masonry stone where a tram is parked. Two wheelbarrows and two men wait. The level track to the waste scree tip is in the foreground. The fence was realigned on several occasions as the quarry expanded. Richard, Nancy's father, was a rockman and would have worked on an rope and bosun chair on the overhang drilling so that explosives could be placed. *Nancy Francis*

Ladies climb the lower incline at Penstowed on a Sunday from the chapel for a picnic *circa* mid-1920s. The view shows the double track with the roller guides for the haul steel ropes and the corrugated roof of the engine shed (*to the right of the incline base and partially hidden by trees*) as well as the base turntable and the bridge for stone to cross the tramway to the tarmacadam plant. The rail siding is not clear.   *David Pugh, Newtown*

Delivery from the quarry started to switch from rail to road as the web of roads with a weight bearing base increased. J. Peter Jones was a major contractor and had both a Robey and a Foden high speed tractor on pneumatics hauling four-wheel trailers holding 12 tons plus from around 1928 onwards. Sid Williams was the son of Penstrowed quarryman, Albert. Rigid-framed vertical boiler Sentinel steam lorries started to be used from 1935. Sid became the junior stoker and he and his driver would collect Rhayader quarry granite grit delivered by rail to Llanidloes, Dolwen and Caersws sidings in 1938/39.   *Gordon Lloyd, Newtown*

Scafell station looking towards Caersws. The original line was by the platform and had just been lifted in 1963. Snow remains on the roof where the slates are in the shade and cooler.

Elwyn V. Jones Collection, Newtown Library

The Haynes Family at Scafell. The two seated figures are Granny Haynes, station and siding duties, and Grandad Haynes, Moat Lane to Newtown ganger. The now older children are, *from left to right*, Eddie, Sally, Bernice, Joe, Mary, Susie and John. Joe was the only one to join the GWR. He became an engine driver at Shrewsbury and the West Midlands. *Ann Evans, Mochdre*

surface building took from 1895 until the final smaller lanes were metalled in the 1950s. A road in 1898 would have a bottom layer of unbroken stone, then a build up of layers of graded stone topped with a fine grit. Each layer was slowly traversed with a steam roller. The use of the car and lorry with faster speeds from 1910 would raise summer dust and a fine droplets of slurry in winter. The original 'macadam' then was surfaced to become 'tarmacdam' as these roads were metalled.

Stone was hauled to Newtown station by horse and wagon and caused some congestion. Both the Cambrian Railways and the county council considered that a siding was desirable in 1899 and increasing demand changed this to essential so the siding was built in 1903. Stone haulage was around 4,000 tons in 1904 and increased to 8,000 tons with the first full year of siding operation in 1906. The head of the siding was redesigned in 1912 within a large cutting so that most material flowed by gravity from the rock face until the final chute into the rail wagon. A full internal tramway system expanded including two drum-controlled gravity inclines. Much of this equipment came from the local foundries of Mills of Llanidloes and Turners of Newtown. The stone crusher was made by Baxters of Leeds and the portable steam engine was Ruston & Hornsby, replaced by a Marshall in the 1930s. A tarmacadam plant was installed for asphalt production but was marginal on both economic and quality performance.

So stone started to be delivered from 1905 to local sidings such as Abermule, Dolwen, Llanidloes, Carno, etc., plus Kerry and the Van sidings. A 1910 record records masonry stone for road bridges to be delivered to Llanbrynmair and Cemmaes Road. Delivery by road started to increase after 1920 and the siding facility was withdrawn in 1936 and lifted in 1943. Only coal was delivered in about once per month in the final year. The quarry closed in 1950. It was re-opened in 1965 by a private consortium to use the scree for grant aided farm roads. The Mid-Wales Development from 1967 led to major local requirements for base core stone for factories, access roads and housing estates. The quarry is a site for a construction company in 2008.

Scafell station

The only station built between Moat Lane Junction and Newtown was placed on the land north of the River Severn between two substantial underbridges called Doughty's and Sgafell Road. It is within the township of Hendidley (Hendy-dylife means homestead by the torrent). This is the western township of Llanllwchaiarn of Newtown north of the Severn. Ysgafell means ridge and Sca Fell in the Lake District may be from the same Brythonic derivation. There were and still are only a few farmsteads. People further to the east would walk to Newtown and the people of the nearest settlement at Aberhafesp would walk to Caersws or cross the footbridge over the Severn built around 1887 to Moat Lane Junction. The station was not on the first timetables of the Llanidloes & Newtown Railway in 1859 and a service started in 1863. A siding was placed there and had to be shunted by the up train from Moat Lane. Some timetables show passenger stops only on Tuesdays and Saturdays and the service ceased in 1891. The station was called Scafell. The station opened again on 9th June, 1913, soon after the line was doubled in 1912. No platform was placed on the down side and this has led to the story that one could only catch an up train. The 1923/24 timetable showed only two up trains calling (on request) and the station was not even listed in the Index of Stations.

Ann Evans, née Roberts, was the daughter of Bernice Roberts, née Haynes and Ann recalls visits to the station when she was a small child in the late 1940s. The Haynes lived at Scafell station from around 1905 to 1950. Grandad was a lengthman and then

Les Bradley, on the right, surveys the damage on Dulais bridge in the immediate period after the June 1936 cloudburst. The tall man on the left is one of the Freeman brothers, again from the Caersws Bridge Department. Vertical sleepers were placed with a steel span so a single line was in place within the week. The stumps of the temporary piles can still be observed in 2007.

Vivian Bradley, Caersws

Caersws Bridge Department making progress on the new bridge at the Dulais/Severn confluence in November 1936. The bridge of vertical abutments and steel girders is rapidly being assembled. The Vaynor occupation bridge is in the background and the men and the crane are just in front of the Vaynor cattle creep. The temporary bridge needed provision near Ysgafell for signalmen with two signals either side of the damage plus ground frames and a token needed to travel the 200 yards of single line.

Montgomeryshire Express

the ganger between Newtown and Moat Lane. He retired around 1938 but continued to live as a pensioner in the GWR house. Granny looked after any goods up to about 1940 and any passengers. The goods were an occasional full wagon of coal, bricks, stone, lime or slag for collection and some timber may have been loaded.

There was a small portable steps and handrail for any passenger alighting or setting down on the down side with no platform. The passenger service was used by the Haynes children that passed the scholarship. There were eight children, one sadly drowned in the Severn. Only the children that passed to the grammar school had a season ticket, the others had to walk to the boarding school.

The only group of houses with any traffic potential was on the southern bank of the Severn. Ann would walk from Glan Dulais Grove along the bank of the Dulais under a cattle creep and then cross the Severn to Scafell station on the footpath bolted on to the Scafell bridge. There was a large country house called Glan Hafren. The Lewis family were great entertainers in the early 1900s. One of their frequent guests and a close friend was J.M. Barrie, the author of *Peter Pan*, *The Admirable Crichton* and other works. He would get down, with granny having arranged to have the steps ready, and then walk across the bolted footbridge. Meurig Mostyn of Scafell Cottage recalls that the up train stopped about eight in the morning but the stopper used on return with a request to the guard was about 7.30 in the evening. Most people returned on the bus that passed the siding at about half-past four in the afternoon. Meurig's father had a special pass to walk across the Doughty's bridge as he was a quarryman at Penstrowed quarry. Ron Jones recalled that any passenger in the late 1940s would board the train at Scafell and purchase their ticket at Newtown booking hall. Although last used by the public in 1952, the station did not officially close until 7th March, 1955.

The adjoining Dulais bridge was swept away in a flood in 1936. Edward Haynes, ganger, and his daughter had observed the huge cloud building up over the Dolfor Hills and the torrential rain. They both walked over the Ysgafell and Dulais bridges as the cloudburst started to ease. Suddenly a complete tree, roots trunk and branches swept down and crashed into the Dulais masonry so that the stones just disappeared into the swirling water leaving the metal tracks and sleepers suspended. Edward immediately instructed Bernice to hurry east to Newtown signal box. Edward crossed the Dulais road bridge that would soon close. The Aberystwyth excursion could proceed no further. The mail train was held at Moat Lane. Communications could continue between the two signal boxes as the telegraph/telephone lines were still intact. The national press took on the story and it became a little exaggerated including a version that Bernice had ripped off her red skirt to attract attention and halt the train that had already left Newtown. Both Edward and Bernice certainly helped to prevent a potential railway accident.

Bernice became a schoolteacher in the mid-1930s and had a motorbike. She was to go a friend's wedding so she went on the motorbike to Moat Lane Junction and changed into her finery in the ladies waiting room prior to travelling south. Somehow she managed to jam the lock and had to shout for help. Ann has several documents dating from the 1920s and 1930s including an invoice when grandad hired a Cookson's taxi to take someone to Moat Lane on behalf of the GWR. Another is for day-old chicks to be collected at Newtown. The halt had a very frail economic need and the Haynes may have been the final railway family to live in the house. Both grandparents were very keen gardeners. Ann can remember an immaculate allotment, beautiful roses set along the platform plus chicken and a pigsty. The station still stands and is now a private home alongside the now single track.

Gordon's father, Fred, eases the Sentinel over the emergency lattice steel bridge on the class 1 road. This was the weight test. The flash flood had damaged one of the then two masonry arches. The Roman road and ford is situated between the rail and road bridge over the Dulais river.   *Gordon Howells, Guilsfield*

Dulais signal box stood for about six months with token, flags and signals, to control the single line temporary bridge. Bernice Haynes has dressed up in GWR attire. She would not have been permitted to operate the system. Porter-signalmen from either Newtown or Moat Lane worked the box.   *Ann Evans, Mochdre*

DULAIS SIGNAL BOX.

Chapter Three

Moat Lane Junction

The origin of the station name is contained within the Moat Lane. The lane leads to an intact motte and bailey maybe less than half a mile from the junction station. The Moat was fully described in the 'The Montgomeryshire Papers' in the late 1860s soon after the station was opened. The camp has three distinct parts. The first is the high conical circular mound with a surrounding fosse to the south. There is an almost rectangular closure to the north with remains of ramparts and an outer ditch. The site is then split with a lane and the modern Moat Farm. The larger field towards the railway still has boundaries marked as low embankments. Such moats are associated with the Norman period as part of a defence system. It is considered that the site was a post-Roman Celtic camp where the Welsh pastoralists had a meeting point for trading. The building would have been of wood. The site has a view over the flood plain of the Caersws area so it would easy to understand why the Normans reused the site. So Moat Lane has been part of a communications system long before the advent of the railway. Thomas Pennant (Tour of Wales) visited the site in the late 1700s. It was reputed that 'D.K. 1796' was engraved in one of the stones in the farm house. This refers to a David Kinsey. The name of Kinsey is within details of of land transfer in the early 1860s between the land owner, contractor David Davies and the railway companies. The field areas adjoining the Moat were the traditional scene of a Welsh tribal battle between the men of Merioneth and Ceredigion. The feud was healed by one of the daughters of the tribal leader called Galena. Galena is the technical word for lead ore so one ponders any connection between this lass and the lead deposits in the area. The first railway bridge between Moat Lane and Newtown is an accommodation overbridge leading to Bron-felin where there is a second smaller moat.

The Moat area has a history of the movement of a valued commodity. One could have looked down from the Moat to the junction in the 1930s and 1940s and observed a Dean pannier (ex-saddle tank) heading east with cattle wagons. The pannier tank was used for the Kerry branch goods but, on Mondays, it worked the stopping livestock service at each station with cattle docks taking cattle and sheep for auction at Welshpool Fatstock. The lorry quickly took all this trade as the fuel shortage eased in the early 1950s.

There are names that give a clue to livestock movement before the railway. This area would have witnessed drovers moving their stock towards one of the main exit routes of the Kerry Ridgeway. The trade increased with the urbanization and growth of large cites such as Birmingham. There are several isolated houses above the Moat towards the then open moorland now called Little London but earlier references are Llundain Vach. This almost certainly refers to a jest from drovers who had a long way to walk to Llundain Vawr. The broad route climbs and passes Cefn Lladron. Lladron refers to thieves suggesting a place of skullduggery where rustling was a risk on the 'up' journey and purses could be snatched on the 'down' return. This problem caused two early banks based at Llandovery and Aberystwyth to issue the earliest of cheques. The farm just above the junction is called Porth-gwibedyn. Porth is a gateway such as a start to a new section of a route. Gwibedyn indicates a swarm of gnats and small flies. Anyone who has ever herded cattle on a sultry late summer day will understand the problem of a plague of flies. The railway quickly gained this

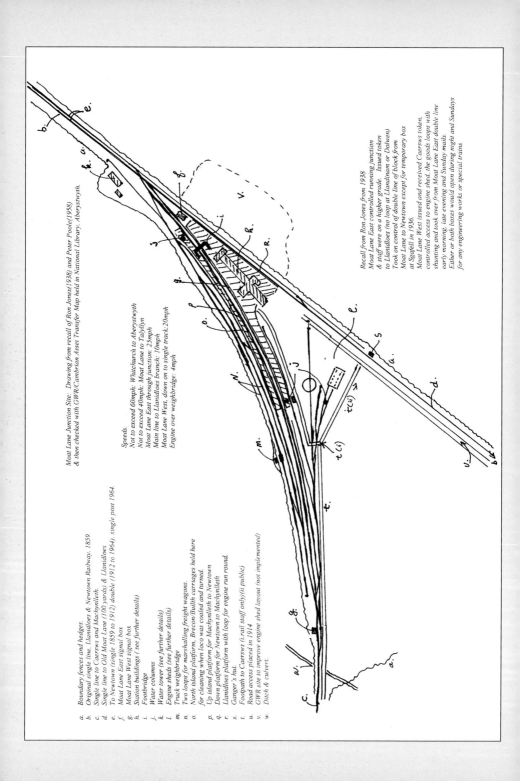

Moat Lane Junction Site: Drawing from recall of Ron Jones (1938) and Peter Poole (1958) & then checked with GWR/Cambrian Asset Transfer Map held in National Library, Aberystwyth.

Speeds
Not to exceed 60mph: Whitchurch to Aberystwyth
Not to exceed 40mph: Moat Lane to Talyllyn
Moat Lane East through junction: 25mph
Main line to Llanidloes branch: 10mph
Moat Lane West, down on to single track: 20mph
Engine over weighbridge: 4mph

a. Boundary fences and hedges.
b. Original single line, Llanidloes & Newtown Railway, 1859
c. Single line to Caersws and Machynlleth.
d. Single line to Old Moat Lane (100 yards) & Llanidloes
e. To Newtown (single 1859 to 1912) double (1912 to 1964), single post 1964.
f. Moat Lane East signal box
g. Moat Lane West signal box
h. Station buildings (see further details)
i. Footbridge
j. Water columns
k. Water tower (see further details)
l. Engine sheds (see further details)
m. Track weighbridge
n. Two loops for marshalling freight wagons.
o. North island platform, Brecon/Builth carriages held here for cleaning when loco was coaled and turned.
p. Up island platform for Machynlleth to Newtown
q. Down platform for Newtown to Machynlleth
r. Llanidloes platform with loop for engine run round.
s. Ganger's hut.
t. Footpath to Caersws (i. rail staff only)(ii public)
u. Road access placed in 1914
v. GWR site to improve engine shed layout (not implemented)
w. Ditch & culvert.

Recall from Ron Jones from 1938
Moat Lane East controlled running junction & staff were on a higher grade. Issued token to Llanidloes (no loop at Llandinam or Dolwen) Took on control of double line of block from Moat Lane to Newtown except for temporary box at Sgafell in 1936.
Moat Lane West issued and received Caersws token, controlled access to engine shed, the goods loops with shunting and took over from Moat Lane East double line early morning, late evening and Sunday mails. Either or both boxes would open during night and Sundays for any engineering works or special trains

trade (cattle not flies) from the early 1870s and many a cattle wagons would have been marshalled through Moat Lane with staff trained to load, inspect and water the beasts in transit.

The first railway building was a station owned by the Llanidloes & Newtown Railway, opened on 2nd September, 1859. It was called Maesmawr in the first proposal but appears on the 1859 timetable as Moat Lane with four trains calling each way. It sometimes appears as Caersws or Moat Lane for Caersws. It will now be referred to by the current local name of 'Old Moat Lane'. Its working life as a station was just over four years before being replaced on 5th January, 1863 by Moat Lane Junction necessary for the Newtown & Machynlleth Railway. Why did a railway company build a station with such a short working life? No local research gives an adequate answer but deduction may be possible. Although the Llanidloes & Newtown Railway opened in isolation, it was also within other projected systems when proposed in the early 1850s. A number of smaller companies were to provide track facilities and running rights for the Manchester & Milford Railway with Llanidloes as a focal point. Two proposed routes to Aberystwyth would have continued on from Llangurig with a junction for a branch to Aberystwyth at either the now terminus of the Vale of Rheidol Railway or at the station of Strata Florida (see *The Mid-Wales Railway* (Oakwood Press) for details of this complicated story). The lead mines may have had some influence with potential traffic on these routes with greater gradients and engineering requirements. There was also another approach to the coast on what was to become the Ruabon to Barmouth GWR route. The proposed LNWR route from Shrewsbury, via Criggion, Welshpool, Newtown and on to Machynlleth and Aberystwyth was not passed by Parliament in 1853 when only the Llanidloes to Newtown passed. So the Newtown to Machynlleth plan came on to the scene around 1857 as an alternative and the chosen route. A junction at Newtown was considered with an extension of the Shrewsbury and Newtown route (which ceased at Minsterley) to Machynlleth.

The 1864 timetables show the line to Aberystwyth open with Moat Lane Junction as the only station with five services to Llanidloes and three to and from Aberystwyth plus freight. There was a ferry service from Ynyslas to Aberydovey, Tywyn and Llwyngwril. The station of the now 'Old' Moat Lane became the crossing keeper's cottage for nearly a century. The last keepers were Dinah Lewis, wife of Danny, a Moat Lane porter during the 1950s and Mrs Jones, wife of retired engine driver Reg 'Cwmbelan' for several years until passenger closure at the end of 1962. It makes little difference in time or distance to travel from Newtown to Aberystwyth by road via either Machynlleth or Llanidloes. The current National Express coach route to London travels via Llanidloes.

The late Mr Perry and his wife Doris purchased a section of Old Moat Lane from British Railways in 1966. The railway had made two cottages 100 years previously. The station house became No. 1, Crossing Cottage. Doris lives in No. 2 which is the old booking hall, waiting room, station office, etc. The building from the track/platform looks like a single level but there is a substantial lower ground level on the west side so the huge cellar is also part of No. 2. The foundation is almost certainly Penstrowed coarse rubble wall. The Perrys purchased a ¾ acre triangle so this may have been the area for sidings that never materialized. The tied railway staff moved into Caersws or elsewhere soon after closure in late 1962. Doris has a collection of items dug up from the garden. There are a Mid-Wales Railway and a Llanidloes & Newtown Railway button in corroded condition. There is a brass label for Buttington North. Doris recalls that the families in the two tied cottages were saddened when the main Moat Lane Junction station was stripped and vandalized

Moat Lane staff 1900. *Standing at rear, all left to right*: Arthur Evans, A.E. Mills. *Standing in central row*: George Rogers (wheel examiner), Tom Mills (telegraph clerk), J. Mason (booking clerk), G. Hopper, J. Hughes, D. Davies (all porters) and Richard Evans (wheel examiner). *Seated*: John Jones (guard), Lewis Hamer (signalman and father to Nat), J. Roberts (station master), Thomas Trow and Richard Parry (signalman). *Montgomeryshire Express*

From the collection of the Revd Rokeby, an Anglican priest serving in Galloway and then Norfolk. He would spend his holidays in Wales. His extensive collection contains both his own photography and purchases dating from 1930 to 1950. Pictures of freight movement are not common. The train is coming in from Llanidloes. Note three staff seated on the bench in front of the screen panel of the gents toilet.
Revd Rokeby/Royal Commission on the Ancient & Historical Monuments of Wales, Aberystwyth

through *circa* 1963. This may well have been the reason for demolition. The track has grassed and brambled over. In 1969, just after closure, the ballast was exposed and warm. Lizards would bask every summer day but they have not been seen for many a year.

Moat Lane Junction

Gwyn Briwnant-Jones has written the history of the Newtown & Machynlleth Railway under the title of *Railway through Talerddig*. He states that no reference has yet been discovered relating to the commencement or completion of the junction at Moat Lane. Further local archive research can add little to this quote. The line was supposed to start at Moat Lane but this coincided with the Davies and Savin split and the complex rivalry between the GWR and the LNWR that would lead to such people as Engineer Piercy supporting the concept of the Cambrian Railways. Traffic flow was supposed to start from Moat Lane by January 1860 to Talerddig at the 'tunnel' entrance. The first through timetable was published in January 1863 showing Moat Lane Junction. It is not known if the station was a temporary building with construction to follow. Originally the station was an interchange facility only, but on 31st December, 1865 it was recommended that a public access path be provided. The first engine shed must have been built during the early 1860s and such facilities as the water tower and the first site of the turntable would follow later. The first shed was a single through shed similar to the shed at Builth that closed in 1958. The three locomotives serviced were the overnight freight from Oswestry for early morning return, a similar arrangement with the Brecon passenger service plus a locomotive held at Moat Lane for ballast and other material delivery to site. The twin-gable shed was opened in 1890 after the Cambrian had taken over the Mid-Wales Railway in 1888 when Moat Lane became the main engine shed with Builth relegated to a support role.

The transfer map from the Cambrian to the GWR in 1923 gives some dates. David Davies purchased land from John Pryce Davies dated 19th July, 1860 on the east and north station area with a further purchase on 29th October, 1865 that looks to incorporate the siding area. Land was purchased from Thomas E. Kinsey dated 18th May, 1860, that is the south-west area of the engine shed, etc. Land was purchased from Evan Kinsey for the access road from Old Moat Lane to the station with completion in 1914. A site for turntables and other facilities at Newtown was abandoned but the site can still be discerned close to the Brimmon bridge. Local research is not helped by the fact that the first local weekly paper called the *Welshpool and Newtown Express* did not start until the late 1860s. The junction with freight exchange was certainly well under way with the following notes from the copy of 18th May, 1869. A fatal accident happened at Moat Lane Junction to a porter called Thomas Hunt. Hunt was usually employed at Llanidloes but he was detailed off as a guard of a special goods train. It appears that the unfortunate man leapt off the van to check his train and turned his back on a train behind him with their wagons passing over him. He was killed instantly. The body was carried to the waiting room awaiting inquest. Two other guards, Tomas Griffith and Reese Lloyd, observed that Hunt stepped out just as three shunted trucks were about 16 yards away. The accident took place near the junction box (assumed to be Moat Lane East).

Local documents within Powys County Council Archives relate to agreements on bridges and crossings. The following item relates to road access to Moat Lane

One must assume that this was taken with at a different time from the previous view as the Bovril advertisement is missing from the screen in front of the gents. The new concrete panel footbridge replaced a wooden structure on 21st November, 1935. The track on the left plus the loop was for use of the Llanidloes/Builth and Brecon trains. The coaches on the right would be on an up train from Machynlleth heading to either Buttington Junction for Oswestry or Shrewsbury. The large information board is recalled as 'Moat Lane change for Machynlleth, Aberystwyth, Barmouth and Coast' reflecting the origin from the Newtown & Machynlleth Railway.
Revd Rokeby/Royal Commission on the Ancient & Historical Monuments of Wales, Aberystwyth

The opposite side of the board with the coaches of a southbound train in the platform. There are several similar images in the Caersws locality.   *Don Griffiths*

The 'Cambrian Coast Express' will stop at the water column to take on enough water for the climb to Talerddig. A banker would be attached in the summer months when the coaches increased from seven or eight to up to 14. *Cambrian Railway Society, Oswestry Museum*

Brian Hutton was a staff member of Birmingham Central Grammar School. The school had a camp at Bryn-tail near Llanidloes so the train was used until 1962. Passengers are entering the train at Moat Lane to travel to Llanidloes only on 13th July, 1962. This engine would have been coaled and watered at Llanidloes shed. *Brian Hutton, Birmingham*

Central Grammar School boys change at Moat Lane to travel and change at Shrewsbury and then on to Birmingham Snow Hill on 27th July, 1962. The engine is 'Manor' class 4-6-0 No. 7812 *Erlestoke Manor*. The trolley has taken the luggage from the Llanidloes platform to the up island platform.   *Brian Hutton, Birmingham*

No. 7823 *Hook Norton Manor* eases the up 'Cambrian Coast Express' into Moat Lane so that the tender will stop by the water column on 18th September, 1962. The carriages for the southbound service are being cleaned, hence the bucket. Porter, Brian Wilde, looks toward the train. The lady is talking to the cleaner who can be discerned with his broom handle. A major increase in inter-town gas capacity was taking place in the early 1960s and this may be the explanation for the large pipes held in the siding.   *Brian Hutton, Birmingham*

Junction within a Parliamentary Session in 1896. Access was by train or footpath only for this exchange station set in the middle of the fields. The need for certain internal goods, for some local passengers to come in on their pony and trap plus other services, including in emergency, warranted road access. It was therefore proposed that the company be authorized to construct a road leading from the Newtown-Llanidloes highway at a point 52 miles 59 chains from Whitchurch known as Llanidloes Road level crossing and terminating in the station yard 15 yards from the south-west corner of the workshop. This road was not built. (The map confirms that the original turntable was by the water tower and that the engine shed would later be resited. A further loop siding would be added.) There was a considerable traffic increase both prior and during World War I including maritime steam coal to the fleet at Scapa Flow in the Orkneys. These trains were called 'the Jellicoe specials'.

Negotiations were to take place with E. Kinsey of Maesmawr for both the road site parallel to the footpath and the deviation line (the extra land taken during construction and then restored to be returned to the farm). The road access was built in 1914 from Old Moat Lane and is still in use today for access to the various units that are sited on the old junction.

Several notes were placed in the local papers in 1930. Caersws Rural Council received a letter from the GWR announcing that the road to the junction was a private road for railway business access and not a public road. The public access was by several footpaths. It was suggested that the GWR should erect a notice stating the section that was private. There was also a request from the GWR staff asking that five of the proposed council houses could be allocated to five married Moat Lane staff. These men lived at either Newtown or Llanidloes and they had to cycle in all weathers to start an early morning shift or return after evening shift.

Most of the memories that now follow date from the late 1930s to closure with only traces of earlier stories. There are only a few people in 2012 who have a working knowledge of the junction that closed in 1962. The largest cohort would be that of the young engine cleaners/firemen and they are now pensioners.

Moat Lane Memories

Ron Jones, 1937 to 1939

Ron Jones commenced as junior clerk at Abermule and was moved to Moat Lane after about 12 months. He was based in the booking office but there was not much ticketing to do as 'Remote' Lane Junction was mainly an exchange station and Caersws had the far larger passenger booking potential. Some Caersws villagers would walk to Moat Lane if travelling south on the Mid-Wales line. Some would walk across the Victoria Jubilee footbridge from Aberhafesp. Much of the work was by telegraph from and to the district office in Oswestry with all the connections to Machynlleth, Aberystwyth, Builth and Brecon.

Paybills for wages was another important duty. There was a travelling safe on the passenger trains and this took all the daily takings from every station to Oswestry. The wages were returned with the same security on pay day. There was no freight invoicing at Moat Lane, the nearest coal wharf, cattle docks and goods shed were at Caersws. The only goods unloaded were coal and sand and the only product loaded was ash waste (from the engines).

Ron had to think hard of the number of staff on site. He was then 18 and he suspects he is the only one left. Most jobs required two people as the junction

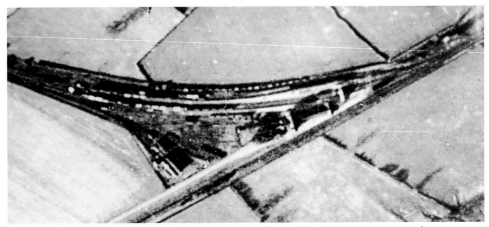

RAF Frame 4001, 9th March, 1948. Enlarged from a photograph taken from 10,000 ft. The engine shed with twin gable roof may have two locomotives parked. There is a freight train in the down curve about to depart towards Machynlleth. Both transfer loops have goods wagons for marshalling. The water tower is to the left, the footbridge and the main station building are clear but Moat Lane East signal box roof is a sun reflection blur. The short road built by the Cambrian from Old Moat Lane in 1914 can be clearly seen. Moat Lane West box is just out of view.

Central Register of Air Photography for Wales, Cardiff

There are very few images of marshalling work on the goods loop. The late Peris Evans, older brother-in-law of Philip, stands as duty shunter with his pole. *Philip Gethin, Caersws*

Peris Evans has a hug on the main down platform to Machynlleth at Moat Lane. The photograph would have been taken from Moat Lane East signal box. Note the sectional footbridge erected by the Bridge Department in 1935, only to have a life span of just over 25 years.

Philip Gethin, Caersws

worked two shifts and cover was also needed for illness etc. There were 25 on the traffic side and this would include signalmen, platform staff, shunters and guards. There were eight sets of drivers and firemen. There would also be train crew coming in from Llanidloes, Builth and Brecon as well as men waiting to return west to Machynlleth and east to Oswestry. There was a carriage & wagon examiner. The engine shed had a chargehand and a coal loader with two or three engine shed cleaners plus several lads just starting their careers. There were two carriage cleaners. There was a gated crossing at Old Moat Lane and this was staffed by the wife of one of the signalmen. There was a chief inspector and his clerk. The station master lived on the premises and was 'the boss'. Finally there were two booking clerks. The refreshment room was staffed by two ladies. This had been an independent business in Cambrian days and continued to be so. However, the ladies were part of the fabric of the 60 plus staff at the station.

Ron would cycle from Newtown and the journey took about 30 minutes. His bike would be parked with many others. The first clerical shift was from 8.00 am to 4.00 pm. The late shift was 12.30 to 8.30 pm or when the last passenger train had cleared if running late. The senior duty porter issued the few tickets for any boarding on the mail/newspaper trains around 5.00 am. The two staff overlapped and this was when duties such as preparation of time sheets and wage envelopes were done. Herbert Evans was called up in late 1939 and Ron did a double shift. He was then moved to Oswestry for a year until he also was called up. Ladies took on the clerical duties for the duration of the war.

There were up to 60 train movements including light engines through the station per day. Summer excursion traffic plus the Saturday holiday exchange must have been close to capacity with the Clatter loop being added. There were several through trains from South Wales such as one from Treherbert (Rhondda) to Aberystwyth and the coaches had to be taken on to the Newtown line beyond Moat Lane East, where they reversed, as there was no south to west junction there. Both the Kerry and the Van branches still operated from the Moat Lane shed. The Kerry branch was worked by the Dean '2021' class (Nos. 2032, 2068 and 2075) already converted from saddle to pannier tank and they were also used for shunting at Moat Lane, Caersws, including the Bridge Department, and Newtown. The Van branch had a light Manning, Wardle, No. 819, plus a rarely used standby, No. 824, for either the branch or the pumping engine. Tender locomotives worked the Mid-Wales line and were either Dean Goods or Cambrian Neilsons as the Beyer, Peacocks were too heavy to work south of Llanidloes. There were additional block freight trains as the war duties commenced and this would include South Wales steam coal to Coleham shed (Shrewsbury) and Crewe freeing other routes for troop movement. Older staff still recalled the World War I 'Jellicoes' working coal to Scapa Flow. There was a daily freight to and from the Tregwn Admiralty store in North Pembroke routed either via Aberystwyth or the Mid-Wales and Central Wales lines via Llandeilo Junction.

The refreshment room was close to the booking office but the office had its own tea brewing facility and men usually brought their own sandwiches. The room had a beer licence and this would be the main reason for most railwaymen (plus local farm staff to visit). There were chocolate vending machines on the platforms. One of the railway staff would have this little franchise and would restock as necessary taking his margin from the accumulated pennies. The same small perk was also at Abermule. [The author recalls that some of the older people of Aberhafesp would recall an Edwardian child's treat walking across the footbridge over the Severn to the station to buy a penny bar of Nestlés chocolate on a Sunday between services.]

Moat Lane East signal box in 1950 with a clear view of the rails of the junction and the water tower. The then recently planted conifers on the right horizon were planted alongside Penstrowed quarry and were clear felled as mature trees around 2004.   *Ron Jones, Newtown*

Ron remembers this Oswestry-based 'Duke' class 4-4-0 No. 3255 *Excalibur* working through both Abermule and Moat Lane to Aberystwyth in the late 1930s. It worked a Llanidloes to Blackpool excursion when Ron was at Moat Lane. The engine was too long to be placed on the Llanidloes turntable. It therefore pulled the empty stock from Oswestry to Llanidloes around 3.00 am. It ran tender first back to Moat Lane to be turned, coaled and watered and then ran tender first back to Llanidloes. Such excursions would leave Llanidloes around 7.00 am to be in Blackpool around 11.00. The departure return would be around 8.00 pm to be at Llanidloes around midnight. Some Moat Lane staff would have to change to an extended 12-hour shift to accommodate such traffic.   *Graham Lloyd, Churchstoke*

Men were paid at a flat rate according to their grade. They would fill in a weekly time sheet that extended to enhancement columns for additional pay to their standard week. This would include 1¼ for ordinary overtime, an additional ¼ enhancement for any hours worked between 10 pm and 6 am whether standard or extra hours and finally 1¾ for Sunday working. This would be for ballast and engineering trains, the Oswestry-Aberystwyth mail and the occasional excursion. Wages came back from Oswestry in bulk so the clerks had to make up the net sum for each individual. The National Insurance stamps had to be purchased and the office held the staff record with their weekly stamps stuck in. The men came to the booking office to collect their wages. A second man had to be in the office with one to act as a witness with the duty clerk. Some men were working away and could not collect for up to several days. The latecomers had to sign the unclaimed wages register to receive their money. Everyone had a uniform or an overall supplied except the clerks. Everyone was paid in 'coins of the realm', no cheques were issued. The local pensioners, including those who had Cambrian Railways service, would call to collect their pension monthly. Most retired to remain within the local area, anyone that moved could collect their pension at their nearest GWR station. Ron could not answer how anyone from Caersws could collect at St Ives, Huntingdonshire but there would be no problem at St Ives, Cornwall!

Staff were entitled to free passes. This would vary from one per annum up to four for those with long service and higher grades. Many could not afford to take a week of holiday so they took day trips. Staff and family (wife and children) could also have a ¼ rate privilege ticket once they had used their train passes. These were not limited in number but an application form had to be countersigned by the station master or other superior officer. This information had to be forwarded to Oswestry for recording.

Ron returned to the GWR after World War II and spent much time working at Newtown until being the senior man on site; station masters had ceased to exist and the area came under Shrewsbury after transfer from the Western Region to the Midland Region. The status of clerical work had altered from pre-war due to a variety of factors. A rural railway job in the earlier part of the century was almost an elite. It was an achievement to get on to the railway ladder at Moat Lane.

An example of an excursion using Moat Lane engines was advertised on 22nd June and took place on Sunday 30th June, 1935. It was from Newtown and surrounding district to Merthyr Vale (4s. 6d.), Abercynon & Pontypridd (5s. 6d.), Cardiff (6s.) and Barry Island (6s. 6d.).

Ray Morris recalls aspects of the railway career of his father
John Morris joined the Cambrian Railways in 1897. He was issued with a pass to attend an interview at Oswestry from Llanfechain station on the Llanfyllin branch. He would have travelled on the newly-opened loop (1896) at Carreghofa. He started as a junior clerk at Llansantffraid, then Oswestry and then Machynlleth. He was moved to Rhayader from 1903 to 1906 to help with clerical duties of the extra traffic on the Elan Valley branch when the fixed equipment was delivered for filter beds, pipes etc. as the dam complex proceeded placing the infrastructure necessary for water flow to Birmingham. Much material was forwarded through Moat Lane. John transferred to Newtown in 1906. Ray is the last surviving child of seven children and spent time with his father in the booking office in the early 1920s. One older brother joined the railway at Pwllheli and then moved to the LMS at Birmingham. Ray has

A train on the run-round loop adjoining the platform to Llanidloes in the 1930s. The train is headed by a 'Dean Goods' locomotive. The porter is in front of Moat Lane East signal box and the first bridge to Bron-felin farm and Motte can be seen in the background.

Olwen Williams, Caersws

A 1930s view of the twin-apex engine shed that would be badly damaged by a storm in the early 1950s. It has two locomotives waiting for, or having received, attention by the cleaners. Coal trucks and ash truck are stabled and the coal on the loading wharf is alongside the track. The left-hand engine is on the turntable pit. The lamps would have been paraffin. Penstrowed Hill is in the background.

Olwen Williams, Caersws

two railway nephews, now retired, with Malcolm at York and Godfrey at Birmingham.

Moat Lane seemed to be part of Dad's language as trains moved west to Moat Lane. Ray can recall the Penstrowed siding with the shunt being timed into the day's work. Dad was on duty on the day of the Abermule accident. The fatalities sadly returned around 4.00 pm to be placed in the station room and dad and a local policeman checked personal property and other details. The Cambrian Director, Vane-Tempest, died at Newtown hospital that evening.

Some of the family would go back to see Nain (granny) at Llanfechain and this would involve a change of train at Llanymynech. Ray may be one of the last who can remember seeing the Ford 'Rattler' railcar operated by the Shropshire & Montgomery Light Railway drawing in from Shrewsbury when he was about five years of age. Moat Lane Junction was an important part of a total system.

Olwen Williams née Bound

Olwen spent her childhood on a small farm on the outskirts of Caersws. Olwen may well be the last local person to have travelled on the Van branch. The children would open the Carnedd gates and hope that Ewart Thomas would offer them a lift in the guard's van. Olwen passed the David Davies Scholarship and therefore travelled daily on the train from Caersws to Newtown between 1935 and 1940. Olwen can remember the track still in place on the Penstrowed Siding. It was of interest to her because grandfather had the contract with horses and waggons to haul stone from the quarry on both short haul work and to Newtown Sidings before the quarry siding was placed in 1903. Her first job was with the mail order company of Pryce Jones at Newtown. She also worked hard at home as wartime Birkenhead evacuees were billeted at the farm.

There was a request from Moat Lane to apply for a vacancy. Olwen was interviewed and accepted the duty of general clerk. There were already two ladies on site and they were Megan Davies (telegraph clerk) and Gwyneira Corfield (clerk to the chief inspector). Soon other ladies came on to site as men were called up. Most were lady porters and included Mrs Evans, the wife of the curate, Miss Beti Jones, Mrs Betty Jones and Mrs Edith Stephenson. Most were made redundant at the end of the war.

Olwen's main duties were booking clerk, telegraph duties using morse code and the paybill for both Moat Lane and Llandinam staff. Olwen was also moved to cover other posts and worked at Caersws, Aberystwyth and was in charge of Pontdolgoch (two staff). Specials were a feature of the wartime traffic and the telegraph section could be very busy. There were extra troop trains to and from Tonfannau. Some of these worked through the night so that Moat Lane West signal box was staffed throughout the 24 hours. The box also had a warning siren and a shelter. All trains stopped to take on water. The engine shed, cleaners and chargehand, Mr Davage, worked through the night. Olwen also had to work the weighbridge. A huge bottleneck that required 24 hour staffing took place on several occasions when the Ruabon to Barmouth line was closed, usually for bridge inspection after a flood. This also happened in September 1945 when a breach occurred in the bank of the canal near Llangollen that tore away the railway line.

The war ended but traffic remained heavy as holiday traffic started to replace military needs. Alternative Saturdays were worked on a 12 hour extended shift. The 'Leamingtons' were the nickname for the Birmingham trains (maybe from the home

Right: Olwen stands outside the booking office on the Llanidloes platform of Moat Lane.

Olwen Williams, Caersws

Below: Some of the station staff. *Rear:* Gwilym Williams (shunter). *Front, left to right:* Jack Aldridge (shunter), Danny Lewis (porter whose wife kept the Old Moat Lane gates), Sidney Griffiths (clerk) and Dai Lewis (porter).

Olwen Williams, Caersws

engine shed). All were packed and all needed bankers. The engine would whistle and wait for the banker to come off shed. The booking office was usually quiet in terms of decibels as the up trains cruised to the east water column and the down trains braked to stop beyond the station for the west water column. Only the banker thundered outside the office as the long push started to Talerddig. There were still through trains from South Wales, certainly in late July and August. The Mid-Wales line had spare occupancy but the main line between Buttington Junction and Dovey Junction struggled to fit every path in. The South Wales train had to wait for over 30 minutes before proceeding over Talerddig. The result was that 400 plus passengers got out and swamped the station and the refreshment room. There was no problem on the return as it could proceed quickly to Llanidloes and the south.

Olwen left in 1956 for family reasons and helped her husband, Frank, to establish his garage business at Penstrowed. BR had offered her promotion to Shrewsbury in 1955 but she declined the offer. The junction was still busy in 1956 so Olwen left just before the car and the lorry started to make a major impact. Sidney Griffith was a fellow clerk in the late 1940s. He was promoted and moved to Paddington. He was a bachelor and he retained either ownership or tenancy of his parents' home. He retired to the village and died around 1990. The photographs from Olwen are from Sidney's camera. The known Moat Lane/Caersws collection of Sidney cannot be traced.

Olwen now reflects that it is over 55 years since she left employment at Moat Lane Junction. It is now 80 years ago when she and her friends would sit on a warm stone outcrop looking down on Caersws watching freight trains or excursions held in the loop. Caersws only had a single platform to hold either the up or down stopping train. Olwen would soon have a full understanding of these problems from working in the telegraph room in the late 1940s. The double line between Moat Lane and Newtown and the double section between Forden and Buttington Junction helped the situation. However, there would be trains held in the loops at Montgomery, Abermule, Caersws, Carno, Talerddig, Llanbrynmair and Cemmaes waiting for single line clearance. Therefore trains with limited scheduled stops stopped at most loops on a peak Saturday. It was little wonder that passengers stormed the refreshment room for the five minutes when the tenders were replenished with water. Both passengers and engines needed their beverage. The opposite was a winter week day that could be so quiet. The driver of the Brecon locomotive would take one of the duty clerks for a ride in the cab from the platform through the complex to the engine shed/turntable area or the reverse trip when coaled up ready to travel to the far south. Gossip would be exchanged. Guards/firemen/drivers on the Mid-Wales line, whether Moat Lane, Llanidloes or Builth were part of the family. Oswestry, Machynlleth and Aberystwyth crew usually stopped for only a few minutes and were fleeting glimpses rather than close daily friends. Sadly Olwen is one of several who have passed on between research and publishing.

Relief clerical duties

Reg Thomas was a Llanidloes lad. Dad started with the Cambrian and retired from BR in 1954 as station foreman at Llanidloes. Dad started as a porter, then signalman and then guard working anywhere between Brecon and Whitchurch. Reg joined the railway after completing National Service as clerk at Abermule and this would include the paperwork necessary for the Kerry branch. He became relief clerk anywhere between Welshpool and Aberystwyth. This would include many months

Above, left: Harold Jones, carriage cleaner, working on a carriage on the Llanidloes loop. The train is almost certainly the 2.30 pm Moat Lane to Brecon. Ethel, his widow, recalls Harold's work. Harold was a prisoner of war held in Prussia and returned to Llandinam in 1945. The family smallholding was not viable without extra income. He became a postman at Newtown. His duty was the Dolfor Llaithdu route. This is an astonishing loaded cycle route for those who do not know the area as Newtown is around 400 ft above sea level and the route rises to over 1,100ft across moorland with severe winter weather. Harold cycled to and from Llandinam for the shift. There was a hut at Llaithdu to shelter for an hour prior to returning via post boxes in walls, etc. for return mail to Newtown and onwards. This is an example of Rowland Hill's 'Penny Post' as this shift would take all day for about 70 households that would only take 30 minutes in a town. Such routes were replaced by van in the early 1950s. Harold joined Moat Lane staff as one of the carriage cleaners, the other cleaner was Pryce Evans. Harold started to struggle with his health so he left to work on the smallholding. Even this was too much. He was a very independent man but it was almost certain that his ill health was triggered by his experiences during the war and he would have qualified for war pension assessment. The tradition of a smallholder known as 'tyddynwr' with the man working out at quarries, roads, railway, etc. and the wife looking after the farm animals during the day was very common in upland Wales. *Olwen Williams, Caersws*

Above, right: Owen Jones was the wheel tapper and looked after the pump to the water tower. Owen preferred a draught beer from the refreshment room rather than Virol. Virol was a barley malt drink not to be confused with Vimto which is a soft drink. Note the Butlin's promotion behind. Owen came from near Penychain, near Pwllheli, and was nicknamed Billy Butlin. Much Saturday exchange traffic went through Moat Lane on the way to Butlins at Penychain. *Olwen Williams, Caersws*

at Moat Lane. The ASLEF (drivers and firemen) strike of 1955 took place when on Moat Lane duty. These strikes did not help the industry because freight customers made alternative arrangements and their business did not return. Duties at Moat Lane included booking clerk telephone/telegraph communications all the way to Brecon including Bill Power at Builth and son, Glyn, at Newbridge. The original engine shed at Moat Lane still stood with huge gaps in the roof so working conditions for engine cleaners were deplorable. The new prefabricated shed was quickly erected in 1957.

Work at Welshpool would include clerical duties for the Llanfair branch in the final years of operation and included several journeys on the line. Reg must be the only current member of the heritage society who worked the line for British Railways.

Reg lived at Llanidloes and travelled daily to wherever required. He spent many hours 'on the cushions'. An example would be to catch the Llanidloes to Whitchurch train to be at Abermule at 7.00 am for an 8.00 am opening. Journeys home were equally tortuous with many an interval spent in Moat Lane refreshment room. Reg's great friend was Llew Watkins, the Caersws lad, who worked at Newtown Goods. Reg was at Moat Lane when the 'Blue Bird' special was arranged in 1956 when AFC Caersws played Buckley Wanderers at the Racecourse ground in Wrexham in the Welsh Amateur Cup Final. He left the industry with all the cut-backs in 1963 and worked for many years for a light engineering company in Welshpool where he set up home.

A partnership at Moat Lane Junction

Peter Poole moved from Wolverhampton to Llanidloes as a very young lad in 1939. His father had been an engine driver and failed his eyesight test. The GWR moved Dad to be the engine shed chargeman at Llanidloes. There had been a second engine shed for the Mid-Wales Railway at Llanidloes but this was closed around 1904 so no one has oral recall of this. Peter attended Llanidloes schools. He opted to serve three years, rather than two years, National Service in 1952 and was demobbed in 1955. He worked for the Post Office. He then married Ruth in 1957 and they needed a house. They applied for a railway vacancy at Moat Lane with tied accommodation. Peter's duties included that of clerk. Ruth became the refreshment room manager. There were two booking clerks and Peter worked with Mrs Jean Campbell and then Elaine Coates, daughter of Llew Watkins. Duties were similar to those described by Ron Jones and Olwen. The wages now not only included Moat Lane but also the Bridge Department. The two had become four when the family moved to Llandinam station in 1961 as the refreshment room duties were not easy with a young family. Peter now cycled daily to Moat Lane to work until closure. There were now only about 20 bikes and even as late as 1960, men cycled in from every direction including Newtown, Carno and Alfred Bebb (signals/telegraph) cycled in from Llanidloes.

Moat Lane staff faced redundancy from January 1963 but Peter opted to move to Paddington. He was faced with a completely different volume of work with more customers in a peak hour than a winter week at Moat Lane! Peter lodged in the hostel at Old Oak Common with the railway paying towards this and the return fare home to see the family. This arrangement was for a certain period of time, maybe nine months. Peter just could not get a house in London so he applied for a vacancy at Caersws at a lower pay grade. So he became the final clerk at Caersws until the

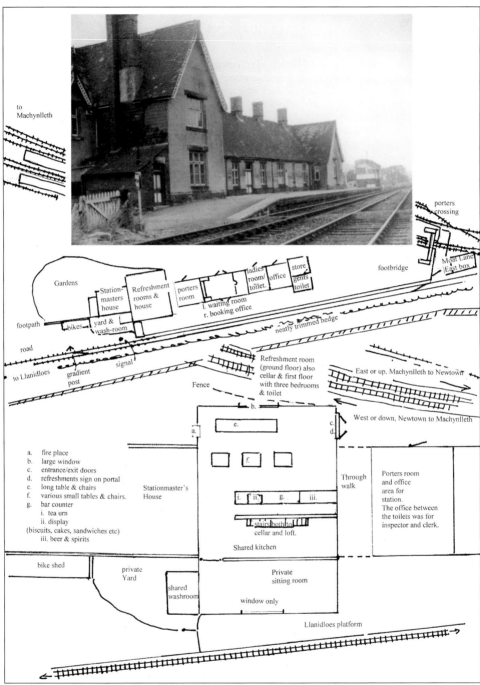

The layout of the refreshment room and main station at Moat Lane. Drawn from the recall of Ruth and Peter Poole. The original photograph was taken by Elwyn V. Jones in 1964, just prior to the station's demolition in 1965. Just imagine what the value of this real estate would be today!

Ruth Poole & Elwyn V. Jones

railway made it an unstaffed halt. It was a close call that the station remained open. He moved to Clywedog in 1965 and finally worked for Russell Bradley, the largest local garage, as storeman/clerk, until retirement. Russell is the grandson of Charlie, son of Cliff and nephew of Les Bradley.

Peter recalls some extra facets of clerical work at the junction. The very busy switchboard was one of the reasons for two duty clerks. The lines now connected with Oswestry and Shrewsbury and the Mid-Wales line to Builth Wells and through to Brecon. It also worked closely with Aberystwyth, Machynlleth and Pwllheli. It was a railway internal telephone by 1955. The telephone was in contact with signalmen and crossing keepers all along the lines. The single needle morse machine was still in the booking office but no longer in use. There was a GPO telephone and line was on site; this was available for staff and passengers but they had to pay. A ledger book was kept for this purpose. Both duty clerks had to cover all duties.

The leading porter issued any tickets before 8.00 am. There was little demand to catch the mail/newspaper/milk trains very early in the morning. There was a float of £5. It would be rare for someone to pay by cheque. Military lads including those on National Service had a travel warrant issued at the barracks, airfield etc. An exchange station in the middle of fields did not have too many passengers requiring tickets. Maybe £30 would be taken in a day while Caersws would take four to five times that amount daily. A trade had started with cars coming in from the surrounding areas to be parked for several days. People, usually for London, could get on the 'Cambrian Coast Express' as it was there about four minutes for the tender to be refilled. Otherwise they would have to travel to Newtown as this train did not stop at Caersws. The booking office doors closed to customers at the end of December 1962.

Peter continued on site for a further four weeks with inventories of furniture, tickets, etc. and the lists were forwarded to Shrewsbury. Peter then worked at Paddington before the transfer to Caersws. He was on a return journey from Paddington when he observed that demolition of the station was taking place. The final few years of service south from Moat Lane was not customer friendly. The service was slow. The journey to Cardiff involved a change at Bargoed Junction and a return, within reasonable hours, could not be done in a day. It was said that a journey from Pwllheli to Cardiff took so long that some started with their milk teeth and arrived at the final destination with dentures! The stopping freight left Moat Lane for Talyllyn around 10.15 am and the return came back about 7.00 pm. There was still a challenge during the summer timetable especially on Saturdays when most loops were still in use. A banker was still used from Moat Lane to move the 13-coach 'Cambrian Coast Express' to Talerddig in 1962. The only facility retained at Moat Lane was the two water columns. Many heavier trains were now double-headed from Machynlleth to Shrewsbury. Goods services had virtually ceased to local stations prior to closure in early 1965. Unbraked freight of coal, timber and building materials continued to the larger stations for only a few years. The final freight was block oil/petrol to Aberystwyth from Stanlow oil refinery. Peter returned to Caersws to find a service of diesel-multiple-units (dmus) being phased in until only the school train and finally the 'Cambrian Coast' were steam-hauled.

So wife Ruth took on the duties of the refreshment room. Access was from the down Newtown-Machynlleth platform. The gablehouse was both the refreshment room and the private accommodation. It was rent and rate free. Coal, milk, sugar and tea were an added bonus. The room opened at 8.00 am and operated until the last train to Llanidloes around 9.30 pm with the licensed bar operation continuing

Stephanie in her pram. The Newtown-Machynlleth platform with view of east water column, footbridge and Moat Lane East box. The carriage would be from the Moat Lane to Brecon service, stabled at the island platform for cleaning while locomotive went to engine shed for coal and turning. The crossing for the porters is just beyond the footbridge. The hand-drawn trolleys were placed close to the anticipated stopping point of the luggage/brake section of the train so that parcels could be quickly moved across platforms. *Peter & Ruth Poole*

Stephanie on rocking horse on the Llanidloes platform. The three coaches may be the Moat Lane to Brecon train with the locomotive just out of view to the right. *Peter & Ruth Poole*

Family album with daughter, Stephanie, taken around 1959. The west end of the Llanidloes platform; the exit right of the signal led to footpath and terminus of the road access from Old Moat Lane. *Peter & Ruth Poole*

until 11.00 pm. The premises were therefore open for 15 hours. No cooked meals were provided. Sandwiches were made fresh to anticipated demand. Cakes were either purchased or home made. Other foods were within snack packs such as crisps, chocolate bars and biscuits. The 1950s saw the growth of brand-named chocolate biscuits such as 'Penguin' and 'Wagon Wheels'. The latter was a most appropriate brand for a station sale. The beverages were tea, coffee, orange squash and some bottled 'fizz' such as lemonade. Draught mild and bitter were available tapped from oak barrels. Brandy, whisky, rum, sherry, etc. were sold using a cup measure. If anyone had asked for a cappuccino or red wine, they would still be waiting in the rain and the ruins in 2013!

Connection time to and from the Mid-Wales line was fairly short, maybe five to 15 minutes, so this was the reason why meals were not an option. This would give a flurry of activity for a short period. There were only two to three trains travelling beyond Llanidloes and four to five trains terminating there, plus the first train heading to Whitchurch and the last train of the day returning from Whitchurch.

All trains stopped on the Cambrian route including the express. The trains heading west stopped with the carriages on the platform beside the refreshment room entrance door. A guess was made for demand with 15 to 20 cardboard cups of steaming tea and coffee. The stop was for about four minutes so passengers rushed out, grabbed their tea and jumped back into the carriage. The cups necessary for the normal passing trains could be made with some accuracy but a gamble had to be taken with excursion trains. The up trains stopped on the island platform so a customer had to be a 'greyhound' to get over the footbridge and back within the short time interval.

An extra service developed with the Newtown schoolchildren returning to Caersws, Pontdolgoch and Carno. Crisps and 'Wagon Wheels', each item priced at 3d., were laid out and the children dashed out, collected them and then returned to the carriage to complete their journey. The last one out would show his or her thumb. The guard would also check.

The refreshment room was used throughout the day by various railwaymen, both those on site and those passing through such as the three staff on a freight train. Many usually had their own 'bait' but would have a warm drink and also replenish their enamel covered teacans. The lads from the Bridge Department always looked frozen in the winter and a wink was a request to put in a measure of brandy.

The final section of the trade that made the franchise viable was that of the licensed premises. It was popular with local rural workers and men at the end of their rail shift. The room had been popular for generations due to skilled interpretation as locals used the refreshment room as a local tavern to avoid the local temperance hotels. The Saturday evening was a focal point. A dart board was set up, the dominoes came out and a meat pie would be baked. Any surplus cheese and ham sandwiches made in the day were sold to this trade.

The working day was very long. Ruth would look after everything until 4.00 pm and she would then devote her time to the two children. Peter took on duties after 4.00 pm once his clerical shift had finished. It was not the best place to bring up a young family. The rooms had no electricity so all lighting was by paraffin. The house had no bathroom, just a toilet. This was one of the reasons for the family moving to Llandinam 12 months before closure leaving another person to operate the rooms.

Moat Lane was a community within the community. The other staff all helped. The station area could flood with the first sign of water seeping into the lower brickwork of the cellar. There was a severe flood in Caersws and Newtown in 1960.

View of Moat Lane buildings taken from island platform. View from right to left shows garden, two-storey station master's house, gable end refreshment room (ground floor) with Peter and Ruth's residence on gable rear and first floor, then the station with footbridge then Moat Lane East signal box and the water tower on left. This may be the final image of the station before demolition as the goods exchange loops have already been lifted.   *Elwyn V. Jones/Peter Poole*

Station friends *circa* 1950. *Top row left to right*: Mum and Dad (refreshment room), Danny Lewis and Charlie Jones (porters). *Lower row*: Sidney Griffith (clerk) with Gyp, Dai Lewis and Jennifer and finally George Davies, the station master.   *Jennifer Rimmer née Breese, Newtown*

The locals came out of the bar at 11 pm to find that the island platform opposite was not the only island. Peter bedded them all down for the night as if they were cattle but they had all gone by the morning. They had used first light to wade their way home and should have all received a telling-off from their wives for staying out so late!

The porters were very good in helping to look after the then toddlers and would also help to clean the room in addition to their platform duties. Once Stephanie and Stephen were following passengers on to the train and told the porter they were going to London. They could have had no concept of such a place. Several of the staff would help if either child needed attention. They were all very kind. The place was vibrant, sometimes full of fun and sometimes of sadness. Fred Claffey (porter) once blew his whistle as all the passengers entered the room so they immediately returned to the westbound train leaving steaming cups of tea on the counter. It may have been 1st April. Another porter called Cliff Slee would fuss over the gentry to try and get a better tip. One 'toff' fisherman was transferring to the Wye for salmon fishing. Cliff got the trolley moving quickly in the wrong direction and succeeded in snapping an expensive rod. Such stories are almost endless with such themes that must take place at every work place.

So Peter and Ruth lived at Llandinam station from late 1961 to May 1964. The only train from 1st January, 1963 was the goods service to Llanidloes. The family moved before the Clywedog dam trains started. The two now older children would sometimes have a ride to 'Llani' in the guard's van. Two large lumps of coal would land on the platform as the train pulled through. Railwaymen always looked after their own. It must have been an unusual childhood having parents that worked and lived in the middle of a rural junction. Sadly, the whole station section of Moat Lane was knocked down two years after closure. The station was well built with wonderful wooden floors. Renovation could have made a very good large private house or up to three smaller dwellings. Ruth always remembers the superb views of the Llandinam area hills viewed from the upstairs window. There may have been a reason for demolition in 1964. Fashion changes and such stations as Pondolgoch, Llandinam and Dolwen are now highly attractive and valuable private dwellings.

Moat Lane refreshment room remains part of the folklore of the area. The chapel membership was very kind and generous but they were strong teetotallers, including David Davies. The temperance movement was strong. The Licensing Act of 1904 brought legal complications. Application made to sell intoxicants on railway premises were granted on the understanding that it would only be sold to passengers and close after the departure of the last train. The station master was told to be watchful. The resourceful people of the temperance villages would buy a return ticket from Llandinam, Caersws or Pontdolgoch to Moat Lane to enjoy a pint of beer. So the wayward brother of a good baptist or calvanist family found a legal loophole to 'sup the fluid of the devil'. Moat Lane best bitter was preferred to a glass of sarsaparilla or root-beer.

Jennifer Rimmer recalls

Jennifer Rimmer née Breese moved to Moat Lane at the age of four to live in the tied accommodation. Her father, Ernest, had taken on the refreshment franchise, assisted by mother who had worked for Hughes, the caterers, at Welshpool who had inherited the local role of Spiers and Pond. Jennifer lived at the station from 1948 to 1955. She attended Caersws Primary School while her older brother and the youngest son of Howell Morris, who succeeded George Davis as station master, took the school train daily to Newtown Secondary Schools.

The description of the refreshment room is similar to that given by Ruth Poole. The adjoining corrugated lean-to with a tall chimney was the shared private wash house with a coal-fired boiler. It was the bathroom using a zinc tub.

There was a tremendous gale in the early 1950s. The empty beer barrels and other debris were on the Llanidloes track and Jennifer recalls dad and the porters trying to clear everything before the Llanidloes train came in around 6.00 am. The storm caused much damage to the twin apex engine shed and most of the roof and sides had come down. The final photographs of Moat Lane station show the different shades of slate as some of the roof had to be repaired.

Jennifer's childhood would have been paradise for a young railway buff. Much time was spent with staff and, on reflection, they may have spoilt her. The porters would pull the trolley with Jennifer having a ride. She would often spend time with the duty cleaner in the carriages parked on the north side of the island loop. Time would be spent sitting on a chair in East signal box. A ride would be arranged with the guard to Llanidloes. There was no shortage of certain foods in such a rural area during the period of rationing with bacon, lamb chops and eggs cooked on the shovel. Sometimes Jennifer would sit with Olwen Bound and was fascinated by the telephone and plug connections sending messages along the lines to stations and signal boxes. It may sound most unsafe to live on a station but Jennifer would query the safety of children walking to school with cars parked on the pavement etc in 2013. Jennifer would walk to Caersws school along the same footpath used by the station staff. She learnt to ride a bike with solid wheels endlessly cycling along the Llanidloes platform, then turn along the Machynlleth platform and then through the

Jennifer stands on the Llanidloes platform ready to walk to school at Caersws.
Jennifer Rimmer née Breese, Newtown

Jennifer helps the Llanidloes guard, Bill 'Clod' Edwards, with the token. The nickname 'Clod' came from his parents/grandparents cottage along Clydfannau Lane near Dolwen station. It was one of the last homes with a turf (or clod) roof.
Jennifer Rimmer neé Breese, Newtown

covered alleyway to complete the circuit. Jennifer would watch the operations through the day. All the station woodwork was brown and cream as were the carriages until the gradual change to BR maroon. Owen Jones would check the wheels and look after the steam pump below the water column. He was a dapper man with one nickname of 'Clark Gable' but he was always very kind and amusing. The whole house seemed to shudder as long freight trains moved out to start the long climb to Talerddig early in the morning. Everyone was very busy on a summer Saturday with the coast traffic and this would include mum and dad in the refreshment room. Jennifer's husband was a Newtown lad and he can recall travelling direct on the Newtown-Llanidloes special without the usual need to change at Moat Lane for the Boxing Day derby between the football clubs. Over 1,500 supporters would turn out to watch a local Mid-Wales derby in the post-war period before TV and other cultural changes took place.

Spiers & Pond

Mrs Margaret Blakeley of Newtown was given literature and some pottery of Spiers & Pond from her deceased neighbour who was a railwayman. Spiers & Pond were refreshment contractors to the Cambrian Railways. They provided rooms at Oswestry, Llanymynech, Welshpool, Moat Lane, Llanidloes, Builth Road, Three Cocks, Machynlleth, Glandovey (Dyfi) Junction, Borth, Aberystwyth, Towyn, Barmouth Junction, Barmouth, Portmadoc, Afon Wen and Pwllheli. Many of these were at junctions or the larger seaside towns. An order could be given to the guard at a preceding larger station for tea baskets or luncheon baskets (summer only) and this would be signalled ahead to Moat Lane (for example) so that the basket would be prepared by the refreshment staff as the train drew in. The tea basket would contain tea, coffee or cocoa with bread & butter (option of toast) and a piece of cake. A substantial lunch basket could be pre-ordered by letter or telegram giving reasonable time for preparation at any time of the year. This would be cold fowl and ham or roast beef with salad, bread, cheese and claret or beer or wine or mineral water. There was also a system of food hampers being provided for first class passengers. Two Spier & Pond ladies were very lucky to survive the 1921 Abermule crash as guard Shone, who may have just left the dining section, was killed. Jean Lloyd née Davage recalled that her mother worked in Moat Lane refreshment room in the 1920s prior to marriage to the shed foreman. Hampers and baskets would collect at certain stations and empties had to be returned. There was a story that two Spiers & Pond ladies loaded surplus empty hampers to return to Oswestry on empty stock carriages that were also being worked back. The train took off with them still on board and the first stop was Welshpool. The two ladies then came back on the local 'all stations'. A South Wales to Aberystwyth train came in during their absence so they found the one remaining tearful staff member exhausted beside a mountain of washing up.

The Nicholas family

Contact was made with Wally Nicholas (aged 81) at New House Farm near Moat Lane in the autumn of 2007. It is easier to trace the Aldridge, the Bradley and the Nicholas families rather than the Evans, Hughes, Jones, Morgans, etc. Wally's father was a younger member of a large family. Wally's mother loved music and his

Christian name is Walford after the musician. Walford Davies worked with the two Davies sisters at the Gregynog Arts helping to establish the centre of music. He was and remains a classical composer of renown. He was also Professor of Music at Aberystwyth University based at Savin's failed hotel.

Grandad, John Edward Nicholas, was a young stonemason in 1860 and was employed on the Newtown-Machynlleth contract. It is known that he worked on the goods and engine sheds at Machynlleth and almost certainly helped to build the goods shed at Caersws. Wally would have no recall of him but he can remember the older siblings of dad. Three of the family are on the 1908 Moat Lane photograph.

Levi was a porter/signalman. He moved to Cilfrew on the Neath & Brecon line within the South Wales coalfield and returned to retire in Caersws.

Fred was killed in 1918, aged 24, working with the Railway Operating Division of the Royal Engineers. He was buried at Sangatte near Calais, so the young lad who helped marshal trains at Moat Lane is buried near the railway yards that serve on the French side of the Channel Tunnel. The picture, unknown to the family, becomes their only image of Fred after a period of nearly 90 years.

The three other railway brothers follow. Eddie was the wheel tapper and looked after the pumphouse at Moat Lane in the 1920s. William Jacob started at Caersws, then worked at Welshpool. The GWR moved him to Bath where he retired as a senior inspector. Joseph George worked in the Caersws area prior to World War I, then served in the army and he returned to work for the railway in South Wales. His wife was a Caersws & District midwife so he returned after the 1924 strike when Aunty became the matron at Llys Maldwyn hospital. Joe trained as a male nurse and became the master (the male equivalent of matron).

Edward Wilson married the sister, Miriam Nicholas. He was the station master at Cemmaes Road and was promoted to be station master at Moat Lane. Dad looked after the small farm at New House.

Ian Nicholas is the younger brother of Wally. Ian became the cleaner/junior fireman at Moat Lane in 1959. He was moved to the Cardiff sheds and then opted to leave around 1962 to return to the Caersws area.

Moat Lane Staff, 1908. Standing (left to right): Richard Morgan, Jack Hughes, Three Barmaids of Messrs. Spiers and Pond's Refreshment Rooms, Sam Evans, Levi Nicholas. Seated: Lewis Hamer (booking clerk), Fred Nicholas, Edward Wilson (stationmaster), J. Pryce Jones, and T. E. Francis (telegraph clerk).

The photograph of staff at Moat Lane in 1908 includes three un-named barmaids, Note the name of Nicholas. Ian Nicholas would have been one of the last cleaners/firemen trained in the late 1950s and he knew several of his grandfather's cousins and brothers may have worked at the station. *Montgomeryshire Express*

Wally has researched the local Home Guard history. He confirms that there was a fire wall and stand for Lewis machines guns in case the Germans tried to cross the bridge over the Severn from east to west. There was no anti-aircraft gun. The Home Guard shed was by the Llanidloes Road level crossing and the footings can still be discerned. It was used by both the Llandinam and Caersws Home Guard so they had the nickname of Moat Lane platoon.

Bombing the refreshment room

The local paper, the *Montgomeryshire Express* described the German air raid on 27th July, 1940 with bombs being dropped on a rural parish but with no futher identity given. The parish was the Caersws area. Revd David Francis of Pontrobert recalls the event as described by his mother. Dora Francis worked with Ethel Higgs looking after the Moat Lane refreshment room during World War II. Dora and Ethel were sleeping in the upper floor bedroom over the refreshment room and both ladies woke with a start as the building appeared to tremble with an explosion. The nearest crater was on the fields at Maesmawr. Several of the windows of both Llanwnog church and the vicarage were shattered. The attack was likely to have been on Moat Lane Junction as opposed to aircraft lost on the route to Birkenhead/Liverpool or Belfast depositing bombs to ensure that the aircraft had enough fuel to return to Germany. This is because incendiaries were laid to flare a route and preceded the explosives. Bert Davidge and his cleaners were on their night-shift duty so they dived into the engine shed pit under a 'Dean Goods'. A few of the older parishioners of Caersws can still recall this hushed-up incident.

David was born in 1945 and his childhood was spent in Llanidloes. Ethel was a child brought up at the Garth Crossing cottage at the Van. It is likely that both families had ancestors who worked within the lead mines during the Victorian period. Dora's stepfather was one of the gangers between Moat Lane and Tylwch.

David would often travel through Moat Lane as a young child in the late 1940s. There was the annual Sunday School trip to Aberystwyth and David can recall being carried by his mother through the corridor by the refreshment room at Moat Lane. All the young children were exhausted by the final hour of a long day out. The other journeys were to Newtown for shopping, especially at Christmas, or to the Shrewsbury Flower Show.

David comes from a noted family of musicians and is a skilled player of the organ, the piano and the harp. He has an original copy of Nicholas Bennett's *Collection of Old Welsh Airs*. Nicholas Bennett was a very close friend of 'Ceiriog', the Van Railway poet.

David worked at the Llanidloes leather works that sent many parcels of finished goods out by rail via Moat Lane. He trained later as a Wesleyan Minister before transferring to the Church of Wales. One of his parishes was Borth where it was necessary for worshippers to cross the railway line from the village to the church that stands on a ridge within an island of bog. It was of some concern for a large weekday funeral when the mourners were either side of the gates but everyone crossed and returned safely.

David visited Moat Lane site in 1994. He was astonished by the reversion to nature and placed his thoughts on to paper. It conveys the haunting ambience:

One of the shattered windows of Llannwnog church.

Montgomeryshire Express/Geoff Charles Collection, National Library

Dora Francis returning from work in Llanidloes around 1938. Many ladies were unaware that they would soon be working in railway-related duties or munitions by 1940.

Revd David Francis

The first large crater was below the bank sloping down to the Severn east of the village. The man is thought to be Mr Bound of Tygwyn who farmed this area. The second crater was closer to Moat Lane Junction. These misses would have a degree of accuracy within the bomb aiming technology of 1940.

Montgomeryshire Express/Geoff Charles Collection, National Library

In memoriam to the Cambrian junction in the fields
Moat Lane, Caersws, Montgomeryshire

From Northern Dales to Midland towns
We journeyed on past black canals and hills of scrap
Until another realm was reached
And dismal grey gave place to green.

And on that western curve of track
Midst fields that never knew the plough
A crumbling edge of platform showed
All wet with Autumn evening dew.

Sad, lonely remnant of those former days
When plastered walls and steep pitched roofs
Stood proud, and decked in barge boards fine
Twixt Aber and the Mid-Wales line.

Where 'Deans' and 'Manors' roared and hissed with lively steam
And whistles blew, and engines barked, like monsters in a dream
While over on the other side, the porters called out reams
Of long forgotten stations on a line of different scene
Where engines pulled carriages of strawberry red and cream.*

And on the wind swept platforms, people waited there and gazed
At walls arrayed with adverts, Virol, pills and 'Scenic Wales'.
Or if time allowed, to seek refreshment there
With tea or Camp† and sticky buns, or a pint of bitter beer
In rooms, where blue clad railwaymen sit playing cards and raise
Their glasses all to barmaids fair in a alcoholic haze.

This gateway to so many worlds, where now the rabbits play
Where many stood and caught the trains to other worlds and ways
Bright youth with hope to England went, while some departed in shame
And war time soldiers sang their songs before the battle flame
While on Christmas nights stood children with toys on this island of foggy damp
And perished parents stamped up and down in the light of the Tilley lamp.

And exiles of that part of Wales in later years returned
By steam express from far off towns to scenes no longer spurned
And hardened business men whose lives no sentiment had known
Stand near to tears on platform one, then board the train for home.

But now is another era, and there's thirty years of more
Since porters trucks were trundled in haste to the open carriage door
And four Scotch Pines still guard the site and the Eastern wind blows cold
While Severn mists now blur the view of brambles round ruins old
So fewer and fewer remember the Cambrian Junction of yore
For dark the night, long gone is the light
FOR THE TRAIN TO BRECON IS NO MORE.

---

* Coaches were crimson and cream (known colloquially as 'blood and custard') for a period after nationalization.
† Camp was a wartime and post-war syrup essence of chicory with some coffee.

Moat Lane East signal box viewed from the Newtown approach *circa* 1955. The Llanidloes branch is to the left of the box. A down train to Machynlleth or Aberystwyth is just beyond the footbridge. The Brecon coaches are left for cleaning while the locomotives is coaled, turned and watered at the shed. Derek disliked the duty of replenishing passenger carriage toilet and hand basin water, having to stand on the carriage roof with a long hose. The track on the right is the siding to the water tower and steam driven pump. Note the very tall signal post for the driver to get a view from the up train as he looked towards the footbridge.   *Ron Jones, Newtown*

Doreen Bunney is the youngest sister of Derrek. She has three photographs of their father, Arthur, as guard. The tall Arthur stands as the young guard, second in on the rear row in 1924 at Builth Wells. The oldest man may well have started with the Mid-Wales Railway. Arthur would have known the route from Brecon to Moat Lane and on to Whitchurch. He had some problems with his eyesight as he approached retirement so he spent his last year working at Newtown on clerical duties including the weighbridge. The then young Dennis Glasscodine can recall a journey in the mid-1930s from his grandparents home at Oswestry to his station master 'dad' at Builth. The train could be full to Llanidloes from Moat Lane so Arthur would put Dennis in the first class compartment. They would then share a cup of tea once things were quieter south of Llanidloes.   *Doreen Bunney née Llewellyn, Newtown*

Signal duties at Moat Lane

Research is too late to have direct recall of a senior duty signalman. One man has been located who was a porter/relief signalman at Moat Lane East from 1949 to 1951. Derrick Llewellyn's father was a Llanidloes-based passenger guard. Arthur Edward Llewellyn worked his life on the Cambrian, GWR and final few years with BR starting on the Moat Lane to Brecon route. He was appointed passenger guard at Llanidloes so his shift duties would have expanded to include work to Whitchurch. Dad was based at Welshpool in the early 1950s working from Shrewsbury to Aberystwyth including the 'Cambrian Coast Express'. Derrick joined the GWR in April 1942 and worked various local duties until moving to Maidenhead East signal box in 1955 and then to various senior clerical duties at Paddington until retirement in 1984. He continues to live at Maidenhead.

Derrick was appointed junior booking clerk at Newtown in 1942 where he was to learn the single needle telegraph so that he could receive and send out messages. He then became trainee signalman at Abermule box during 1943 to learn single line operation with token and the Kerry branch worked under 'one engine in steam'. Derrick has answered one question. Several trains were required on the Kerry branch during the annual sheep sales. The problem was eased by double-heading a long train, so a junior would travel up to Kerry in the guard's van and then cycle back to Abermule with the train staff so a second train, if necessary, could proceed to Kerry. This was a good task in the morning when the cycle ride was down hill but a different matter in the afternoon when required to cycle up the gradient from Abermule to Kerry. The station had a railway bike.

Pontdolgoch in 1944 to 1947 was already a one man operation. The duty included walking to the Clatter loop to change the signal oil lamps. The whistles were heard from Moat Lane shed on VE Day at 3.00 pm to celebrate the conclusion of war in Europe. The next move was to Forden as senior porter. An important duty was to load 10 gallon milk churns from W.R. Griffith's farm to his own-brand milk bars in the larger towns of the Midlands and North Wales and as far east as Birmingham. The milk arrived at 7.00 pm and the up mail was allowed eight minutes for loading. Up to three cattle wagons were loaded with sheep and cattle for Welshpool on the Caersws via Moat Lane train hauled by the Kerry tank. There were several noted pedigree herds in the locality and these required horse/groom wagons for shows such as Smithfield and other national shows. These wagons were attached to the passenger trains.

Duties at Moat Lane were as porter/signalman from 1949 to 1951. These involved manning the East signal box from 11 am to 2 pm daily or taking a full shift during holidays or illness cover. Derrick then returned to Forden as signalman from 1951 to 1955. The night shift was boring. There was an evening freight around 10.15 pm and then nothing until the 2.10 am Welshpool to Machynlleth freight followed by the 3.15 Oswestry freight and finally the morning mail to Aberystwyth. The arrival of this train at Moat Lane caused a flurry of activity as mail, newspapers and parcels transferred to the Builth train. Four trains only in an eight hour night shift! Derrick studied various railway correspondence courses, not only signalling but also station working and accountancy not then knowing that this would later lead to a senior clerical post at Paddington. So Derrick took up duties, in 1955, at Maidenhead East where 200 trains would pass on the day shift.

Derrick is remembered at Moat Lane for his own form of transport that was peculiar to a short period around 1950. He would phut-phut along the footpath to

Moat Lane Engine Shed as remembered by Bill Jones
(nightshift junior cleaner 1946, fireman 1952-1962)

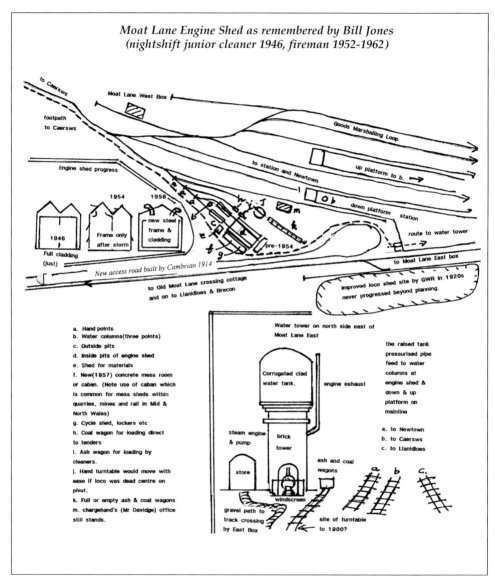

a. Hand points
b. Water columns(three points)
c. Outside pits
d. Inside pits of engine shed
e. Shed for materials
f. New(1957) concrete mess room or caban. (Note use of caban which is common for mess sheds within quarries, mines and rail in Mid & North Wales)
g. Cycle shed, lockers etc
h. Coal wagon for loading direct to tenders
i. Ash wagon for loading by cleaners.
j. Hand turntable would move with ease if loco was dead centre on pivot.
k. Full or empty ash & coal wagons
m. chargehand's (Mr Davidge) office still stands.

Water tower on north side east of Moat Lane East

the raised tank pressurised pipe feed to water columns at engine shed & down & up platform on mainline

a. to Newtown
b. to Caersws
c. to Llanidloes

Moat Lane Junction was built to accommodate the Newtown & Machynlleth route and the engine sheds became necessary for the Mid-Wales extension south of Llanidloes. All was in place by late 1860s. The two-track dead-end engine shed was timber built with twin slated gable roof. It was in poor condition by 1945. All cladding & roof was removed by a storm in the early 1950s so it looked like a derelict skeleton. Working conditions were poor. The shed was reconstructed with steel frame, single pitched roof with cowlings plus corrugated sides and roof sheets. The shed closed at the end of December 1962 and remains the only substantial junction building still in use in 2013 as a timber workshop. Steam locomotives continued to take water until early 1967 and it is thought that diesel power replaced steam engine for the pump.

the area of the bicycle shed with the bike powered by the 'Cyclemaster'. This was a small engine that fitted into the hub of the rear wheel of a bike. He also was one of several who had a motor bike at one stage.

Bill Jones

The main information for this research comes from the then cleaners and junior firemen. Sadly, the guards and drivers, with a few exceptions, have passed on. Many of the younger drivers and fireman opted to move to other railway depots rather than take redundancy in early 1963.

Bill Jones was an Aberhafesp lad. He joined the traffic department of the GWR at Newtown on leaving school in 1946. He transferred to Moat Lane as a cleaner as soon as he was 16. He would either cycle to work the long way round via Caersws or walk across the Jubilee (Victoria), rebuilt Festival (1951) bridge This footbridge is the only public route across the River Severn except for the now closed Ysgafell bolt-on footpath section bridge between Newtown and Caersws. He left after 18 months to go to Old Oak Common (Paddington), after completing National Service returned to Old Oak Common. In 1952 he came back to Moat Lane as the junior fireman. This duty was a night shift getting locomotives coaled up and watered ready for traffic and to move any locomotive around the yard. Engines were stone cold on Sunday evenings and raising steam would take extra time. He moved on to cover Moat Lane to either Builth or Brecon, the Kerry branch and sometimes the Whitchurch run. The Saturday duty would include banking to Talerddig. The usual driver was Reg 'Cwmbelan' Jones and sometimes Charlie Claffey. The fireman was required to train for driving so the driver would drive down to Brecon and fire back. Bill had served the necessary time and would have moved up to driver except the whole system was going to close so he opted to leave in 1962 to enter the building trade.

The journey to Brecon even after all these years is remembered for its scenic attraction. Many of the staff at both stations and signal boxes had a very quiet day so had become good gardners and hen keepers. This led to both the guard and the footplate staff acting as an exchange for vegetables, eggs and other countryside goodies. One had some special pullets at point of laying but nothing happened because the first 'on shift' were helping themselves until they had to explain the joke. The goods train was remarshalled at both Builth and Talyllyn. There was a wait at Talyllyn for the Newport train to clear through. Bill can always remember the refreshment room where the old lady still smoked a clay pipe.

The train was made up at Moat Lane by the duty shunter and various locomotives, including the Kerry Dean pannier tank until 1950, through the day. Dai Edwards was the the one of the shunters. The wagons were assembled on the loops on the north side of the station and the train could be placed in the Llanidloes loop ready for the tender engine to back on and then down towards Llanidloes to Brecon.

The night shift junior fireman duties included looking after the steam engine to power the water pump. An old engine boiler was set on a plinth recessed below ground level within a brick tower with the water tank set on the top. It was stoked to have steam ready for the day shift when Owen Jones kept the unit going. The water was pumped to the high storage tank where pressure delivered it to the engine shed and to the head of both through platforms to Caersws and Newtown. The engine had a connecting rod to the pump and a steam locomotive could also take on the duty in an emergency. There was a siding for both coal and ash by the pump.

The first of two views of the water tower. The hidden stationary steam engine, for the water pump, exhausts steam through the tall pipe. Part of the tin office can be seen on the left. The stabled wagon contains the coal. *John Jones, Builth Wells*

Owen stands with his wheel hammer. The water gauge can be seen beside his head. This measured water in the tank without the need to climb the fixed ladder. Note the pipe and the St Bruno tobacco. *John Jones, Builth Wells*

The railway staff (nicknamed the 'Bullocks') on holiday in Jersey: Nathaniel Hamer (Caersws station), Wilf Smith (Bridge Dept), Reg 'Cwmbelan' Jones (driver), Percy Smout (Bridge Dept), Tom Aldridge (engine driver). The bullocks may be a corruption of a Victorian nickname as there are several Bwlchs (place name) on the hill to the north of Caersws. *John Jones, Builth Wells*

There were only about five trains leaving Moat Lane to travel beyond Llanidloes (5.45 am passenger/mail to Builth, 9.55 am passenger to Brecon, 10.15 am freight to Talyllyn, 2.45 pm passenger to Brecon and 5.30 pm passenger to Builth). It was a very relaxed system.

Old Oak Common was a hierarchal structure. Once there was no spare fireman in the mess room except Bill and someone was required at short notice for the 'Cheltenham Spa Express'. The driver rudely refused to contemplate Bill but finally had no choice. He made minimum conversation with Bill, both down and up and Bill had to find his own way to the Cheltenham mess room for a cup of tea. Bill shovelled eight tons of coal in four hours for just a grunt of thanks. He was told later 'on the grape vine' that the elite driver said the young Welsh lad had fired really well and he would be delighted to take him if there was another emergency. A young lad from Llanfyllin based at Oswestry shed travelled with Bill to Old Oak Common and they met at Shrewsbury. Jack was desperately homesick and disappeared home. He was back within a few days having received a real scolding from his father. He settled down. It was a tremendous cultural shock moving from Montgomeryshire to London around 1947. The hostel at Old Oak was composed of redundant corridor coaches with each compartment being an individual room. It was comfortable. There was a canteen on site plus toilets/wash rooms. The footings were already in place for a permanent three- to four-storey hostel that must have accommodated the Moat Lane and other Cambrian lads from 1950 onwards. There was a long skew bridge over the tracks between Old Oak and Paddington. The cleaned empty coaches would cross this long girder bridge on the way to the Paddington departure platforms. There was a steep gradient either side. There was no bridge of this length between Moat Lane and Brecon.

The Caersws of the 1950s was based on local work of railway and farming so it was a close but very warm community. Such villages are still very pleasant but a commuting village, while gaining certain facets, has also lost much of value and that is true for everyone.

Wagon examination and care of the water tank at Moat Lane Junction

The local paper recorded the funeral of William Henry Jones on 17th October, 1942. He had spent his working life with the Cambrian and GWR. He commenced work as flagger for the Caersws permananent way gang. He later moved to Moat Lane to become a fireman. His next move was to Oswestry works. He returned to Caersws when he was appointed wheel examiner at Moat Lane, a post he held until his death. He had received a gold medal for work with St John's ambulance brigade. Various railway staff attended his funeral including the Home Guard, Moat Lane Platoon.

John Jones (no relation) recalls the last wheel examiner on site. John is a police officer who has retired to Builth Wells, the home of his maternal grandparents. John was the only child of Owen Jones. Dad started his railway career at Porthmadoc around 1930, duties unknown but may have been porter/clerk within the goods yard. He moved to Aberystwyth until promotion to Moat Lane in the late 1930s. Owen served in the Royal Engineers during World War II and returned to Moat Lane on demobilization. John was born in 1946 and spent his childhood in Caersws.

The duties as John remembers were vehicle and wheel examination plus the duty of looking after the water tower complex. Owen would spend some time at

Oswestry updating his carriage and wagon knowledge. Owen was one of many Joneses so he had a number of other names. The commonest was 'Tojo', the reason is unknown. The second was 'Billy Butlin', the well known owner of Butlin holiday camps. Owen had a physical similarity to Billy Butlin and Owen's childhood home was also close to what was to become the Penychain holiday camp after 1945.

He was also known as 'St Bruno' as he always had a pipe with St Bruno brand tobacco and also 'Clark Gable' because of the moustache and fondness for chatting to ladies. John would go with Dad on the crossbar of the bike on many Saturdays. One reason was to have a questionable haircut with hand clippers by Owen Evans in the washroom by the bike shed.

The water tower was powered by the boiler of an antique locomotive. The fire was stoked by the shed staff during the night and dad looked after the unit during the day. The coal was a finer material than that used for the locomotives. Maybe this was for slower burning. Dad went into the pit and fired as required, so John has also put coal through the fire doors. The small shed beside the tower was the office, store and kitchen and this was kept in immaculate condition. The water system to the up and down main line was necessary after the Junction station closed so Dad plus several signalmen were retained. A stationary diesel engine took on the duty of powering the pump. Dad died suddenly in 1966 just before final closure of the site.

Dad was a keen football supporter and had various official duties with Caersws AFC. Both he and Noel Manual (Bridge Department) arranged many railway trips for the village. This included the specials when Caersws reached the Welsh Amateur Cup Finals at the Racecourse, Wrexham. John got to know many of the staff. One was Danny Lewis who had been an excellent footballer. Danny had only a thumb on one hand (maybe a shunting accident) and worked at the Llanidloes road crossing. He managed everything with one good hand and a stump plus a large smile. Dad would often greet John on the return from Newtown High School and would have a packet of crisps purchased from the refreshment room for him.

Both parents spoke Welsh but it was difficult for John to retain this once he was at primary school. Like many, he now regrets the loss of fluency. He was exposed to French and modern Caersws Latin (Italian) when Dad decided to make use of free rail travel. So Mum, Dad and John set off to Alassio on the Golfo di Genova in around 1952 when such a holiday would be very unusual. The journey from Caersws included seat and couchette reservations from London Victoria to Dover, ferry, the Calais to Paris Nord, then Paris Lyon to Ventimiglia. John still retains the reservation for this journey. Dad was also a member of a group of railwaymen who would spend a 'lads' week together, always in Jersey, using the British Rail packet boat from Weymouth to St Helier. John's maternal grandfather was a ghillie (water baliff) on the Wye. John would take every chance to spend time along the river. Dad would put John on the train even when he was about six and one of the guards would look after him to Builth Wells. John is thrilled to retire back to Builth after years with the police, including CID work in the West Midlands conurbation.

Dai y Pant, the guard's story

Dai (David) Edwards was brought up in Llandinam. He left the then all-age school at 14 to join the staff at Moat Lane in 1944. His first duty was porter/lamp boy. He primed the wicks and filled the lamps with paraffin. The lamps were used at the head and rear of each train and signals also had lamps. The station was not connected to electricity so there were lamps within signal boxes and the station. The guards also carried lamps for any emergency. The duty changed to junior porter, usually on the morning shift starting at 4.00 and finishing at mid-day. There was much work transferring mail, newspapers, parcels and perishable foods from the Whitchurch mail to the Llanidloes, Rhayader and Builth train. Newspapers and mail for further south came in from Craven Arms with transfer at Builth Road. Goods such as Llanidloes leather had to be taken across the wooden crossing on a four-wheel trolley. The next stage in Dai's career was to be shunter. This work was on the loops on the north side of the station. The duty was to uncouple and marshall the wagons so they could proceed south, west or east. The Steetley Quarry train still came through with dolomite limestone on the way to Dowlais Steelworks near Merthyr. This would have 15 wagons with some being taken off at Builth Road to work to Gorseinon near Swansea.

There was a very steep grade between Doldowlod and Rhayader working to Moat Lane but any banker was normally provided by Builth or Llanidloes shed.

The shunting engines included the Kerry Dean pannier until 1950. Other locomotives had a time interval for shunting between line duties and would include Llanidloes, Moat Lane and Machynlleth engines at various times of the day. Reversing with a 'Dean Goods' would see everyone, shunters, fireman and driver, soaking wet during a south-westerly gale even with the canvas sheet in place. Dai became a grade I shunter in 1950. This would include working at Kerry terminus on sheep sale days. The young firemen such as Bill Jones were sent off to Old Oak and then a course at Swindon to become drivers. The shunter stopped where he was learning the rule book and taking various tests under the supervision of inspector Dan Jones from Aberystwyth. Dai moved to Rhayader during the peak flow of materials to the Claerwen dam construction.

Builth staff brought two types of load into the yard. The cement from Aberthaw Works (Glamorgan coast) was held in an early bulk form with two steel containers per wagon. The other load was a green facing stone cut by the forwarding quarry for using on the dam face. Again there would be two on each flat wagon. A small mobile crane on rubber wheels was at the yard for the duration with Ifor Lawrence as the driver. The items were placed on a lorry and the lorry returned with the empty cement containers.

Promotion took Dai to be senior shunter at Builth Wells from 1952 to 1958. There still some cattle wagons on a weekly basis but volume loading from both sheep and store cattle took place each autumn. Feedstuffs and fertilizer came in. Artificial fertilizer was called Fisons by many farmers even if it was ICI or another brand. Much wool was loaded between June and September and forwarded to Bradford. Farm machinery came in on flats and included the little grey Ferguson tractor. Timber was loaded through the year, including pit props but also trunk timber, loaded on to 'Macaw' bogie bolster wagons. Empty wagons were sent about 800 yards to Llanelwedd quarry loop around 10.45 am and returned with the previous day's wagons full of roadstone around 11.30 am. Builth was such a contrast with the exchange station of Moat Lane with all the necessary loading and unloading and interface with the customers.

There was a one-bay engine shed at Builth. It closed in 1957 and the reduced need for a locomotive could be met from Builth Road until that closed around 1962. Dai thinks these were the only two engine sheds in Radnorshire as the Knighton shed was just over the border in Shropshire. There were four sets of enginemen at Builth and they were Ted Davies, Bill Egerton, Terry Crimmond and Harold Richards and

Right: Dai, aged 25, taken at Y Pant, Llandinam when he was the shunter at Builth Wells.

Dai y Pant, Edwards, Newtown

Below: Wrexham Central was the final Cambrian station from Ellesmere. Dai stands next to the shorter Keith Stayley. Both had worked in the Caersws area many years previously. The other staff are Reg Green (porter) and Jack Lewis (driver). Marchweil siding remained in use for several years after closure to Ellesmere to service a creamery and an oil depot. It was a huge wartime complex with an ordnance factory.

Dai y Pant, Edwards, Newtown

they worked with firemen Neville Williams, Reg Loveridge, John Watkin and Vincent Lawrence. There was a combined cleaner/coal loader also called Ted Davies. The engine shed had a brick base with corrugated sides with an awkwardly-sited turntable and coal loading siding.

Dai returned to Moat Lane in 1958 as a guard. Dai was often on sick or holiday cover working to Aberystwyth, Pwllheli, Whitchurch and also Aberystwyth to Carmarthen. The normal duty was on the Brecon line either the Moat Lane-Llanidloes shuttle or to Builth or the whole way to Brecon. There were very few passengers during the winter months between Llanidloes and Builth except on Saturdays. The guard/luggage section on one coach was usually placed next to the full passenger coach on the two-coach train so that parcel loading and unloading was within the central area of the station close to the canopy. This was very wise on many a winter day. The daily stopping goods worked down to Talyllyn and then back to Moat Lane. There were only shunters at Llanidloes, Builth and Talyllyn so both the guard and the fireman worked the various ground frames into the local sidings placing the necessary wagons, usually coal, and hauling out the empties. Single wagon freight to rural stations was in rapid retreat by the late 1950s.

Dai opted for transfer rather than redundancy in 1962 and was moved to Croes Newydd at Wrexham. This was a freight duties-only location as Chester and Shrewsbury guards now staffed the passenger services. Trains worked included from Stanlow oil refinery to Shrewsbury for crew change. Steel was taken from Shotton to Hockley Sidings in Birmingham. Coal and empties were taken up the steep little branch to Brymbo and the gradients and curves were not unlike the Kerry except for the industrial setting. The Brymbo steel wagons were marshalled at Croes Newydd. Dai was never stuck in the snow on the upland routes through Wales, but their train became firmly stuck in a snow drift at Neston on the Wirral in early 1963.

Dai could be the guard taking coal in and cement out of the Tunnel Cement Works at Padeswood at the Penyffordd siding. Some were marshalled at Croes Newydd to be sent to Coton Hill Yard at Shrewsbury before proceeding past the now childhood home station at Llandinam, their destination the Clywedog Dam construction. Another duty was to work on the Wrexham-Ellesmere branch as far as Marchwiel where oil tankers were collected and returned to Stanlow oil refinery. There were several viaducts just south of Wrexham Central that would have been maintained by the Caersws Bridge Department. Croes Newydd had four English Electric class '40' locomotives allocated for freight. The need for a guard's van on block bulk trains was retreating so Dai opted to leave the railway in 1970. He had a lovely home in the uplands south of Newtown and did not wish to spent any more time in lodgings. He secured work in a local factory until retirement at the age of 65.

A succession of engine cleaners

This section is a précis of several careers that started at Moat Lane. There are very few relevant photographs available from these then young lads. This is hardly surprising as their work was on the night shift.

Gerald and Aneurin Jones of Llandinam. Gerald started at Moat Lane with the GWR on 10th November, 1947 and vesting day for British Railways was 1st January, 1948. An older friend, Elvet Gethin, had just been promoted. Gerald immediately went to see the station master for the assumed job vacancy and was told in a stern voice 'no vacancy'. Grandfather worked in the Bridge Department stores and was known as

'John the Tools'. So 'Taid' (grandad) immediately phoned the station master at Moat Lane saying his grandson was with him. He returned to be taken on as junior porter as he was too young for night shift. Work at Moat Lane was valued and it was always a help to be part of the GWR local (nepotic) empire. Porter and lamp duties continued for about 18 months until a cleaner's vacancy arose. The locomotives were Dean or Cambrian 'Goods', the Kerry tank plus a rebuilt 'Duke' with the Cornish name of *Tre Pol & Pen*.

Soon a request came to transfer to Llanidloes engine shed. So Gerald cycled from the village to Llanidloes but usually returned home in the guard's van. The next stage was to train as junior fireman and he was sent to Wolverhampton. National Service followed until 1952. He returned to spend the remainder of his railway career in the West Midlands completing 49 years of service. He progressed from fireman to driver. Much of the work was at Bescot yard on freight. He later drove diesels working freight to Crewe, Bristol and London. Another duty was the relatively short journey taking coal to the Ironbridge power station. Gerald also worked the electrics to Euston.

Younger brother, Aneurin, joined Moat Lane as an engine cleaner in 1951. His duty only lasted four months. A vacancy for fireman for Wolverhampton was posted in the mess room and Aneurin applied. This was very rapid advancement. The problem was that a nationally agreed wage was very competitive in rural Wales but faced staff retainment problems in the then booming Black Country. The result was that Wolverhampton (Low Level) GWR almost became a Welsh colony from the 1930s to the mid-1950s. Aneurin progressed within a period of time to driver at Oxley on shunting duties and then to Woverhampton (Stafford Road) for steam passenger services including the Paddington to Birkenhead and the 'Cambrian Coast Express' to Shrewsbury. Steam finished in 1967 and the ensuing redundancies caused Aneurin to become a secondman in the electric cabs to Euston. The unions finally agreed on one man in the cab so a move was made to permanent way maintenance to train as a heavy crane driver on the new Midland Division that included support for bridges on the previous Oswestry Division. There was a request to go to Clatter and no one knew such a place existed. One of the lads was so excited that he phoned Euston saying Aneurin knew where to go.

Both brothers finished in the mid-1990s, Aneurin before the sub-contracts with Railtrack started and Gerald finished a few weeks before Virgin commenced so his career virtually coincided with the life of British Railways. Both recall the older men travelling to Moat Lane to visit the room with a beer licence. So the temperance hotel was by-passed and many a happy smile got off the last train from Whitchurch to Llanidloes. Moat Lane had acquired an alternative name of the 'Pig and Whistle'. Gerald would transfer many a parcel at Moat Lane in 1948 when he was a porter. A definition of a parcel had a wide interpretation as it would include day old chicks, racing pigeons and a single small farm animal such as a ram, a goat or a calf tied on a strawed sheet. Even greyhounds were forwarded during the fuel crisis of 1947/48. There was and still remains a trade of selling trained sheep dogs from the skills within an upland farm. Aneurin recalls a classic at Wolverhampton when a sheep dog ran loose. A very strong Welsh accent was heard, 'Stop that dog, he is a parcel'.

Both boys stopped in a very comfortable hostel in Wolverhampton. Many large interchange stations had to provide such facilities for drivers, firemen and guards who often had to work back to their home base the following day. This may be the reason for the very large station at Llanidloes to accommodate staff on the aborted Manchester & Milford line. There was also a draft plan for a small hotel and hostel at Moat Lane around 1875, but it remained only an idea.

Gary Jones was another Llandinam lad. He joined the Moat Lane staff in 1953 at the age of 16 so he commenced as a night shift cleaner. This duty only lasted five months as there were desperate requests to move to certain industrial areas so Gary opted for junior fireman at Wolverhampton. There were also some West Indian immigrants there helping especially as cleaners and coalers. No doubt some of their grandchildren now speak with a Black Country hint of dialect. The basic duties were Wolverhampton to Chester via Shrewsbury or Crewe and Wolverhampton to Bristol both before and after National Service (1955 to 1957). The occasional roster to London would have a crew change at Banbury and work back. Some of the extra holiday specials worked via the Shrewsbury curve rather than drawing into the station. Heavier locomotives could work the joint LMS/GWR line to Welshpool when the lighter locomotives and Machynlleth or Aberystwyth crew took over. Other specials and the 'Cambrian Coast Express' would call at Shrewsbury and the Machynlleth crew and lighter engine took over. There was flexibility according to engine availability. Gary had to fire once to and from Machynlleth and was not used to non-stopping double-headed trains on single token lines. He had not acquired the art and finished the shift with huge bruises on his arms. The second locomotive carried the token. The freight workings were from Oxley yard mainly to Banbury. One duty was to haul the iron ore train back to Bilston works. The ore came from that corner of Northamptonshire and Oxfordshire where there was a considerable network of now lost ironstone railways. It was a very heavy train back to Bilston. Banbury had a recently installed humpyard that was floodlit at night so Gary would watch this marshalling activity as they waited to roll out with the Bilston train.

Gary took the chance to return to Moat Lane in late 1959. His regular driver was Arthur Evans. Gary recalls several incidents. The service was running late to Brecon due to the late arrival of the through train to Aberystwyth at Moat Lane. An attempt was made to gain some time. There was a road crossing near Llyswen and the signals and gates were normally set for the train when on time. Gary shouted to the driver that the signal was against them so the brakes were applied but it was too late and they sailed through the wooden gates. The driver and Gary were suspended and had to attend an interview at Oswestry, Gary had three weeks suspension and Arthur, who was then 64, was placed on shed duties until retirement.

Gary's home was at Neuadd-llwyd beside the track just south of Llandinam. He had overslept one morning so the mail train left Moat Lane with the night fireman on board. The driver was Reg Cwmbelan and he stopped outside the house and tooted the whistle. Gary scrambled on board to take on duty without his toast and tea but with his pyjama bottoms under his trousers. The night fireman got off at Llanidloes and Gary had to endure much leg pulling.

The bridge over the Severn at Llandinam took a tremendous battering with floods and the 1960 flood closed the bridge. A staff swap took place so that Llanidloes lads worked south and the Moat Lane crews worked to Oswestry and Whitchurch. Gary was offered a move to London in late 1962 but opted for redundancy. He moved to Ciliau Aeron in 1982 to work, continuing to live on a smallholding supplementing income with lorry driving. The route out would cross the long closed level crossing by the station on the Aberayron Light Railway. Gary looks back with much nostalgia to his short-lived railway career of only 10 years. There was a skill and a thrill working steam locomotives.

Rodney Evans started at Moat Lane Junction as a cleaner in 1951 under the tutelage of Mr Davage, the chargehand. He started on the Monday and a Den Thomas had left the previous Friday to join the Rhodesian Railways. Den was often recalled in the mess room especially when he sent a letter to his old pals. Rodney can remember the first engine cleaned was 'Dean Goods' No. 2449. He completed around 18 months, became a passed cleaner ready to move forward to fireman and then was called up for National Service. He was re-posted to Shrewsbury on demobilization and qualified as a fireman. One duty would be to work the old joint GWR/LMS line to Welshpool. His older brother, Robert, would have previously worked from Moat Lane to Whitchurch based at Welshpool and would have included the Welshpool-Llanfair branch rota. Another duty for Rodney was the Minsterley goods. The whole shift was to take coal plus empty wagons to Minsterley and return with creamery produce. The other closed line worked was the Severn Valley through Coalport to Bridgnorth. It was said that the Severn Valley was for rabbits and pheasants but Minsterley for mushrooms, swedes, honey and eggs. Rodney would return to Moat Lane on summer Saturdays usually travelling 'on the cushions' to Aberystwyth and bringing a heavily-loaded double-headed passenger back. This had to stop at Moat Lane for water. Robert was firing with Albert Jones. The first locomotive had two Oswestry lads, Doug Lawson and Ben Ruff. Doug told Rodney they would shift through Forden and to be smart with the Montgomery-Forden token. Rodney leaned out and placed the token neatly on the catching hook and it spun round like a catherine wheel. Doug leaned out from the front locomotive and clapped with appreciation (boys with giant toys!). The line was double between Forden and Buttington Junction and then again was single with token exchange at Breidden and Westbury before the double line resumed again at Hanwood. Severe cutbacks commenced from 1960 onwards with line closure and withdrawal of rural stations including Buttington Junction in 1960. Rodney faced redundancy as the dmus started to come in so he opted for transfer to Southern Region and passed as a driver for both electric third-rail multiple-units and the diesel-electric locomotives with third rail pick-up. His duty was to work from Victoria to Haywards Heath and Brighton passing through the rapidly-altering Gatwick.

Rodney just could not afford accommodation. He did not wish to spend time away from his family so he opted to finish in 1968 and returned to Newtown. He sometimes regrets this decision which may have been made in haste and could have waited for an opportunity for transfer to Crewe or Wolverhampton. Rodney started work cleaning a vintage GWR 'Dean Goods' at Moat Lane. One of his final steam rosters was with a BR 2-10-0 only a few years old working a heavy oil train out of Ellesmere Port refinery. It just coasted up the Rossett Bank between Chester and Wrexham steaming and pulling like magic. The first bridge east of Buttington Junction on the joint line at Cefn was and remains on a sharp bend. There often was yet another fence gap with a car parked in the adjoining field awaiting recovery. The Central Wales line was also worked as far as Llandovery. They got hopelessly stuck in a snow drift at the Sugar Loaf summit in 1963. The track had an underbridge over the Mid-Wales line at Builth Road. It was only a few months after closure when the track to Llanidloes was lifted and this was observed crossing the bridge. The Central Wales line was busy with night freight of coal and steel until around 1960. Sometimes Shrewsbury was so congested that they would get permission to use the triangle loop to turn rather than book the turntable.

Rodney recalls a duty cleaner's task at Moat Lane around 4.00 am. The knocker-up walked or cycled to Caersws along the footpath, often in appalling weather. Some would leave out a stick to tap the upper window, others were alerted by an aimed pebble.

Charlie Caple was the problem. He was a heavy sleeper so his wife would acknowledge that she was awake by a blow on a whistle. Gruffydd Jones' house had to be approached through back yards. On a pitch black night, Rodney managed to knock a zinc bath off the hook, dogs howled and the whole terrace was awake. Jack Davies was an older driver due to retire and it could be two to three minutes before he signalled that he was awake. Jack was a junior cleaner at Llanidloes in January 1921 and he was one that was asked to return to work immediately around mid-day. Llanidloes had the nearest spare locomotive on the down side so this locomotive plus wagons, axes, hacksaws, etc. was at the crash site at Abemule within 60 minutes.

Rodney is again one of many that looks back with considerable nostalgia at a railway career. Railways were within the blood of the lads of the Upper Severn Valley centred on Caersws for just over a century.

It is not known how many young men qualified as junior fireman to work from Moat Lane. The final lad in this illustrious line is *Trefor Owen of Tir-brwnt, Caersws*, who commenced as junior fireman/cleaner in 1959 at the age of 16. It was now realized that it was unlikely that the services south would continue to run so staffing with necessary new recruits was difficult. A Mr Jones was the engine shed boss who would call twice a week from Oswestry so one of the older men looked after the night shift. Huw Smout decided to leave to join the police force. Mr Jones asked Trefor if he would take on the duty. Trefor went to Oswestry for a two week course and passed as the last fireman at Moat Lane. He normally worked with Jack Hatton who lived in Ceiriog's house. Trefor applied for an engineering apprenticeship with the Royal Ordnance factory at Leeds making 'Chieftain' tanks. He commenced in September 1961. The technical school class also contained lads from John Fowler Ltd who were still making diesel shunting locomotives and the 'Challenger' crawler tractors. Fowler was a division of Thomas Ward which was awarded the contract to lift the line from Llanidloes to Brecon. In April 1959 Trefor was a pupil on the school train from Caersws to Newtown, he never realised that within the year he would be firing the train for scholars attending the new Further Education College between St Harmons and Moat Lane.

Two neighbours at Ael-y-bryn, Llandinam recall their railway interludes

Gwynne Jones opted to leave school at 15 in 1952 to become the lamp boy/junior porter at Newtown station. He transferred to Moat Lane as soon as he was 16 to work as a cleaner on night-shift for 11 months. He then went to Old Oak Common as a junior fireman. He returned to be a fireman for around 12 months firing for Arthur Evans, Charlie 'hit em' Claffey and Jack 'Oily' Hatton. He opted for three years' enlistment rather than two years' National Service. There was no vacancy at Moat Lane on return to 'civvies' so he was asked to move to Paddington. He gave his notice and worked afterwards in local forests, then on building sites and then a factory night shift. It was obvious that the rural line was under threat from car and lorry competition. He still had many friends at Moat Lane and it seemed a strange decision to erect a new engine shed in the late 1950s.

Dad worked at the Bridge Department. His duty was to carry the ladder for the bridge inspector. The pair would travel on the passenger service to a station, then walk to another station further along the line to catch a train home so Dad must have walked every inch of the GWR/BR Oswestry Division. An older brother of Gwynne, the late Emrys, joined the railway as a platelayer. He took every opportunity for study until he became a salaried permanent way engineer based at Manchester. BR consultancy took him to both Zambia and the Canton Railway of Hong Kong.

The brand new engine shed dates from 1957. The small shed on the right was a store. The two bays into the shed also had an outside service pit. The Mogul tender is beside the water column on our right and the coal truck on the left is for direct loading. The turntable on the fourth road is hidden behind the truck. No photograph taken by local staff has been located.

Welsh Railway Research Circle, Stratton Collection

Tom Kinsey stands in front of the right line of the engine shed in January 2007. The rail track can be discerned embedded in the concrete and filled-in pit. This area is leased to a forest company. Tom's ancestors sold the site to the original railway companies in the late 1850s. Tom's father re-purchased the site around 1966 after the station building had been demolished so he cannot give a reason why such a substantial dwelling was knocked down.   *Brian Poole*

The two coal loaders at Moat Lane have long passed on. They were Goronwy Price of Llanidloes and Sid Corfield of Caersws. They worked alternate weekly shifts of day or night. The coal truck was parked out in the open. There was no intermediate loading platform so the coal was shovelled directly to the tender. Although it was not the duty of the cleaner, Gwynne would help the older man on this physically demanding duty. Work proceeded in all weathers whether dry or humid, still or a howling gale, or rain, or heavy ground frost, or a blizzard. The shovelling eased once a third was unloaded so they could shovel from the floor planks and open the door. The usual night fireman who moved the locomotives was either Jack Davies or Ken Davies; Mr Davage (Gwynne would never have used his first name) was the chargehand.

Emrys Evans lives next door to Gwynne. Both attended Llandinam school starting around 1942 in the final few years as an all age-school. Emrys went to the technical school at Newtown while Gwynne went the opposite way to Llanidloes for secondary education. Emrys' father worked for the railway as a porter at Llandinam station before and during World War II. He was also on guard duty for the Observer Corps in a shed up the mountain so Dad must have worked up to 16 hours every day. Emrys sadly noted the uncle he never knew. Albert Evans (known as Penri within the family) was the fireman on the down train from Whitchurch working to Llanidloes on the ill-fated day in January 1921 at Abermule. It will never be known why Penri or the driver failed to double-check the incorrect token handed to them. Dad thought that Penri was so busy putting coal into the firebox on the incline that he may never have known that the fatal impact was immediate. Ernie Trow had been station master at Llandinam since their childhood. He seemed to be a permanent feature but he finally retired. Emrys took on duty at Llandinam for three years from 1960 to closure in December 1962. He was everything, book-keeper, gatekeeper, looking after freight, etc. As manager, he could not tell the junior off for not cleaning the platform as he was also the junior. It was a very quiet job compared with Ernie Trow and Dad's work during World War II. There was so much through freight during the war and Mrs Trow received pay for opening the gates during the night so Ernie could sleep on until the mail came in around 6.00 am. Peter and Ruth Poole lived in the station house. Peter cycled to Moat Lane while Ruth looked after the two children. A Bill Pryce and his wife took on the Moat Lane refreshment room for the final year of operation.

The next station down the line was Dolwen. There was a low bridge but only cars and vans could pass underneath. Lorries and tractors with a trailer load of hay had to cross the adjoining level crossing with the gate shut to road traffic. The lorry driver had to go to Dolwen station so the duty (usually) lady would secure the signal and open the gate. Full wagon freight only was propelled by pilot from Llanidloes and not a shunt on the stopping goods. The station had become a halt around 1956. Mrs Harrison, the widow of the station master, kept the gate key. She had become immobile so one of her daughters returned to live at the Dolwen station house. Cover had to be arranged sometimes. Gangers worked on the line with a small Wickham powered trolley.

The really big event of Emrys' tenure was the Severn flood of 1960 that took out part of one pier at Llandinam. This left the rail bridge with a sag. The bridge was closed for about 10 weeks. Lovatts of Wolverhampton were contracted to drive in new piles, fit a replacement pier, jack up the sag and strengthen with cross members. A Crosville bus operated from Moat Lane to Llandinam. The bus could only stop on the main road because the first road bridge built by David Davies had a weight restriction. Any passenger had to walk about 50 yards from or to the station over the Severn. Newtown railway depot took on the parcels, newspapers and mail. Heavy

Gwyneth Morris would visit Moat Lane station to see her grandparents with her late father. Howell senior was the last station master. Granny was terminally ill in 1962 so poor Howell had some pressure with both illness and station closure. Gwyneth was only three and her main memory was climbing a large Victorian wooden staircase to the bedroom. Howell moved to live with his maiden sister at Bwlch near Brecon until his death in the early 1970s. Howell Morris's oldest son is Frank who started at Machynlleth with Archie Fleming in the mid-1930s. He moved to Banbury and spent his railway career in the Midlands. The then young Frank Morris is leaning out of the lead 'Earl' class 4-4-0 locomotive. It can be difficult to place a photograph because of tree growth since the demise of steam. Note the coping stone just visible in the right-hand corner of the picture. This is part of skew bridge 197 (Dolgoch No. 1) with an upstream wing of five chains plus (over 100 metres) to contain flood erosion from both the Afon Tyn-y-rhos and the larger Afon Iaen. Bridge No. 198 is a side occupation bridge and the accommodation crossing is by the fifth coach. Bells bridge, No. 200, is out of view 300 yards further down the track and also incorporates a long culvert under the embankment known as Dolgoch No. 2 (bridge No. 199). The up train has only a short distance to travel before it enters the Talerddig cutting.   *Ifor Higgins*

Howell Morris, the last station master, welcomes the Lord Mayor of Cardiff when he makes a fact-finding tour of the threatened line on 13th February, 1962. The other dignatories include local councillors. They are on the Llanidloes platform. *Gwyneth Yeoman née Morris, Llandrindod*

goods were diverted via Builth Road. The local heavy freight such as coal and animal feeds was collected at Newtown sidings. The railway delivered much dry sugar beet pulp into the area during the winter months. The bridge was dismantled soon after the last cement train to Clywedog crossed in late 1967. So ended the history of one of the more difficult bridges for maintenance for the Bridge Department with the depot only a mile away across the flood plain.

Broneirion House was close to the station. This was the house built by David Davies for his family home around 1864 as his wealth started to increase. It became a centre for girl guides around 1947. It soon was not only a centre for Welsh and British guides but attracted members far and wide. This house generated much traffic although not much revenue; the most work was checking their return tickets. Emrys recalls the problem with some Swedish guides. They had travelled on an express that split somewhere like Hamburg with half the train going on to Milan and the remainder to the Hook of Holland for the ferry to Harwich. Somehow, the girls were on the correct section but the luggage proceeded to Milan. The girls spent their week in borrowed clothes and their luggage arrived the day after they had left. Such were some of the varied duties of the station in the final years of operation.

Both men recalled their childhood when the railwaymen would leave the village for their shift at Moat Lane or the Bridge Department with their heavy-framed bicycles. The temperance hotel ceased around 1959. Both can recall the last through train from Whitchurch to Llanidloes with the men with their one stop return ticket to and from Moat Lane and their happy ruddy faces. Both men sampled their first draught bitter at Moat Lane. It had a lovely taste. The author recalls an older farm worker, long deceased, who thought paradise may be a pint of beer from the oak cask at Moat Lane. It really had become part of the folklore of the community.

The last stage fare duty

Bernard Ashton was born and bred within the Pontdolgoch/Clatter community just west of Caersws. Taid (grandad) was a Cambrian guard and his duties included both the Llanfair and Rheidol lines. Uncle Idwal was a general labourer and Uncle Richard or Dic was a mason, both within the Bridge Department. Richard was the father of two signalmen, Lewis and Wyn. Uncle Jack was a lengthman between Moat Lane and Talerddig. Another older cousin, Walford, was a relief signalman and he lived at Weeg crossing where his mother, Auntie Bessie, was the crossing keeper.

Bernard joined the railway in February 1952 as a cleaner at Moat Lane. He had spent some time on local farms and was 21 years of age. He lost exemption rights so he was called up for National Service within eight months. He returned to Moat Lane for a fireman vacancy on demobilization in August 1954. He was still a fireman in December 1962 when closure took place. He fired the last full round trip train with Arwyn Price on 28th December, 1962 leaving Moat Lane at 9.55 am to arrive at Brecon at 12.40 and then return at 1.25 to arrive at Moat Lane at 4.03 pm. The guard gave him a pile of used tickets which Bernard has retained as a memento. The weather, with heavy snow drifting, was closing in.

Bernard recalls several previous incidents. The train entered the Marteg tunnel from the Rhayader side when he sensed sheep were in the darkness. The driver slowed down and sounded the whistle. They came out into the daylight to see boy scouts scrambling up the batter.* On another occasion when proceeding to cross the Wye bridge at Boughrood, they suddenly realized that two lads were on the track

---

* Packed earth on the steep slope at a tunnel entrance or the wing wall of an over- or under-bridge.

Taid (grandfather) smartly dressed in Cambrian uniform as a guard *circa* 1900. His guard rota would have included the newly-opened Llanfair Light Railway and holiday rota on the Rheidol line soon after the Cambrian takeover in 1916. Three sons and a son-in-law worked for the Cambrian/GWR from around 1910 to 1930s. Four grandsons including Bernard worked with the GWR/BR in the locality. *Bernard Ashton, Frodsham*

Photograph taken by the duty guard failed to get Reg 'Cwmbelan' Jones fully in the picture. Fireman, Bernard, and driver, Reg, take a short break around 1955. Bernard cannot remember the site but thinks it was either at Builth Wells or Builth Road. *Bernard Ashton, Frodsham*

Photograph taken in 2007 by the tombstone of John Ashton, 1861-1940, in the now closed Siloh cemetery at Clatter. John was a little boy when the Newtown & Machynlleth Railway constructed the line near his Clatter home creating the chance for him to join the Cambrian Railways around the late 1870s. Most inscriptions in this corner are in Welsh. So John's spirit can look into the valley as the four-coach train will soon cross bridge No. 178 over the Afon Carno and pass the long deserted Clatter Loop. *Author*

and the boys had to hang on to the side of the bridge to escape. It was thought that they may have been salmon poaching. Both groups of young boys were very lucky as it was was a stupid and dangerous venture.

Bernard worked a football special from Newtown to Llanidloes with Jack Jarman as driver. They noticed football supporters on the platform at Moat Lane as they passed through and wondered whether they had misread the diagram working. They therefore decided to stop at both Llandinam and Dolwen but found no one at either station. All was well as the special was not booked to stop at Moat Lane and the disappointed supporters had turned up too early because they should have caught the normal service due to follow the path of the special.

There was a stopping freight all the way to Talyllyn Junction.(The train went on to Brecon with crew change at Talyllyn.) The smaller sidings had a ground frame operated by either the guard or the foreman with a key on the electric token. The line was close to a large quarry south of Rhayader and the signalman had to check with the quarry so no detonation of the rock face would take place when a train was due to pass.* There was a good time interval at Builth Road for freight transfer and Builth Wells for any marshalling.

Bernard opted to continue with his railway career rather than take redundancy in January 1963. He transferred to Shrewsbury as a fireman, later a secondman in diesel cabs. The duty would include Saturday holiday specials on the Cambrian with footplate exchange usually at Welshpool or Machynlleth. The train had still to stop at the now partially-demolished Moat Lane during the summer of 1965 to take on water before the long climb. They should have stopped longer at Moat Lane to build up steam so the driver had to stop at the recently closed Pontdolgoch station. Aunty Lil had married the now retired signalman, Emrys Wilson, and they lived at the station house. Aunt Lil appeared with two cups of steaming tea as they waited to get sufficient steam pressure to continue to Talerddig summit. An odd event took place when Bernard was secondman on the York-Aberystwyth night mail working from Crewe to Shrewsbury. The boiler fitted on the locomotive heated the carriages where mail men were sorting letters. The boiler started to overheat so they stopped to turn the boiler off. They moved on to find a signal, where they never usually stopped, against them. Police cars were at the crossing in case there had been another audacious mail train robbery.

Bernard was moved on. The Southampton docks was an interesting interlude with passenger working to the Ocean Terminal for the last period of the large liners such as SS *United States*, SS *France* and the Cunards. Bernard then moved to Liverpool for Speke Junction and finally Garston. Bernard was now qualified for both electric and diesel locomotives and multiple units. The passenger trains to Euston changed drivers at Rugby to work the Euston back to Liverpool. Garston came up for closure in 1994 so Bernard took early retirement at the age of 63. Bernard then looked back to previous decades to add to the legion of Moat Lane stories when he was a cleaner and fireman.

The engines really were cold on a Monday morning. Kindle sticks made into a frame came down from Oswestry. Cotton waste soaked in paraffin was used to start the fire. There was no pressure for a short period until the blower came into action so the initial fire produced a cloud of acrid smoke. The fire draw was quick once the blower came into action. One driver had not appeared so Bernard was asked to get on his bike and he cycled along the cinder track to Caersws. The driver had woken up and had chosen to cycle along the Moat Lane so they missed each other. Bernard arrived at the cottage

* This quarry is at Cerrig Gwynion and was used for roadstone with road transport. The Cambrian placed a siding and loading stage during the construction of the dams in the Elan Valley around 1897. It is only a mile from the Elan Valley Junction.

Arwyn Price recalls double heading when a light engine was worked back for a duty at another engine shed. The two Moguls pull two coaches into the Builth Wells complex from the south in 1960. Llanelwedd Church is in the immediate background and the work faces of Llanelwedd quarry show up with the snow and frost in the background. Roadstone from the quarry was a valued revenue source. *Mrs Pat Power/Les Mayall Studios, Builth*

The last service train, Brecon to Moat Lane, at Builth Wells on the last Saturday in December 1962. Arwyn Price was the driver. The temperature had fallen well below zero celsius increasing the effect of condensing steam. The locomotive had not been turned at Brecon so it was working tender first. *Dennis Glasscodine, Abermule*

to knock at the window. The poor lady had just got off to sleep again to find Bernard, the knocker-up, below at 4.00 am. He may have had the contents of the chamber pot on his head if this had been the medieval village. One of the staff on the Moat Lane payroll had a side enterprise of barber. Bernard did not realise how good the barber was until he enlisted for military service when he had some sympathy for the sheep that had been sheared and grazed the pasture surrounds of Moat Lane. A locomotive was kept in steam on New Year's Eve. The whistle then sounded through the valley at midnight. Maybe this was a tradition at many sheds.

Bernard became the Moat Lane staff representative for the GWR Engineman & Fireman's Mutual Assurance Sick & Superannuation Scheme. This was eventually wound up and members were invited into the BR pension schemes in the late 1950s. The retired Machynlleth man on his list was Wmffre Humphreys noted as duty driver on the Corris line. One duty was to receive a wagon load of sleepers from Oswestry for retired fund members. Bill Gethin of the Bridge Department had an engine-powered portable saw bench. The wood was unloaded into piles, cut into logs and collected by the older men in wheelbarrows to take home for either logs or to split into kindle sticks. Maybe Moat Lane to Brecon had no place within a modern transport system but it truly was a wonderful experience to have worked the line. Both Bernard and Arwyn plus many others recall an aspect of working the roads even at night. Every culvert, every underbridge or overbridge made a different sound so one knew where one was on the route irrespective of visibility. Any slight problem with the track could be sensed and the next signalman would be informed to pass on to the ganger. The local lengthman would have taken the necessary action such as packing of ballast, often before the return journey.

Arwyn Price, the driver of the last round working from Moat Lane to Brecon and return already mentioned, was interviewed at his home at Llanwrda, Caernarfon in December 2006. His childhood was at Carno. His father was a coal loader at Moat Lane and then became one of signalmen/crossing keepers at Carno. Arwyn joined Moat Lane as cleaner in early 1943 under the wing of Mr Davage with duties as already described. He was asked to move to Tyseley (Birmingham) as junior fireman in 1944. The RAF defences were such by this stage that any Luftwaffe attack was unusual. He caused his landlady to face a fine for not drawing the curtain and infringing the black-out regulations. First duties were shunting in the yards. Duties then expanded usually moving empty stock to Birmingham (Snow Hill) and then freight radiating out to Banbury, Worcester, Kidderminster and Wolverhampton. The contrast of the Black Country and the Upper Severn Valley was immense.

Harold Hawes was promoted to driver at Moat Lane so this gave Arwyn the chance to return to Moat Lane in 1946. Oliver Gittins was the usual driver of the duty Dean pannier that worked to Kerry. Oliver gave Arwyn a small bugle he had retained from around 1910 when he retired in about 1950. This bugle was used at Oswestry at night in place of the shrill piercing of the steam whistle when night shunting. This was due to complaints of waking the town. People could sleep through the noise and clanging of shunting but found the higher frequency of the night whistle to be a different proposition. Oliver could have started his career as cleaner and then junior fireman in 1905. The system changed in 1950 when the Moat Lane freight to Oswestry changed crew, usually at Montgomery, to worked a 'Dean Goods' to Kerry. Arwyn has fired both pannier tank and tender engine to Kerry.

Promotion to driver took place in 1956 after attending a course at Swindon. He was on driver's pay (passed fireman) for 18 months before becoming a regular driver. The Ivatt and BR Moguls were starting to take over duties. Two Cambrian 'Goods' (Nos.

Faces of Moat Lane past. The source of the photographs on pages 102-105 is from the families or a cutting from the *County Times/Montgomeryshire Express*. Some date from the early 1900s but most from 1935 to 1965. A selection has been made to further illustrate the importance of railway employment.

a. Richard George retired in 1938 with 37 years' service. He was a cattle wagon loader based at Builth Wells. His duty was to attend the main markets plus the main sheep and cattle sales. He was well known to farmers and dealers as well as his railway colleagues. There were also specialist timber loaders.

b. William Jones retired in 1938 after 44½ years of service. He began his career at Builth Wells engine shed in 1893, then Brecon and lived at Llanidloes from 1904 onwards. He was a driver from Llanidloes to Whitchurch and south to Brecon. His father was one of the first Cambrian drivers. William had four brothers with the railways including a signalman at Moat Lane, a GWR driver at Wellington (Salop) and two with the LMS at Bradford and Liverpool.

c. William Thomas was a goods clerk at Builth Wells for four years. He was then promoted to clerk-in-charge at the goods at Oswestry. His work would have included monitoring the progress of wagons through the exchange at Moat Lane. In 1938, he left to work for the Ferrocarriles Antofagasta Bolivia (in the Andes) then owned by a British company. A number of men moved abroad with some locals recalling a lost great uncle in India, Rhodesia, Canada, the Argentine and one letter to Newtown Historical Society to ask how an ancestor from Penstrowed became a road/bridge maintenance engineer in the late 1890s on the Milwaukee Road, USA. The earliest example must be the foreman contractor for David Davies in the 1860s. Morgan Jones moved to the USA and was responsible for much railway construction in Texas.

d. Bert Davage moved from Bristol to Moat Lane as chargehand of the engine shed. His eyesight was not good enough to continue as an engine driver. His work is described in detail by the young cleaners. He married a Caersws lass. He enjoyed cricket and he was Mr Caersws Cricket Club for many years. His daughter was the first railway queen.

e. Arthur Evans started his career as a cleaner at Laira (Plymouth) and worked at Leamington Spa, Exeter and Banbury. He came to Moat Lane as a driver in 1938 and retired in January 1963 with the closure of Moat Lane shed.

f. Charlie Claffey started at Oswestry as a cleaner and came to Moat Lane as a fireman in 1920 and was promoted to driver in 1941. His daughter, Christine, was railway queen in 1960. He also retired in January 1963 when Moat Lane shed closed.

g. Tommy Webb was duty signalman at Moat Lane West. He was a native of Rhayader and joined the Cambrian at Builth Wells in 1915. The photograph, taken in 1962, celebrates 40 continuous years with the first aid movement.

h. George Jones received his gold watch for 45 years of service in 1962. He worked at Machynlleth, Llanidloes, Moat Lane, Oswestry, Kerry (fireman until passenger service ceased in 1931) then Welshpool as both fireman and driver. His rota would have him working on the Llanfair line goods service during and after World War II.

Albert Freeman started work with the Cambrian as lamp boy and served the Cambrian, GWR and BR for 48 years until Moat Lane closure in 1962. The illustration is from the *County Times* in 1970. Albert had taken the signal from Montgomery station and erected it in his garden between Llanidloes Road level crossing and the bridge over the Severn at Caersws to remind him of his days as signalman and guard. Another brother worked for the Bridge Department.

849 and 855) were disliked as the vacuum brake was worked by direct steam and not from a reservoir pump. Arwyn cycled to work in the 1940s but acquired a Triumph Twin motor cycle. He was aware that the young cleaners would have a spin on this bike along the straight road to Old Moat Lane. He helped to fire the Llynclys to Dowlais Top dolomite freight working to either Three Cocks or Talyllyn Junction for crew change. It was a heavy load leaving Moat Lane around 2.15 am (this time explains why the author has failed to locate any photograph of this working). They would work a passenger service back returning to Moat Lane around 9.05 am. The steep gradient between Doldowlod and Rhayader was enough to cause a heavy freight to stall. The older men could remember a Builth engine would simmer at Doldowlod to bank both heavy freight and excursions over this difficult piece of road. It would be a rare event to have heavy freight after 1955. The problem of a stalled train was solved by splitting the train at the now unstaffed loop/station leaving a section of the wagons with the brakes pinned down at Doldowlod. The front section was then stabled at Rhayader, then the engine and guard's van returned to collect the remainder. Only a line with huge under-usage could employ such a system.

Arwyn was asked to recall the bridges. Different sounds would tell where they were on a pitch black winter morning. They could also open the fire box door which would create an eerie floodlight so they could recognise a hedge or gate feature. There were no long stretches across flat pasture as the route alternated between cuttings and embankments with many over and under accommodation lanes and cattle creeps. There were numerous culverts as well as stream and river bridges. A stream could be just a trickle one day and would turn into a raging torrent within hours after heavy rain. The first major feature after leaving Brecon would be the tunnel prior to entering Talyllyn Junction. This tunnel was on the flat so it had little smoke problem. Underbridges were frequent around Talgarth. The train swung west at Three Cocks to cross the first Wye bridge at Boughrood. The train then ran along the east side of the Wye crossing several side gorges. The train passed under the Swansea line at Builth Road. The next river bridge was over the Ithon as it flowed into the Wye. This bridge was in a dip with an approach slope on either side. Caution was needed as wagons on a heavy train would push hard and then snatch as the gradient on the opposite approach was tackled. The Wye was crossed just north of Newbridge, then again near Doldowlod and finally on the gradient approaching the Rhayader tunnel.

The Elan Valley line was now obliterated with vegetation. The main line looked down on Rhayader and continued on the west side of the valley until crossing the Wye for the final time before entering the Marteg valley. The Marteg tunnel was on an incline where steam could be so bad that a wet handerkerchief was placed over the mouth to try and reduce smoke discomfort. The train burst out to cross a bridge over the Afon Marteg. This bridge was crossed one morning when under a severe flood spate. Arwyn and his fireman were the last to cross until the river flow slowed and the Caersws boys carried out inspection and repaired dislodged masonry. There were several overbridges either side of the summit at Pantydwr.

Reg Cwmbelan and Ken Jones were stuck all night in a snow drift at St Harmons in 1947. Ken tried to walk to Pantydwr with the tablet. The snow drifts had merged the line into a whiteout and Ken fell into a culvert and lost the tablet. There was no chance of placing detonators as the snow drift filled the cutting. Morris Jones and Arwyn took staff from both Caersws Bridge Department and the permanent way gang at Llanidloes to dig the train out. Weather conditions were truly awful but they finally reached the stranded train. Trains must have crossed the Afon Dulas four or five times winding down through the valley through Tylwch to Penpontbren Junction. The section between Builth and Llanidloes must have been one of the most scenic routes in Britain.

The approach to Llanidloes was under two road bridges and the only inter-platform footbridge on the total length from Moat Lane to Brecon. The journey from Llanidloes to Moat Lane was a gentle run with the two main features of Morfodion and Llandinam bridges over the Severn. The passenger train would sometimes let passengers off on the Llanidloes platform at Moat Lane and place the carriages in the

Mr and Mrs Mills celebrate their golden wedding. They were married in Caersws Chapel in 1891. Mr Mills' father was a guard for the ballast train at Moat Lane. Mr Mills joined the Locomotive Department at Moat Lane in 1885. He worked for the Cambrian and the GWR. He returned to Moat Lane from Llanelli in 1932 as first class engine driver. He took part in many St John's ambulance competitions. He held numerous offices within the Amalgamated Society of Railway Servants for the Moat Lane & District Staff.

loop or would move to the north side of the island platform. This was convenient for parcel exchange as the train was timed to connect with the up Cambrian train. The locomotive was then taken to the shed to complete the shift. The fire was damped down so little firing took place from Llanidloes and hand-over to the engine shed staff was quick. Sometimes this engine would be required for banking to Talerddig and a message was given at Pantydwr to keep the fire up.

The Whitchurch early morning service started at Moat Lane during World War II and then reverted to a Llanidloes start with Llanidloes crew. Moat Lane would then work this train infrequently if there were difficulties at Llanidloes. A locomotive would work to Oswestry for any repair or exchange. Sometimes a locomotive would work through 'light' during the night from Oswestry if an engine was immobile. A double-headed train with only a few coaches would have a second engine working between sheds.

Arwyn opted to stay with the railway after December 1962 and was transferred to Slough passenger depot. He had two immediate tasks, to learn the road into Paddington and to drive a dmu. The main work was the suburban route from Reading to Paddington. He would see more passengers trying to get on at one station than would be seen over the whole distance from Moat Lane to Brecon and there was certainly more than one footbridge. The family stayed in Carno and Arwyn stopped in a hostel. It was no life and it was difficult to see how house purchase could be achieved. He gave in his notice during 1966 and Arwyn obtained work in a Newtown factory until that closed in 1980. He then took on a vacancy as level crossing keeper at Carno so he returned to the site where his father had worked in the 1930s. The gates were automated in November 1989 but a vacancy became available at Pwllheli for a conductor selling tickets. This was followed by duties combined with guard. This line could be very busy with many seaside halts during the summer season. Arwyn was 65 in 1991 and therefore retired.

He recalled two extra little difficulties. The train from Moat Lane to Whitchurch stopped at Ellesmere. A lady tumbled after stepping out and turning on to the sloping end of the platform. Maybe the train had stopped a few yards shorter than usual. The lady was in some discomfort but the train had to press on so a station porter gave the necessary help. She had broken her leg. A full report was necessary so both Arwyn and the driver were questioned by Jack Thomas, the footplate inspector.

The next occurred between Bourne End and Marlow around 1964. Arwyn was driving a single unit diesel. He sounded the horn but realised that the car was still proceeding. He braked but hit the car pushing the road vehicle sideways into the ditch area. The line was out of service, the train was taken back to depot and the necessary reports and interviews took place. Arwyn decided to call to see the driver in hospital out of courtesy. The fault was a road accident that involved a train. In the middle of the outer London green belt within stockbroker country, Arwyn had managed to hit a fellow Cymro (Welshman) from Bae Colwyn.

Arwyn was the junior passed driver at Moat Lane in 1962. He may be the last available for interview. His story is an inheritance that started in the early 1860s and stands as a tribute to many drivers who acquired the skill to work this difficult route.

Chapter Four

Working to and from Moat Lane Junction

This chapter divides into sections that recall some of the places east, west and south of Moat Lane. Trains continue to pass the remains of the station, working daily between Birmingham (International) and Aberystwyth/Pwllheli. A rich source of material has come forward so examples only have been chosen and placed into certain themes.

The basic duties of permanent way gangs and the relayers gang are recalled within the narrative of two men. The books of rules and regulations contain instructions for permanent way and works. There are several books from the GWR in the locality, one or two from the Cambrian and even one retained from the Oswestry & Newtown Railway. Several details follow from the Cambrian Railways rule book issued on 1st August, 1898. It is signed by David Evans, leading plumber of Aberdovey and endorsed by William Pryce Morris. The regulations include protection of line and staff, use of flagmen, use of lorry and such things as placing both danger signal and detonators at a set distance before taking a rail length out. The ganger is the foreman and his staff are the platelayers. Each ganger has to have the regulations with him and to ensure that his staff follow the procedures. The word 'lorry' in this book has an obsolete meaning. It was a four-wheel hand-pushed trolley that carried material such as ballast or balanced sleepers or overhung balanced rail lengths with men to guide at either end. A series of regulations was necessary to use the lorry and these would be updated to accommodate the line inspection trolleys, whether engine-powered or two-man hand-cranked, that followed. The signalmen in the box either side of the gang had an important part in this team work.

Thomas Elfyn Lewis was born in Gorseinion near Swansea. Dad had worked at the soon-to-close Tylwch wool shed around 1917 and opted to move south to the steel works. The recession around 1925 was tough so Dad decided it would be far better to have poor wages in the Llanidloes area and the family returned. Dad became a taxi-driver with much business to and from Llanidloes station. Thomas Elfyn Lewis was a name more like a sermon so he adopted the name of Bill Llani. Bill left the board school in 1937 to work on local farms. One of the permanent way gang, Pryce George, said there was a vacancy so Bill joined the railway. There were eight in the gang and Jack Swain was the ganger. The length they supervised was Tylwch to Moat Lane Junction. The little office and store was Llanidloes West signal box that was not needed once the grand plans for the Manchester & Milford Railway folded. The duties were varied and included the rural crafts of hedging, fencing and drainage.

Summer grass cutting with a scythe was important to reduce fire risk. The local papers around 1900 would advertise the availability of hay from these cuttings in many station yards in the locality. An example follows:

4th January, 1910. Estimate in tons, to be sold by private treaty, stacks of well made hay to be harvested at undermentioned stations.

Fenns Bank	5¾	Montgomery	3¼	Doldowlod	5½
Talgarth	7¼	Trefeinion	6¾	Cemmaes Rd	2½
Ynyslas	4¼	Borth	3½	Bow Street	5¾
Towyn	5¾	Barmouth Jn	3	Penmaenpool	2½
Pensarn	3½	Harlech	17	Talsarn	13
Porthmadog	3¾	Criccieth	3½	Afonwen	4½
Aberech	12	Some include collection at Kerry			

Permanent way staff working the line at Moat Lane Junction in 1924. The footbridge is the original wooden structure that was replaced by a concrete unit on 21st November, 1935. The identity of the little girl is not known.   *Jeremy Pryce, Llandinam/National Library of Wales, Casgliad Arthur Lewis*

There was much competition to have the prize length for the best kept section of railway. Emrys' father-in-law is the second man at the rear with the signal pole behind him. The engine sheds of Llanidloes are in the left background. Emrys and his wife plus sister-in-law, Gwyneth, made an attempt to recall everyone. *Standing, left to right*: Pryce George, Harry Lewis (father-in-law), Stuart Jones, Bebb Cwmbelan, Reece (with a hand on Bebb's shoulder), Albert Owen, shunter, Harris Roberts and Stuart Campbell. *Seated, left to right*: Permanent way inspector, Jack Davies, Llandinam, ? and ?, and finally George Evans the senior permanent way inspector based at Welshpool.   *Emrys Davies, Caersws*

The older men had tremendous pride in competing for the best section. The gang had a self-propelled trolley with a small four-wheel trailer. These acquired the name of Wickhams which was the name of the manufacturer and this parallels such examples as hoover for a vacuum cleaner or biro for a ball-pen.

Bill was transferred to the Newtown relaying gang around 1946. He had a pass to travel to Newtown so he must have spent many an hour waiting at Moat Lane. Sometimes he would cycle the 14 miles if on odd shift hours. The work was the maintenance and renewal of rails, sleepers and ballast. All such duties were pick, shovel, crowbar, wrench with team lifting for rails and sleepers. It was labour intensive. There was much work on Sundays when sections of rail were replaced. Staff would unload new material to the track side and load the material from the previous week during the week. The engineer's train would move to the nearest siding when necessary. Some duties needed full line occupation. The train drivers were issued with the gang's movements and had to proceed over the working area very slowly, maybe 5 mph. There were several relaying gangs within the GWR Central Wales Division but they would work together on major alterations. Bill has therefore worked the total system down to Pontsticill and Pencader, north-west to Pwllheli and as far east as Whitchurch, plus several branch line duties.

Although their base was at Newtown, their sheds/stores were the vans and wagons hauled around the system. Their bed was either a camping coach or lodgings. One week they were working near Torpantau between Brecon and Merthyr when an emergency call came to go to Lampeter. Their vehicles were attached to the Newport-Brecon passenger train to Talyllyn, then to Moat Lane, then on the rear of the Whitchurch-Aberystwyth train and finally a light engine took them to the problem at Lampeter. A landslide had taken both the track and several coal wagons down an embankment. The soil was stabilized, the drainage was checked as such causes were often a blocked culvert/earthenware drain and the track repaired so that traffic could resume. From about 1950 a Crosville bus started to be hired to take staff to site and this was far quicker than looping around the system hitching lifts on passenger or freight trains. Bill was quite envious of the crew buses that he observed in the 1980s. The gang would have to move from routine to an emergency at short notice. The commonest emergency was floods washing out ballast, sometimes leaving sleepers and rails suspended a few inches above the erosion. The bad spots were either side of Welshpool, Caersws and the Dyfi. The Dyfi area could be complicated by sand blow. Flash floods could hit any part of the system. The winter of 1947 was difficult as it was almost impossible to keep pace with the drifting snow and to unfreeze points.

Bill was asked to move to a gang near Telford for several summers. The little depot was at Hollingswood Goods that is now the site of the modern station at Telford. There were and are some steep-sided cuttings and embankments and the rank grass could cause a fire hazard. Bill must have had Tylwch hill farm blood in his veins for he could scythe away on any slope. The others just could not keep the blade honed let alone scythe all day allowing the swing to do the work. Bill returned to rejoin the relaying gang. There were several Caersws lads including Lester Bowen. They were called out one night on an emergency at Shrewsbury. For some reason either an LMS or a GWR engine had moved slowly by itself and nudged the other on to the points. They worked hard by paraffin floodlight to get the facility working by early morning. Bill left the industry around 1963 when the Western Region, Oswestry area, transferred to the London Midland Shrewsbury/Crewe control. Bill then worked in a local factory until retirement. The railway work was very strenuous with few of the mechanical systems that were soon to take over. The

An early twin-cylinder-engined motor trolley to patrol the lines replacing the daily inspection by foot. Driver E.C. Jones of Llanbrynmair depot drives what appears to be a three-wheeled machine in 1935.
Montgomeryshire Express

The photograph show the goods shed at Llanbrynmair looking towards the station and Cemmaes Road. Taid (grandad) is the third man in on viewer's left. Richard always worked on the railway, maybe from 1900 to 1945. Three sons worked on the railway. John Amos Jehu was the father of Gaynor and worked on light duties as a flagman after an accident with timber during World War II. Ewart Afonwy Jehu worked for the Bridge Department and was sadly killed when on duty at the Llanaber sea wall north of Barmouth. Dic Jehu worked at Machynlleth station and his son Donald Jehu was a clerical officer at Machynlleth. Dai Brunt was the son-in-law of Richard.
Gaynor Tinker née Jehu

team would always be close knit as this was essential for manual lifting and safety. Bill was interviewed in November 2006 and he must be one of the oldest staff in the locality. He was delighted to recall his thoughts and help with the research

Dennis Jones of Abermule

Dennis started work at the Goetre Brickworks on the Kerry branch in 1947. His duties included unloading coal from the siding and taking the fuel to both the kilns and the stationary steam engine. He would also take the cooled bricks and land drains to load on either rail trucks or lorries. He opted for three years' military service instead of National Service. This choice was taken by a number of local men because of higher pay and a gratuity on completion of the time served. Dennis joined the platelayers' gang around 1954. They had a small depot at Abermule with Jack Lewis as ganger and the team of Terry Parker, Jack Davies, George Davies, Bill Richards, Alf Spencer, Ern Brown, Ivor Humphreys (father-in-law) and Dennis. Poor Bill Richards was killed while unloading long length rails. The work area was Forden to Newtown with sidings at Montgomery and Abermule, plus duties on the Kerry branch.

Dennis recalls the other gangs and apologizes for any inaccuracy. They were Buttington Junction to Forden double line with base at Welshpool; Newtown to Moat Lane double line with base at Newtown and large siding complex at Newtown; then Moat Lane to Talerddig with base at Caersws; and Talerddig to Cemmaes with base at Llanbrynmair. There was also Moat Lane Junction to Tylwch heading south.

The platelayers' work was labour intensive with mechanization just starting to appear. The boundaries were inspected and maintained by hand. This would include summer scything, hand hedge trimming, hedge laying plus fencing and drainage work. There were frequent undertrack drainage clay pipes known as earthenware along the way. There may have been 10 such crossings for every bridge. The entry and exit of these had to be clear of sediment and they were also kept clear by rodding. Cattle and sheep challenged the system continuously. Picks, shovels, wrenches, gauge bars, etc. were used to maintain the line. Points and their rodding to either signal boxes or ground frames had to be greased. There were several level crossings over lanes plus farm accommodation gates. The line was walked weekly and inspected daily by slow travel in the Wickham trolley. The powered trolley plus trailer carried staff to the work site, including lads from the Bridge Department working on the Camlad bridge, etc. They also had to look up to ensure the posts and wires of the internal railway telephone communication system had no potential faults. Dennis was made redundant around 1967 as all loops and sidings were removed at Forden, Montgomery and Abermule. He was on duty at the removal of material at both Borth and Caersws when they became unmanned stations. They also made major inroads into clearing rooms no longer required at Welshpool station.

Dennis returned to the railway in 1978 as one of the duty crossing keepers based at Abermule until automated around 1988. Duties also included relief at Carno, Borth, Ynyslas and Llandre until these crossings were automated. He worked as relief at both crossings in Caersws. The Llanidloes Road crossing on the trunk road needed some courage. Most drivers were good but there was a small minority who approached too fast, tried to push through and they were a menace to themselves, other road users and the keeper. Dennis worked on station cleaning including the

Parking plinth for ganger's trolley near Llandinam. David took this photograph in the 1960s as it still had 'Cambrian Railways' on the sign.   *David Hall, Manafon*

The Wickham trolley being prepared to be placed on the carried light turntable and then on to the plinth to free the railway for the train. This is either Dolwen or Llandinam. The men are Dai Brunt, Pryce George and Jack Davies. Gaynor Tinker née Jehu recalls Uncle Dai. He always wore a cap because of a scar on his head caused by emergency work when sent to Birmingham to help after a blitz. A great uncle of Dai left Trefeglwys for Liverpool to sail to the Welsh colony in the Argentine in the 1880s and became a noted grower of wheat and would have sent this produce out on the Trelew to Puerto Madryn metre gauge, line financed with help from the Welsh colony.   *Don Griffith's Collection*

unmanned coast line, checking lights, notices and renewing the white line on the platform. He finally worked night shift cleaning carriages at Machynlleth until retirement in 1998.

Once the Newtown signalman forgot to ring the bell to advise the up train had left. Dennis phoned but got no reply. He knew the train was due so completed shutting the gates just as the dmu came into Abermule with brakes screeching as the driver realized he had passed the crossing gate distant signal at caution. The inspector called later for all the reports. Otherwise Dennis had nothing, neither train or car, impact upon the gates under his control. It was a lonely job compared with the camaraderie of working in the platelayers' gang a decade before. The railway work on the line was changing rapidly.

Mrs Edna Jones née Lloyd of Tremynoddfa, Carno

Edna can recall her grandmother and her memory of the railway family that worked between Pwllhleli and Barmouth in the Cambrian Victorian period. Taid worked at Barmouth on line maintenance before World War I. Tomos Lloyd, her father, worked as a farrier within the railway cartage department at Liverpool. He was a prisoner of war so the young family moved to Fairbourne around 1915. Tomos was a very quiet man, almost introverted, and this may well have been the result of horrific experiences. He joined the Cambrian as a lengthman at Fairbourne in 1919. One of Edna's childhood memories was a trip across the bridge to Barmouth, then catching the ferry to Penrhyn and returning home to Fairbourne on the little railway.

Tomos had travelled along the Friog Rocks on 3rd March, 1933 and everything was in order. He and several others were called immediately to the site when an engine and tender went over the cliff edge on 4th March following a landslide. Sadly both the driver and fireman who were killed would have been well known to the lengthmen. Such a duty is never easy.

Tomos moved to Glandyfi around 1934. Edna therefore spent her teenage years there. They would often sit on the sea wall just west of the station on a summer day. Dad worked between Glandyfi and Cemmaes Road. He walked the total length every Saturday. He died of a stroke around 1950 just before retirement. Uncle Frank was a clerk at Welshpool and became a salaried staff member at Paddington.

Edna was one of 10 children and she is the only member still alive. Three of her brothers worked for the railway. Dennis Lloyd was a signalman and his final duty was at Talerddig. Bob Lloyd was based at Trawscoed or Crosswood on the Manchester & Milford line. Bill Lloyd was within the team of porters/general duties at Aberdyfi. Arthur Lloyd was a cousin at Porthmadog

Edna married Ianto Jones. Ianto was within the team of relayers at the Newtown depot. This duty would include most working weeks away from home in either a camping coach or lodgings. He therefore requested a transfer around 1955 and was placed at Moat Lane East signal box to learn the various duties for relief signalman/crossing keeper. These duties would include Westbury after transfer from Oswestry in 1964. He retired at the age of 65 and was asked to be on standby for sickness and holiday cover, subject to a yearly medical. Edna and the late Ianto must be one of the now rare local couples who have a son working on the railways in 2008. Alun started locally in 1973 on maintenance and then signals, including the radio-controlled installations in the late 1980s. He now works for Network Rail based in Birmingham on modern signalling.

Flood damage examples and emergency repairs in December 1960. Severe flooding and structural damage would occur within the Upper Severn Valley after several weeks of heavy rain on the Cambrian watershed. This shows track damage on the then double line approach to Welshpool from Cilcewydd. This section of line from Welshpool to Forden has doubled again but the hourly service is still pending.   *County Times*

The result of a very high tide with gale surge plus river flow hold-back, causes a huge reverse flow as the tide starts to ebb. The water flow can exceed that of the drain channels and culverts so the flood breaks through the bund and then erodes the track ballast. This is close to Dovey Junction in November 1977.   *County Times*

Left: Tomos Lloyd at Glandyfi in 1948. He would walk from Glandyfi to Cemmaes Road every Saturday to inspect the line.
Edna Jones neé Lloyd, Carno

Below: A time-honoured duty of lengthmen is shown as Emlyn Thomas and Harold Evans, both from Carno, defrost the points on the west side of the Caersws loop on a bitterly cold morning in January 1979.
County Times

The Newtown relayers gang out on site in 1948. The cliff behind is Tremadog so they are working at Porthmadog. Only some of the staff can now be recalled. *Standing, left to right*: Joe Jones (Caersws), Tom Price (Bettws), ?, ?, ?, Don (Butty) Morris (Newtown), Ganger (foreman) Lester Bowen (Caersws), Sid Williams (Caersws) and Idwal Davies (Trefeglwys). *Seated*: ?, Ianto Evan Jones, ?, ? and Idris Price.

Edna Jones née Lloyd, Carno

Ianto Jones on crossing duty at Abermule on 21st August, 1977. The engine is by the parapet of the bridge over the Afon Mule. The bridge spans the railway and the road. The Kerry branch curved south to the right to keep this side of the Mule.

Peter Baughan/Edna Jones née Lloyd, Carno

The Llanidloes shed and working to Moat Lane

Donald Jones was born in 1926. His father, John y Crydd (cobbler) started with the Cambrian Railways in 1917. Dad was promoted within the system and was one of the engine drivers that accepted redundancy in late 1962 when he was nearly 65 years of age. Donald's father would have accepted the coaled and watered engine from Peter Poole's father. Donald joined the GWR on 31st March, 1942 as a cleaner at Moat Lane after working in the local Co-op for two years. The war was causing early promotion and, within the year, he moved to spend nine months as trainee fireman at Tyseley (Birmingham). He then worked as fireman from Llanidloes shed from September 1943 until 1960. Then on to Old Oak Common to qualify as a driver and a return to Llanidloes from August 1961 to February 1963, spending the last two months helping to demolish the system south of Llanidloes. He accepted the offer of a transfer so the family moved to Reading. Much of the work that followed would be driving class '47' and '50' diesels. The main duties were driving from Reading to Taunton or on the route to Birmingham (New Street) via Oxford and Leamington Spa. One duty undertaken was the milk tanker train from St Erth (Cornwall) to Kensington or empties back. Donald retired from the Western Region in March 1986 after 44 years of service. He and his wife retired back to Llanidloes in 1994 and found it a little difficult and strange to return to a very different town and also leaving some very close friends in Reading.

The Llanidloes shed was the original one for main services for the Llanidloes & Newtown Railway plus the staging post for the stillborn Manchester & Milford. Moat Lane shed opened in 1890. A site was cut for a turntable and shed at Newtown but abandoned in the mid-1860s when the various companies formed the Cambrian Railways. The railway companies such as the Cambrian and GWR were pragmatic in switching engines and crew for maximum availabilty. The first duty at Moat Lane was under the tutelage of chargehand Bert Davage. Duties have already been described by others. The small Van tank engine was still on site in 1942 but never steamed and was towed away to Oswestry. The Kerry pannier was held for shunting, the Welshpool cattle train on Monday and the branch. All other locomotives were tender units and included Cambrian '800s' (both Stephenson and Beyer, Peacock) and GWR 'Dean Goods'. There were seven sets of men (driver/fireman) at Llanidloes towards the conclusion of World War II. Maybe the total staff at Llanidloes was around 40. The duty to Whitchurch went back to starting from Llanidloes about 1945 so the first passenger train at 6.30 am worked to Whitchurch and the return was in the evening. The other up passenger services ran only to Moat Lane.

The wartime goods carried substantial loadings and many were double-headed through to Talyllyn Junction with the second engine being added at Llanidloes. The dolomite train from Llynclys to Dowlais Top arrived around 3.00 am on Tuesdays and the locomotive ran light to Moat Lane to assist this heavy train. A banker also worked to Builth Road to assist at the spur on to the Swansea line and would then work a War Department freight back to Moat Lane. Donald assumes this went on to Llanymynech for the munitions stored on the Shropshire & Montgomeryshire Light Railway.* This locomotive ran to Builth Wells to turn and replenish water. There was a 7.30 am train to Moat Lane after the war. The locomotive would then work the stopping freight to Newbridge-on-Wye. This train would have extra wagons with building materials and machinery for Rhayader during the construction of the Claerwen dam. The cement came up from Aberthaw via Brecon and a self-propelled crane was held at Rhayader during this period.

* This may have been the secretive Saltney Junction working to the Chester area.

The *County Times* reported that Donald Jones' father, a Llanidloes engine driver, had recently received a clock for 45 years of service and it was shortly followed by a redundancy notice. Geof Hawkins is the young fireman and he had been a railwayman for just two years.

Donald Jones, Llanidloes

The favoured 'Dean Goods' No. 2327 for the Llanidloes-Moat Lane shuttle stands at Llanidloes with Harry 'Bow Street' Jones (guard), Anthony Jenkins (driver) and Donald Jones (fireman).

Donald Jones, Llanidloes

A train from Moat Lane prepares to leave Rhayader to continue on to Builth. Alun Davies, station master, shakes the hand of Elliston Evans, signalman, as he prepares to retire. Peris Evans, train guard, stands between while Donald Jones, driver, stands on the platform. Gerald Hughes is the partially-hidden fireman in the cab.

Donald Jones, Llanidloes

Donald recalls aspects of the Whitchurch run starting at zero miles zero chains. The Cambrian line quickly curved west from Whitchurch and was soon on underbridge number one over a farm accommodation lane. Railway staff could be quite territorial and it seemed as if the Whitchurch yard men always gave timetable priority to an inherited LNWR turn. British Rail transferred some of the signalling to the main Whitchurch signal box and the Cambrian lines box was phased out maybe around 1949. The line headed in a straight line over the peat of Fenns Bank. Some said the the train weight dipped the line as it transversed the peat but Donald thought that this was a bit of a tale. All the smaller stations would have a handful of passengers getting on and off but this would increase substantially at Ellesmere, Oswestry, Llanmynech, Welshpool and Newtown. A sad event occurred at Fenns Bank on a late train. The station master was slumped on the bench. Sadly George Peel had had a stroke and he never recovered. The smaller under- and overbridges were hardly noticed. The only real gradient was close to Welsh Frankton and Donald thinks the track crossed an area called the Higher Ridge. The train rattled over a girder bridge that crossed the GWR line at Whittington and then another bridge over the main road at a place called Drenewydd. This is also the Welsh name for Newtown. The train then curved into the Oswestry complex. The substantial engine sheds were in a triangle between the Gobowen GWR line and the Cambrian. The train then went under the longest footbridge imaginable. The footbridge crossed from the Ceiriog residential area of the town to the Cambrian workshops. It crossed the running tracks, the goods sidings and the workshop sidings for holding locomotives, carriages and wagons. A huge amount of railway knowledge must have crossed this footbridge every day from 1870 until closure in the mid-1960s. Water was usually taken on at Oswestry, the tender had enough coal for the day from the Llanidloes loading. Several milk tanks were often picked up at Ellesmere on the morning up train to Whitchurch. There was an early post-war train with extra carriages added from Oswestry for returning secondary schoolchildren to Llynclys, Pant and the English side of Llanymynech. This service was covered by Oswestry crew later. The line between Oswestry and Llanymynech was double and then single with passing places to Buttington Junction. The branch service from Llynclys Junction to Llangynog was still in operation. There was a line just north of Llanymynech called Rock Siding and this was the original route to Llanfyllin before 1896. The east side of Llanymynech was busy with War Department locomotives and freight during and immediately after World War II. The Llanfyllin train was timed to move into a siding so that passengers could change for Oswestry on a train from Llanidloes, Aberystwyth or Welshpool depending on time of the day. The connecting passenger train was held at Four Crosses until the Llanfyllin train was clear of the platform. Services were well used until petrol rationing ceased in the early 1950s, then lorries and cars just leeched away the goods and passenger custom.

There were speed restrictions imposed with bridge repairs, the major one being the replacement of the bridge over the Severn at Buttington around 1947.

The shuttle trip between Llanidloes and Moat Lane was an easy trip. The normal 'Dean Goods' chosen would be No. 2327 as this could heat the carriages from both the locomotive and the tender. It only had to run-round the loops at both Llanidloes and Moat Lane. Other locomotives had heater pipes on the tender only so they had to go on to the turntable at both ends in the winter. This was a complex little journey at Moat Lane. The BR Ivatts could work both engine and tender first with their cab shelter. No. 2327 would be turned at Llanidloes according to the weather forecast. It would run tender first in a south-westerly to Moat Lane and face the storm on

This Edwardian postcard view would have pertained until closure in the 1960s. The view is towards Moat Lane with the goods shed on the left and the two-bay engine shed on the right. The single-bay engine shed between the signal box and the larger shed was the Mid-Wales Railway motive power department and this closed around 1904.

Powys County Council, Llanidloes Museum

The July 1962 view shows the large station building of Llanidloes as the train prepares to leave for Moat Lane. The tracks are now the bypass, the siding area to the right of the station is now a light industrial estate. The station is a listed building and houses various offices.

Brian Hutton, Birmingham

return. It would work engine first into the raw easterly coming in from Siberia and the Shropshire plain (the so called 'gwynt coch Amwythig'). The 'Dean Goods' were very open and the canvas shelter helped only a little. Both the station master's wife and the refreshment room family would filch steamed water on washing day as the engine simmered close to the wash room prior to return to Llanidloes (the locomotive, not the wash room).

Donald has worked trains to Talerddig on banking duties, usually on Saturdays after 1950 but also on wartime freight. The 'Llani' train was rostered to take Italian prisoners of war from Newtown to Llanbrymair for forestry and farm land clearance and then worked the grammar school train back to Newtown. Moat Lane or Machynlleth crews did the afternoon roster. Only tender locomotives worked south from Moat Lane because of the long run between water that was only available at Llanidloes, Rhayader, Builth, Talgarth and Talyllyn. Some of these tanks were slow fillers and the larger reservoir tank was placed at Builth in the late 1930s. There was a weight restriction on what could work to Llanidloes and an even stricter restriction onwards to the south. It was not common to work to Brecon from Talyllyn during and just after the war as footplates were swapped with Brecon crews. Drivers Donald Jones and Pellow collected empty coaching stock with two Ivatt locomotives at Brecon just before closure prior to the final Stephenson Locomotive Society run crewed by Oswestry men. Weather conditions were not good with freezing temperatures and swirling snow.

Sadly Donald recalls two accidents. Trains from Llanidloes were timed to connect with the up trains at Moat Lane. The 'Llani' train would work through to Newtown on Tuesday Fair as both trains could be packed. On other days the instruction would be given to run to Newtown only if the coast train was running very late. This was no problem as the line between Moat Lane and Newtown was double. Lengthmen were working near Penstrowed and the flagman must have thought that the train was from Machynlleth and on time. The Llanidloes train reversed at Newtown and was heading back. The late running coast train was at a stand as the flagman had been killed. The Llanidloes train proceeded directly to Moat Lane to report to the station master and to activate the necessary emergency services.

There was an accommodation crossing near Cilcewydd. The last train from Whitchurch ran an hour later on Saturdays to meet the need of cinema-goers and also to enable all the Saturday extras to clear through. The only conclusion that could be given was that the retired farmer must have thought it was a weekday and the last train had cleared through. The engine driver was Bert Ward, the view was clear, the whistle was sounded but the car just continued on to the crossing and the passenger was killed on impact as the brakes screeched with maximum application.

Donald continued to meet Sidney Griffiths at Paddington for a 'cwpaned' or cup of tea and a chat. Sidney had been promoted to a senior clerical grade from Moat Lane. Sidney was a man of considerable intellect and moved to work within the Western Region archives at West Drayton. Donald is one of many that has commented that this research should have been done 20 years earlier when the late Sidney had retired to Caersws.

The retired railway lads of Llanidloes

Two further men recall their railway career interlude. It is a further illustration of the generations of local railwaymen and the almost umbilical link between Llanidloes and Moat Lane Junction.

Tylwch station *circa* 1900. Les Jones' mother took the Cambrian framed photograph with them when the family moved from Tylwch to Carno. The photograph would have been taken from the road overbridge. There were four bridges over the Afon Dulas between Penpontbren Junction and Tylwch. The steel girders of the fourth can be seen where the loop and siding merge into a single track. The parapet of a cattle creep / flood relief can be observed just beyond.

Les Jones, Llanidloes

Gwynfryn was brought up on a local family farm and they used Tylwch for journeys and Pantydwr siding for collecting fertilizer etc. The time is 8.43 am on Saturday 29th December, 1962. The villagers decided to use the train on the final day for a journey to Llanidloes. The train enters into Tylwch from Builth Wells. Both this bridge and the adjoining bridge out of view over the Afon Dulas were built by the Mid-Wales Railway. Both still stand today as a monument to the cash-strapped venture. They are on the B road now owned by Powys County Council.

Gwynfryn Evans, Kerry

Les Jones first saw the light of day or the gloom of candlelight at Tylwch station in 1931. Great-grandfather (hen-daid) joined the Cambrian or the precursor in the Newtown area in the 1860s on the permanent way maintenance and his wife was a crossing keeper, site uncertain. Grandad (taid) was again on maintenance centred on Moat Lane, Newtown, Talerddig and his wife (nain) was the crossing keeper at Oerffrwd so that was the grandparents' home. Dad joined the Cambrian. Les has the GWR certificate when his dad, Richard Thomas Jones, qualified and passed the rules and regulations exam at Builth Wells in June 1924. The result was that Dad qualified to take up duties in charge of Erwood station. Dad then became station master at Tylwch. The GWR moved the family to the larger station of Carno when Les, the baby of the family, was about six.

All three brothers joined the GWR. Derek started at Oswestry as a cleaner, moved to Machynlleth as fireman, then Welshpool and finally Worcester. He may be the final GWR fireman alive who worked the Llanfair narrow gauge line. Kenneth started as a cleaner at Machynlleth, then a fireman at the same depot and continued his career at Old Oak Common, Paddington, as a driver until retirement. Les started as a cleaner at Moat Lane Junction. He qualified as a fireman at Machynlleth and finished his railway duties at Newport, Monmouthshire, when he opted to leave in 1957 and returned to Llanidloes where he established a bicycle retail business. Unusual duties from Machynlleth including firing to Dinas Mawddwy, pushing wagons up the weed-infested Tonfanau quarry sidings and crossing the Caersws-maintained underbridge to the beach on the Aberdovey harbour branch.

Newport duties included the eastern valleys to Rhymney, Tredegar, Ebbw Vale, etc. The heavy ore trains were worked to Ebbw so Les has taken trains under the huge Crumlin viaduct but never over the valley. Duties included main line work to Bristol or Lydney/Gloucester and further on into England. He would observe the Severn Bridge but never took a diversion over the river between Lydney and Sharpness. An overtime bonus would be Sunday specials to Weston-super-Mare. Skill was needed working through the Severn tunnel with unbraked freight, both going down to and up from the sump, to avoid pushing and snatching. Les has worked a steam engine through the tunnel with only himself on the footplate. The front engine had two staff, the rear had two while Les was on the middle locomotive working light back to Severn Tunnel Junction. He has fired both the 'Cambrian Coast Express' and the 'Pembroke Coast Express'. He still has his enamel tea can, timesheets, a GWR ticket punch and a selection of GWR pencils and pen nibs.

Work place and village nicknames is almost an art with so many Jones, Evans, Morgan, Powells, Thomas, Williams, etc. Names could be based from the location, a physical feature or work duty.

Len Hamer started as a cleaner at the Llanidloes shed towards the end of the World War II. He was moved to Shrewsbury as a trainee fireman and returned to Llanidloes after National Service. This experience covers the final busy period before petrol rationing ceased followed by the rapid expansion of the private car and lorry. He moved to Shrewsbury after Llanidloes depot closure but was not happy with lodgings etc. so he opted to return to Llanidloes where he obtained work as a lorry driver.

Dad was a stoker at the Llanidloes town gasworks so this was dependent upon coal delivered by rail. Three maternal uncles worked for the railway. Oswald Bebb was a driver at Moat Lane, Albert Bebb was on the permanent way gang between Moat Lane and Newtown and finally Arthur Bebb was a GWR lorry driver working from the warehouse at Oakengates (Telford). Len's father in law, Tom Pryce, was a member of the relaying gang based at Newtown. Len's two brothers also joined at Llanidloes but both opted out before closure.

Carno station, *circa* 1900. The second home of the youngest son of the station master is on the right. There is an up train departing towards Caersws and Moat Lane. This photograph was used with publications of Laura Ashley. This clothing and textile company started in the station building after closure in 1965. *Les Jones, Llanidloes*

Les Jones' older brother was the then young fireman wearing the beret within the cab of 2-6-2T No. 5541. This is a World War II picture and the engine is in the Machynlleth yard. *Les Jones, Llanidloes*

Driver Dai Lloyd Davies with the taller young Les Jones as fireman await their duty in 'Dukedog' 4-4-0 No. 9000 at Dovey Junction.

Les Jones, Llanidloes

A Moat Lane bicycle in 2008. Sheila Hamer née Pryce and Len Hamer at their home at Llanidloes. The Rudge Whitworth bike was bequeathed to Len by Frank Corfield, the Moat Lane line manager and boss to Uncle Oswald Bebb around 1952. Frank's career would start back before World War I so this bike may be 100 years old! How many times would Frank have ridden this bike along the cinder track to Moat Lane in the 1930s and 1940s? Les took it home on the 5.40 pm and the vintage bike is still in the shed. Ron Jones recalls that the line manager looked after the telephone/telegraph lines, the signal boxes and their staff and managed any changes such as late running or extras so this was an important duty.

Author

The Llani to Moat Lane carriage set is on the viewer's right. This is an excellent *circa* 1959 view of station master Williams' (known as 'the whitewash') immaculately kept station with the goods shed, feed merchants' shed and exit signals beyond. It also gives a close view of the intricate lattice work of part of the station footbridge (MLT19).   *Brian Morgan/Len Hamer*

Driver Harri Benbow and fireman Len Hamer at Llanidloes on the 'best' shift. They had taken the 11.15 am to Moat Lane Junction to connect with the up Cambrian. They returned at 12.15 and have arrived at Llanidloes at 12.32. The locomotive is heading to the yard for shunting duties. This busy shunt in 1950 was down to a few coal wagons only by 1959. The next duty was the school train leaving Llanidloes, all stations to Moat Lane at 4.15 pm to arrive at Moat Lane at 4.35. This would connect with the Shrewsbury-Aberystwyth train and would leave Moat Lane at 4.45 to arrive back at Llanidloes at 5.02. Passengers would include the County Technical School students. The locomotive would then go to the shed and the shift would finish.   *Len Hamer, Llanidloes*

Les must have spent many an hour at Moat Lane. There were three locomotives. A duty to Rhayader could take place with freight especially when the Claerwen dam was under construction. Len was on the footplate of the final Llanidloes/Moat Lane shuttle shift on the Saturday of closure in December 1962. Len only once worked as far as Brecon. Working south was not common and it was usually only as far as Builth when the train continued but the crew changed. The next freight or passenger was worked back.

Len recalls the staff at Llanidloes around 1953. Station master, Mr Williams, was nicknamed 'whitewash' as he kept everything immaculate. He lived in a spacious first-floor flat of the huge station. There were three booking clerks, Dorothy Ward, Brian Morgan and Hugh (surname unkown). The three porters also worked in the goods/parcel shed and they were John Jones, Evan Owen and (name unknown). The three signalmen were Albert Evans, Glyn Lloyd and Harris Roberts. Ken Poole was the engine shed chargeman and Norman Morgan was the coal loader when Len was junior cleaner in 1944. These three worked night shift. Any locomotive movement was done by Ken and a colleague, Gordon Cross, would move to night shift if Ken was not available. The six drivers were Dai Benbow, Harri Benbow, W.R. Jones, Arthur Jenkins, Bert Ward and George Owen. Only five firemen are recalled: Len Hamer, Donald Jones, Wyn Davies, Walter Davies and Meurig Pugh. There were two passenger guards as others were drawn from Moat Lane. They were Trefor Jones and Harry Jones. The two shunters were Evan Jones and Norman Morgan. The final group was the seven to eight men of the permanent way gang with their depot in the former West signal box. The total staff was therefore around 35. Parcels were delived by Dai Cadman and his own lorry. Dai sold his lorrry so John Vaughan took over with a BR lorry around 1950 and then the duty was done from Newtown, leaving only full load traffic at Llanidloes.

A pint of beer at the end of a shift was a delight at Moat Lane. One story was that a Moat Lane lad would take away any stale beer. He offered to take away a full barrel that was off and took it home on the sack trolley and returned the empty cask the following day. His wife informed the refreshment room lass that she could not understand why the two cottager pigs were staggering around their sty and wondered if they had sunstroke. So an example of how to recycle stale railway beer is to use it as gruel for the pigs.

Station master Thomas William Godshall retired from Llanidloes station in 1931, after 49 years of service. He began his career at Barmouth Junction and moved to Criccieth and Minffordd. In 1895 he became the station master at Marchwiel when the Ellesmere-Wrexham line opened. He moved to Carno, Dovey Junction and back to Barmouth Junction before his appointment at Llanidloes. Mr T.H. Evans, station master at Brinkworth (near Chippenham), was subsequently appointed to Llanidloes. He started as a junior clerk at Oswestry in 1894 and served at Buttington Junction, Overton-on-Dee and Fenns Bank until becoming a relief station master based at Oswestry. He became station master at Bettisfield for 20 years prior to the request to move to Brinkworth.

Recalling the Oswestry Empire and sometimes beyond

George Fleming senior started to work at Machynlleth with the Cambrian Railways in 1915 and retired in 1960. His duty within Archie Fleming's memory was a senior coaler, transferring coal from the wagons to the tenders. An elevator system

This image comes from the *County Times* of January 1938 and the photograph was taken by Edwards & Son, Newtown. Ron Jones can recall some of the faces but cannot place a name. The large gangs would often contain the core skills of the Newtown relayers gang plus platelayers from any section of the Cambrian.   *Dilys Williams Collection, Clatter*

Pupils from Birmingham Central Grammar School, ready to return from their camp at Bryn-tail, near Llanidloes. The photograph dates from around 1925. The Llanidloes goods shed can be seen on the left. The locomotive is working tender first so this would be the Llanidloes to Moat Lane shuttle and not from further south. Maybe Mr Godshall was station master on this day.
Brian Hutton, Birmingham

was built, maybe just after World War I, to an enclosed loft so that coal could be fed by gravity. The late George Fleming junior joined the GWR in 1933 as a cleaner and Archie Fleming joined the same shed in 1935. Both boys were promoted to firemen and then drivers. Both brothers are shown leaning out of the cab within the illustrations of various books on Cambrian steam. The service by father and the two boys to the railway totalled 145 years.

Archie and the family would travel through Moat Lane Junction in the late 1920s when he was a child on the family railway privilege ticket on day trips to Shrewsbury or Wrexham/Chester. Archie was promoted faster than usual during World War II. He was then single and worked at Tyseley, Shrewsbury, Hereford, Brecon and Llanidloes prior to return to Machynlleth. Archie was to marry the daughter of Alex Wood, one of the signalmen at Abermule. Rhoda was a nurse at Machynlleth Hospital so it was a coincidence that Archie married into another Cambrian railway family.

The first firing duties commenced at Llanidloes in 1939. The first train left Llanidloes for Whitchurch about 6.30 am. The three staff returned 'on the cushions' to Welshpool to take over from Shrewsbury traincrew and work to Moat Lane. Three other staff also had to ride the cushions back from Welshpool to bring the 6.30 pm return service from Whitchurch to arrive at Llanidloes around 9.30 pm. The landlady wanted the door locked at 10.00 pm so Archie was quite scared if the train was running late. Archie was asked to move to Hereford so that Ronnie Jones could return to look after his aged mother. The GWR made an effort to help staff within a paternalistic framework.

Archie was moved to Brecon from 1940 to 1946 as fireman and relief driver. He worked to Neath and to Merthyr and Newport via Pontsticill Junction. The Hay and Hereford staff were a separate team of ex-Midland and LMS men and only once was he asked to cross territory lines when no one turned up for duty. The roster would include working to Builth Wells and Moat Lane. There were always servicemen on every train. Archie recalled the evacuees train that worked from Liverpool taking the train on from Moat Lane to points as far south as Brecon. The poor children looked shattered with tiredness and worry. One day they had to take a light engine to clear a path through the snow. They cleared Torpantau tunnel but became firmly wedged in a drift near Pontsticill around 6.00 am. They had to wait until 10.00 am the following day before two Merthyr engines smashed a way through to them! The spectacular approach of the snow plough is still vivid 60 years later. Archie returned to Machynlleth in 1946, only moving away for cover for short periods.

Machynlleth was a very busy depot not only for its own duties but also to supplement Aberystwyth and Porthmadog/Pwllheli. Archie must be the last man alive who drove on the Corris Railway as a driver when Wmffre Humphreys was on sick leave. Duties included everything such as shunting, ballast trains, livestock specials, the passenger shuttle from Barmouth to Dolgellau with an auto-coach and the trip to Dinas Mawddwy. Special troop trains worked to and from Tonfanau. One system was to work the engine tender first from Machynlleth to Barmouth Junction (now Morfa Mawddach) and then run round the carriage to haul back to Tonfanau. Archie recalls working Collett Goods 0-6-0 No. 2219 all the way to Chester both via the Dee line to Ruabon and via Moat Lane and Oswestry. A special worked through the night around 1974 to bring the Ugandan Asians expelled by General Amin to Tonfanau as a holding camp and this must have been the final use of this military base.

There were up to five banking engines at Machynlleth and two at Moat Lane to deal with summer Saturday services working to Talerddig. Most ran back light to

'Dukedog' class 4-4-0 No. 9008 crosses the Poolquay level crossing into the station and passing loop towards Welshpool *circa* mid-1950s. This could be the Welshpool school train returning from Llanymynech prior to working to Shrewsbury around 4.30 pm, as described by Archie Fleming.   *Graham Lloyd, Churchstoke*

George Fleming, the older brother of Archie, leans out from the footplate of class '2MT' 2-6-0 No. 78003 at Machynlleth in 1965. The fireman looking out from the window is Eurwyn James. Diesel trials would now be taking place.   *Elwyn V. Jones Collection, Newtown Library*

their respective depots but some would work through, attached to other services, to speed up occupancy. The success of the Talerddig climb was a full head of steam and coast to either Cemmaes in the up direction or Y Weeg on the down before hitting the gradient. It could be a problem moving an up train away from Llanbrynmair where sanding was essential and the permanent way gang would not be pleased with excess wheel slip. It would be rare not to observe photographers on a fine summer Saturday from 1960 onwards. All trains had to stop on the main Cambrian line at Moat Lane to take on water. Either the driver or the fireman stopped with the Moat Lane lad when the tender was filled while the other nipped into the refreshment room or porters' room to top up the tea can. The tea was delicious waiting in the loop at Talerddig.

Archie described the afternoon shift with the school train in the early 1950s. The shift started with a GWR 'Dukedog' class 4-4-0 for the 12.00 noon Machynlleth to Shrewsbury. Both the engine (to London Midland type) and crew (Shrewsbury) changed at Welshpool. The 'Dukedog' went on shunting duties. There was a tar works at Welshpool and tar leakage could cause slippage. The same locomotive then hauled passenger coaches to Llanymynech with the Welshpool secondary schoolchildren stopping at Buttington, Poolquay, Arddleen Halt, Four Crosses and Llanymynech. They then returned to Welshpool to work the 5.20 pm to Shrewsbury and then worked the 7.35 pm back to Aberystwyth with the Aber lads taking over at Machynlleth to end the shift. The other school duty was Machynlleth to Newtown for the technical school (with the change to the further education college) plus secondary schoolchildren for Newtown from Carno, Pontdolgoch, Caersws and Moat Lane.

Every railwayman had a duty to report any line or bridge fault. The road was so well known that any fault could almost be sensed. Care was necessary when the rivers were in full spate. Flood plain examples were the Dulais east of Machynlleth, Caersws and the three Severn bridges at Cilcewydd, Buttington and Poolquay. The bridges would be closed to traffic if water rose higher than a marker stick. The two bridges over the Twymyn and the Dyfi on the Mawddwy branch had a severe speed restriction.

Any shunting duties at Moat Lane were usually quick as it was just remarshalling at an exchange station, and the station master had enough options with various locomotives, so it was often just backing on and drawing away. Caersws in the early 1950s could be time consuming with the goods and feeds shed on one side and the cattle docks and coal wharf on the north side, plus shunting for the Bridge Department. Steel lengths and girders would come in, covered wagons would deliver cement and paint drums, open wagons had aggregate and masonry stone and then the materials drawn from the store would be taken to site. The two cranes, the camping coaches and the tunnel inspection wagons were stored in the Van siding but often moved to Moat Lane when needed for quicker onward movement. The crane was always placed next to the guard's van and one of the crane operators had to be on board. Archie can certainly remember placing the camping coach into a siding at Porthmadog and Barmouth. Archie had pulled the tunnel inspection wagons through most tunnels, including Torpantau, the Marteg and Rhayader, usually on the same shift, plus the four at Aberdyfi. The engine was eased through for inspection and also to reduce smoke for both visibility and comfort. Archie had to go to Oswestry after the final coach of a troop train was damaged on the roof within Aberdyfi tunnel 3. A stone on the roof/side was slightly out of line and the coach cantle was scratched. Senior staff wondered if he had been travelling too fast

The British Railways class '4' 2-6-4T tank was introduced by R.A. Riddles. These locomotives were on both the Cambrian Coast line and stopping services through to Shrewsbury. Some were moved from Southend-Fenchurch Street after electrification. The date is 30th May, 1964 with only months before the Welshpool-Whitchurch line shut. The stone parapet is over the Corris tramway and the girder lattice bridge is over the main road just before the up platform at Machynlleth. These two adjoining bridges were the first built by Savin for the Welsh Coast line after the partnership split from Davies a century before.   *Brian Hutton, Birmingham*

One of the last of the pre-Grouping '43XX' class 2-6-0s designed by Churchward for the GWR from 1911 prepares to leave Shrewsbury for Aberystwyth on 13th July, 1962 on the GWR/LNWR Joint Line before joining the Cambrian at Buttington Junction.   *Brian Hutton, Birmingham*

Ivatt class '2' 2-6-0 No. 46521 shunts at the now freight terminus at Llanidloes in the summer of 1965. This lightweight engine was necessary for crossing the Llandinam bridge and was used to convey 'Presflo' cement wagons for the construction of the Clywedog dam site. The silo is owned by Aberthaw Cement prior to contract change to Tunnel Cement from Padeswood near Wrexham. The engine first worked the school train from Machynlleth to Newtown, then the cement train and ended the day with the return school train. This engine then ran light from Machynlleth to Newtown when the intermediate stations such as Carno closed and the school train ceased. A diesel locomotive was employed from Coton Hill Yard in Shrewsbury when steam finished at Machynlleth in December 1966 until final closure in October 1967.   *Brian Hutton, Birmingham*

Diesel-multiple-units took on duties from 1965 with only freight, the Mail and the 'Cambrian Coast Express' still being steam-hauled. Units pass at Newtown with the down train drawing out to collect the Newtown-Caersws token at the signal box. This photograph dates from the early 1980s before the introduction of the 'Sprinters'.   *Ron Jones, Newtown*

A class '24' diesel brings the ex-Shrewsbury freight into the station and passing loop at Newtown at 10.00 hrs on a cold February morning in 1970. Bridge No. 154, called Brimmon Lane, is partially hidden by station footbridge No. 154A. The 'A' would indicate that the Cambrian inserted the footbridge at a later date. Brimmon Lane was an accommodation level crossing for a very short period in the 1860s. *Ron Jones, Newtown*

Demand continued for holiday exchanges as shown at Newtown in July 1982. There were now only three to four locomotive-hauled trains to either Aberystwyth or Pwllheli (Butlins Holiday Camp) from Euston, Birmingham and Manchester on Saturdays. Some of the steam-hauled trains were routed via Ruabon to Barmouth until that line closed in 1965. These trains were double-headed with class '25' diesels. An up train awaits the road as the down train clears the single line. *Sam Compton, Llandinam*

but the fault was an LNER coach that was banned from the line. Changes at Moat Lane Junction were rapid from around 1960 to 1967. Most staff were made redundant in January 1963 when the Mid-Wales service ceased and the station closed. Owen Jones and several others were retained for water duties. Moat Lane East box was only staffed to allow the Llanidloes freight and the Clywedog cement train on to the remnants of the branch with a 'one train in steam (or diesel)' staff. Moat Lane West box with token exchange remained until rural station closure in 1965. The double track between Newtown and Moat Lane was singled in 1965, so the token sections became Newtown to Caersws and Caersws to Talerddig with the closure of the loop at Carno.

Talerddig was and remains a bleak spot on the watershed between the Severn and the Dyfi valleys. It was necessary to pin down brakes before the descent in either direction for freight without continuous brakes. Steam ceased at Machynlleth in late 1966 leaving only the 'Cambrian Coast Express' to be serviced at Aberystwyth until March 1967. The need for staff at Moat Lane West box and the water column had ceased, so no one was required after a century of service at the junction in a large field.

Staff at every station became well known over the years. The stop at Moat Lane was about five minutes for water so staff would come across for news. This would include the station master or clerk. Sometimes it was just trivia but could also include an important change from the engineering work book that was given to drivers each week and for which they had to sign. It detailed speed restrictions where permanent way, station maintenance or bridge maintenance staff were working. Once the pump for some reason was slow in replenishing the water tower at Moat Lane and a double-headed down train had reduced the pressure to a trickle. Howell Morris, station master, was going to use a spare locomotive that was heading to Machynlleth to get the freight to Llanidloes until he realized the locomotive was not permitted on that route. Archie assumes that the Ivatt Mogul finally had enough water so the freight was very late that evening or arrived the next morning. The driver, the fireman and the guard were responsible for many things including passenger safety. Drivers were sent for a week to Crewe for dmu training and a further week for additional diesel locomotive training in the mid-1960s. Several diesels worked through to gain additional information and then everyone took a two day conversion course in 1965 and steam rosters were rapidly withdrawn.

Archie took a heavy diesel-hauled excursion over the Barmouth bridge in April 1980 and the bridge felt as strong as a rock. He was astonished to hear of the immediate restriction to dmus only and to realize the damage done by the terodo worm. He was one of a number that went by taxi from Machynlleth to drive the Barmouth-Pwlheli three times-daily shuttle to include the schools' traffic. The line re-opened once repairs had been completed (*see Chapter Eight*). Archie recalled an operation 30 years earlier on a Sunday. He had travelled to Shrewsbury on the Saturday evening to bring the heavy steam crane to Machynlleth. They then moved to Llanaber sea wall for the Sunday where huge stone blocks were lifted off the wagons and placed to strengthen the sea wall. Most of the staff were the Caersws bridge men. The crane returned to Shrewsbury on the Monday.

Archie retired as the first generation dmus were being replaced by 'Sprinters'. He listed some of the locomotives used at Machynlleth. Two 0-4-2Ts, Nos. 4865 and 4834, worked the Dinas Mawddwy freight and the auto Barmouth-Dolgellau in the late 1940s. Various 'Earls'/'Dukedogs' and 'Duke' 4-4-0s remained and No. 9017 was used for banking the 'Cambrian Coast Express' to Talerddig on Saturdays. The

The locomotive-hauled direct Aberystwyth to Euston service ran in the 1980s and ceased when InterCity facilities were withdrawn from Shrewsbury around 1991. Five class '37' diesels were allocated to Cardiff and one attended to this duty with a morning and afternoon service, electric haulage being employed from Wolverhampton. This view shows the up train drawing into Caersws at around 08.10 hours.   *Sam Compton, Llandinam*

Goods services receded quickly after Moat Lane and Buttington junctions closed. The final service lasted until the mid-1990s. Two class '20' diesels, probably Nos. 20151 and 20097, approach Rhydwhyman crossing with petroleum tankers from Stanlow refinery, Ellesmere Port to Aberystwyth. The train has just crossed the River Camlad flood plain between the now closed Forden and Montgomery stations.   *Richard Coy, Montgomery*

same locomotive was used for Sunday school excursions from places such as Newtown during July weekdays, as this previously important business dating from the previous century gradually withered away in the late 1950s. The backbone of passenger services were the various 'Manor' class 4-6-0s (*Bradley, Barcote, Compton, Granville, Hinton* Nos. 7802, 7803, 7807, 7818 and 7819) and then BR Riddles locomotives took over for the final few years. No. 7802 *Bradley Manor* was cleaned to perfection on Christmas Eve, 1958 and had Merry Christmas taped on the smokebox. Four 'Manors' were held on the sidings for Royal train duties in August 1963. A snow plough was held at Machynlleth and was bolted to Collett Goods 0-6-0 No. 2204. Archie drove this to Talerddig through drifts on an early morning during several winters and observed no photographers near the summit. No. 7819 *Hinton Manor* returned for a summer steam-hauled experiment in July 1987 and the retired Archie was asked to be on ill health stand-by but he was not required. Archie never worked a train between Ellesmere and Wrexham, Bala to Ffestiniog, south from Aberystwyth to Pencader or the branches at Llanfyllin or Llangynog.

Major developments – 1984

British Rail, local authorities and Mid Wales Development announced proposals to modernize the Cambrian lines between Shrewsbury, Aberystwyth and Pwllheli. Mid Wales Development and local authorities along the route were considering British Rail proposals for jointly funding the modernization of these services. The package of improvements would include a new system of radio signalling based on an operations centre at Machynlleth to control all train movements over 135 miles of track.

All existing diesel trains operating on the Cambrian system would be replaced by then-new class '150' dmus. These two-coach trains currently being built by British Rail Engineering Ltd incorporated power-operated sliding doors, double-glazed tinted windows and secondary air suspension to provide ride quality comparable with InterCity vehicles. In addition, British Rail would operate a locomotive-hauled air-conditioned InterCity service from Aberystwyth on Mondays to Saturdays through the year. It would leave Aberystwyth at around 7.20 and return from Euston at 15.10 with a journey time of 5½ hours. The new services should be in operation by May 1986. Radio control of the coast line should take place by October 1986 and between Shrewsbury and Aberystwyth by May 1987 (it was actually introduced on both routes in September/October 1988).

Royal trains and Moat Lane Junction

The core of the following section is based on a document held by Ann Morgan of Welshpool. Ann has inherited the Special Notice of the Cambrian Railways for Royal Trains to convey the Prince and Princess of Wales from Thursday 25th June to Saturday 27th June, 1896. This was issued for the use of the company's servants only to her grandfather and many others.

Thomas Leighton was born at Vowchurch in Herefordshire by the long forgotten Golden Valley line between Pontrilas and Hay-on-Wye. He was duty signalman at Talgarth in 1896. He was moved to Glandovey in 1897 and then received promotion to Buttington Junction in 1898. The family moved into a tied house in 1900 and this

There was much criticism of the older dmus by the early 1980s on the Cambrian lines. The first improvement both of comfort and speed took place in the mid-1980s with the introduction of the '150' 'Sprinter' class. One of the 'Sprinter' units is seen at Caersws in May 1987 on a down Wolverhampton to Aberystwyth service.   *Sam Compton, Llandinam*

Regional Railways introduced the '158' class. This view shows No. 158780 in tandem with No. 156404 on the first day of the new timetable in May 1991 on the up train at Newtown. These versatile units have become the standard and have carried Regional Railways, 'Central', Wales & Borders and Arriva Trains Wales liveries.   *Sam Compton, Llandinam*

For five weeks an experimental freight train operated for timber between Aberystwyth and Chirk funded by the Welsh Assembly. It was hauled by a multiple-purpose vehicle with a cab fore and aft with seven open-sided air-braked timber wagons in between. The experiment was withdrawn and the unit moved to Scotland. The site at Moat Lane was considered with a siding and loading bay on the first section of the Llanidloes line if the use had expanded. There is a considerable volume of timber traffic from the now mature forests planted in the 1930s to 1950s such as Hafren Forest close to Llanidloes. The unit is crossing Pengraig bridge No. 178 over the Afon Carno between Pontdolgoch and Clatter in spring 2005. *Author*

Diesel-hauled ballast and replacement rail services continue to take place. Two English, Welsh & Scottish Railway (EWS) class '37' locomotives haul ballast wagons while on track relaying duties just west of Newtown station on 24th September, 2005. The front locomotive is No. 37417 *Richard Trevithick*. Tre-owain Estate is hidden behind the trees. 'Tre' is a settlement in both Cornish and Welsh reflecting a long lost cultural connection of the final province of Britannia Prima. *Author*

The Royal Train waits at Talgarth on Saturday 27th June, 1896. Thomas Leighton stands in front of the boiler on the buffer frame. *Ann Morgan, Welshpool*

Thomas Leighton, in Cambrian uniform *circa* 1898. *Ann Morgan, Welshpool*

Thomas Leighton moved to Buttington Junction in 1898. He stands at top of the stairs of the box. *Ann Morgan, Welshpool*

is now known as 'Station View'. The Buttington/Trewen sidings were just west of the station. Buttington brickyard was used for armament storage in World War I with a military guard necessary plus extra railway duties. Thomas remained at Buttington Junction until retirement around 1930. Ann's father, Harold Leighton, was born in 1902 and joined the Cambrian in 1916 as a junior porter at the junction. He then moved to Dinas Mawddwy and then on to Trefeinion between Talgarth and Talyllyn Junction, where he qualified to perform the duties of porter/signalman. The next move was to Moat Lane Junction from 1922 to 1928. He was to marry a Caersws girl. Harriet Carter was born in Manchester but brought up by Ann Lewis, her aunt. Aunt Ann's son, Bill Lewis, was to join the Bridge Department. Harold moved to be a signalman at Newbridge-on-Wye in 1928. He returned to Buttington Road crossing in 1937 and this was the year that Ann was born. He worked as signalman in the same box as his now retired father for a short period. He was then posted to Welshpool signal box until he retired in the mid-1960s.

The Royal Family must have observed the activity at Moat Lane and other stations. The Royal Train continues to pass the remnants of the junction since station closure in 1962 on several occasions, usually to either the National Library or the University at Aberystwyth. The family have alighted at Welshpool on occasions for Powis Castle.

The *Montgomershire Express* in 1935 listed the following. The first ever Royal train on the line was for the Prince and Princess of Wales to the University at Aberystwyth in 1896 and the details follow. The next was the opening of the Birmingham Waterworks at Rhayader in July 1904 by Edward VII.* The Prince of Wales visited Four Crosses in March 1910 for opening extensions to the Liverpool waterworks piped from Lake Vyrnwy. He then travelled as the new King George V with his family in 1911 from Afon Wen to Aberystwyth to the National Library to place the foundation stone. The return journey was via Moat Lane, Buttington Junction and Whitchurch heading to Scotland. A visit was made to Talgarth in July 1920 to inaugurate The Welsh National Memorial Institution (route details not given).

Royal Train, Thursday 25th June to Saturday 27th June, 1896

All junction stations were to have a very busy time. The details of the notice were exact. An example would be for platelayers to stand at level crossings where there was no gateman in charge (all accommodation crossings) and at all tunnel entrances and at siding lever frames. This included Brickyard Siding and Scafell Siding between Newtown and Moat Lane and Old Yard between Llandinam and Dolwen. The Chief Constable of Montgomeryshire was to place constables at certain station approaches during passage of the train and this included Moat Lane Junction. The telegraph office at Moat Lane must be staffed during the nights of 25th and 26th June. The running of *all* trains must be forwarded to Mr Craston at Moat Lane. Mr Belson would transfer from Moat Lane to supervise the marshalling of the Royal Train in the station yard at Aberystwyth. Extra carriages were to be held at various points, including eight at Moat Lane. All staffed level crossing gates were to close 15 minutes before the passage of the Royal Train. Railway staff must ensure that no member of the general public was allowed on to a station footbridge prior to and during the passage of the train.

---

* See *The Elan Valley Railway, The Railway of the Birmingham Corporation Waterworks*, Oakwood Press (ISBN 978 0 85361 517 0).

Gorn Road bridge just west of Llanidloes station, thought to be the July 1904 visit to the Elan Valley and the coaled and watered train is waiting to take over lighter engine duties on the Mid-Wales route to Rhayader once a heavier locomotive has come in from Moat Lane and beyond. One of the men is guard Shone who was killed at Abermule in 1921.

Shone Family Collection, Ceredigion Museum, Aberystwyth

The ex-Van Railway locomotive, by now Cambrian No. 22 has hauled the Cambrian Directors coach to the Van lead mine terminus on 3rd September, 1909. Charlie Bradley was the duty guard, he is the short man standing in this side of the steps. The toff in the plus-fours and alpine hat is Prince Francis of Teck (brother of the future Queen Mary). *Vivian Bradley, Caersws*

The Special Notice for the Royal Train is detailed on 11 pages while the working timetable for ordinary and special trains extended to 40 pages. A copy has been placed in Ceredigion Museum. Moat Lane, Machynlleth and especially Aberystwyth must have had a hectic three days. Specials in the hours prior to the Royal Train passed through Moat Lane on the Thursday and included one for the Montgomeryshire Yeomanry, a catering special ex-GWR and a special passenger that dovetailed in with the General Manager's special and the Directors' special. The Friday morning commenced at 3.55 am with the goods and 5.16 for the ordinary mail. The remainder are all excursions and some would have started at the point of departure at 2.00 am. The list follows with times at Moat Lane:

am	from
5.33	Oswestry
5.40	Newtown (coaches from Dinas Mawdy attd at Cemmaes Rd)
5.57	Newtown (only train stopping at Caersws)
6.20	Welshpool
7.05	Builth Wells
7.40	Oswestry (calling at Llanymynech, Welshpool and Abermule)
8.10	Liverpool/Birkenhead
8.20	Wrexham via Ellesmere
8.40	Brecon (incl. Midland Railway coaches from Hereford attd at Three Cocks)
9.10	Whitchurch
9.15	Builth Road (coaches from Craven Arms and Swansea)
9.30	Ex-Taff Vale Railway, coaches from Cardiff & Merthyr, via Tallyllyn Jn

A total of 14 trains within 5½ hours. The reverse flow took place throughout the late evening.

The 12 excursions through Moat Lane were part of around 24 that arrived at Aberystwyth. The Cambrian had an all stations ex-Machynlleth. The Coast Line via Machynlleth/Dovey Junction fed in two Cambrians: one from Dolgelley with all stations south and one from Pwllheli with all stations only to Barmouth. The LNWR sent a train from Bangor via Afon Wen and the GWR sent in a Wrexham train via Llangollen, Corwen, Bala, etc. The Manchester & Milford saw three local excursions starting at Pencader (2) and Trawscoed, the GWR one from Newcastle Emlyn, one from Cardiff, one from Neath and the Pembroke & Tenby Railway adding to a GWR service at Whitland plus one from Carmarthen. All sidings were allocated to various trains. All railway staff must have worked very hard as there is no record of any major delay over the three days.

Builth and Brecon

The line heading south from Moat Lane Junction, set in the middle of fields of sheep, moved through sparsely populated upland country. Most stations served a scattered community of few people. The only settlements with some density were Llanidloes, Rhayader, Builth Wells, Talgarth and finally the county town of Brecon. Aspects of Llanidloes including the engine shed have already been covered. Ron Jones of Moat Lane and then Newtown recalled that he would often talk to Bill Power at Builth about exchange of train movements but never met him. Mrs Pat Power would have been a work colleague with the author for Coleg Powys. Pat confirmed that she married into the railway family and that Bill was her father-in-law. Bill joined the Brecon & Merthyr

Waiting for the up train towards Moat Lane in 1938 at Builth Wells. The two-storey building was the station master's house and Dennis Glasscodine's home. The canopy extension is an extra shelter in front of the waiting room. The old water tower with low pressure is the nearer and part of the then recently-erected new water tower is on the left. There was a stationary steam engine and pump similar to that at Moat Lane.   *Dennis Glasscodine, Abermule*

Below left: A lady and child stand at the entry to the booking hall on the station yard adjoining the station master's house. *Below right:* Dad, the Builth Wells station master, stands at the gate to the Glasscodine family home.   *(Both) Dennis Glasscodine, Abermule*

Railway in 1905. The GWR moved him to be one of the signalmen at Builth Wells around 1930 until he retired in 1957. The full importance of Builth Wells as the coach and wagons works and the engine sheds for the Mid-Wales Railway never developed as the Cambrian took over operational duties and then absorbed the company. The level crossing gates/signal box at Builth Wells remained unusual as the gates were wheel-controlled from the signal box. Glyn, the husband of Pat, started work as a porter at Builth Wells and was signalman at Newbridge-on-Wye when they married. He inherited 'Dad's' signal box in 1957 until closure in December 1962. Ron Spoonley was the last station master at Builth Wells and he may have been related to Mr Spoonley who retired as head of Caersws Bridge Department in 1930. Pat and Glyn lived in the station house at Newbridge. There is a literary connection with her brother. T. Harri Jones is now considered a distinguished Anglo-Welsh poet. Sadly, he died in his early forties when Professor of English at Newcastle University, New South Wales. There are several books of his work and his work is often within an anthology. Home was a hard hill farm in the isolated Cwm Crogau valley. He would walk the five miles to Newbridge station to catch the train to Builth for the pre-war high school and lodge in town during the week. He became one of several poets or novelists stranded between the Welsh language decline of a community and English of the grammar school. These poets and short story writers of the 1920s to 1960s produced a very vibrant literature.

Pat and Glyn would travel on the rail privilege ticket usually to stay with friends in the London area. Pat recalls the whimberry trip from Newbridge to Marteg during World War II to collect fruit. There are other examples of whimberry harvest such as the Hailstone bus from Churchstoke and Bebbs of Kerry to collect this delicious fruit for jams and tarts on the Kerry Hill in Montgomeryshire.

Pat has made a request. Builth Wells Historical Group has struggled to get a visual and oral record of Builth Wells station as the questions were not asked until it was too late. For that reason the memories of Dennis Glasscodine and Bramwell Evans are included. Builth Wells railwaymen had an important working partnership with Moat Lane for almost a century.

Builth Wells station as a home

Dennis Glasscodine of Abermule recalls his railway childhood and railway work. Dennis's father worked for the Cambrian commencing his career in 1905 in the audit office of the headquarters. He moved at various stages to become the senior booking clerk at Welshpool when Dennis was born in 1922. The family returned to Oswestry when dad was promoted to a higher grade as chief clerk. The family then moved to Builth Wells in 1935 with a promotion to station master there, living in the station house. Dad moved to Welshpool in 1947, then Ludlow and retired as senior relief station master at Shrewsbury.

Dennis joined the railway as junior clerk in 1940 at Rhayader taking over from Sidney Griffiths who moved to Caersws to work at Moat Lane Junction. He moved to Towyn in 1941 when the Talyllyn Railway was still in operation as a commercial railway. The duties needed transhipment between the two gauges and Dennis made the cross-railway invoices and other paperwork duties that were necessary. He served in the Royal Engineers from late 1941 until demobilization in 1946. He was offered and accepted the goods clerk duties at Builth Wells so he returned to have a room in the station master's house. Virtually all traffic was going to either Talyllyn

It is known that there was much troop movement traffic during World War I on the Cambrian, but photographs are rare. This shows troops at Builth Wells yard; note the engine on the right.
Pat Power Collection, Builth Wells

This Edwardian postcard shows Builth Wells station and yards from the now Llanelwedd Quarry area. The single-bay engine shed is just to left of the church tower. Note that the South signal box is still in place.   *Pat Power Collection, Builth Wells*

Ivatt Mogul No. 46511 enters Newbridge-on-Wye. Glyn Power has left his signal box to exchange tokens. This view is *circa* 1958 with the down train arriving from Moat Lane. There were only four down trains: at 6.56 am to Builth only, 11.09 am to Brecon, 4.02 pm to Brecon or 6.30 pm to Builth only. The masonry behind the rear coach shows a road bridge that has been removed, the cutting has been filled in and this area is now a housing estate.   *Pat Power, Builth Wells*

The final year of operation in 1962. Glyn Power stands in Builth Wells signal box alongside his father, Bill, now retired. Note the wheel for the crossing gates; this was very unusual on the Cambrian system.   *Pat Power, Builth Wells*

Builth Wells engine shed in the summer of 1965, 2½ years after rail closure. This shed was built for the Mid-Wales Railway in 1864. The Cambrian moved most facilities to Moat Lane and Oswestry leaving the wagon repair workshops, etc., redundant. British Railways closed this shed in 1957 with facilities retained for one engine, if necessary, at Builth Road.   *Nigel Hadlow, Derby*

Extracted from the *Liverpool Daily Post* in 1957 with Bill Power (*left*) and John Edwards (*right*). 'Two Builth men retire today each after 50 years of service. Their family connections dating back to the 1860s total over 250 years of service. John Edwards started his career at Barmouth with the Cambrian and served at Criccieth, Afon Wen, Pwllheli and Builth Wells. He has been a guard at Builth for 33 years working to Moat Lane and Brecon. William (Bill) Power joined the old Brecon & Merthyr as a lamp boy at Brecon in 1905. He has served as a signalman at Torpantau, Dowlais, Talybont-on-Usk, Brecon and has been at Builth for 27 years. Three sons are on the railway, Raymond is a fireman at Birmingham, Glyn is the signalman at Newbridge-on-Wye and Vernon is at Doldowlod.'   *Pat Power Collection, Builth Wells*

Junction or Moat Lane Junction and beyond. It was unusual to forward wagons for invoicing via the LMS loop at Builth Road. Petrol rationing meant that virtually all goods for Builth and the surrounding villages was still coming in by rail. It was everything such as groceries and parcels for the shops, building materials, bicycles, etc. Domestic and industrial coal was then volume business. The agricultural flow included fertilizer, compound livestock feeds, machinery and sundries in with cattle and sheep going out, especially after fair days. There was a checker, two goods porters and three office staff. Emrys Evans had the delivery contract with the GWR but this changed with nationalization; BR had two lorries and two drivers working from the site from about 1949. Dennis opted to leave the railway in 1950 to work for the port compounder, Levers, who had a farm depot in the Builth yard. Dennis moved with the same company to Montgomery station.

The first train in from Moat Lane was the goods arriving about 4.00 am. This would shunt wagons in and out of the sidings and stable covered vans close to or in the goods shed. The first passenger train arrived from Moat Lane with few passengers at 6.56 am but had the mail, newspapers, fresh fish and parcels. Wagons worked from the nearby Llanelwedd quarry private siding and the necessary invoicing and supply of wagons was administered from the Builth goods office. There were two engines kept at the shed, one was a Dean pannier tank and the other was a Dean or light Cambrian Railways 0-6-0 tender engine. Crew and locomotives worked both directions to Moat Lane and Talyllyn. There was a cleaner, a chargehand, two wheel tappers and often a junior cleaner. There were three sets of enginemen, two goods guards and one passenger guard and three shunters. The staff for the passenger services plus signalmen resulted in over 25 staff at the station. Three or four men with builders' skills were based in the old coach workshop and looked after station fabric from Talyllyn to either Llanidloes or Moat Lane. A team at Machynlleth looked after Welshpool to Aberystwyth and the Coast Line while a team at Oswestry did the same for everything north-east of Welshpool. Station staff wages were collated and forwarded to Oswestry and the money came down in a travelling safe that was in the passenger guard's compartment.

Dennis can recall engineers trains including those from the Caersws Bridge Department working through. Sometimes there was material held in the sidings for them but often their trains were self contained. There was an engineer's shed that held their sundries.

Dennis was uncertain of the platelayers' gangs. He thought there was a group at Pantydwr for Tylwch to Rhayader, the Builth team with Joe Davies as chargehand worked at Builth, then a team at Erwood worked to Three Cocks.

Dennis retired to his wife's home at Abermule. He was aware of all of the problems of the January 1921 crash. His father's older brother from granny's first marriage was S.G. Vowells who was the assistant Secretary to the Board of Directors so he was deeply involved in the paperwork. Dennis's wife had an older brother who was one of the lengthmen between Newtown and Forden.

Dennis would often journey from Builth Wells with his parents on a day off to see the old people at Oswestry. The journey of about 75 miles would take over four hours with stops at every station and a wait at Moat Lane Junction and sometimes at Welshpool. They were returning to Builth in June 1936 just after the Dulas bridge had been swept away by flood so the journey to Moat Lane from Newtown was by bus.

Above: Brecon engine shed, 23rd
April, 1961. This shed was built
for the Brecon & Merthyr
Railway, the GWR closed the
adjoining Cambrian (ex-Mid-
Wales Railway) shed in 1923. The
Ivatt Mogul in the shade of the
shed is being prepared for the
journey to Moat Lane, the pannier
will work to Newport and the
'Collett Goods' 0-6-0 No. 2218
could be either for freight to
Newport or passenger to
Hereford.
                Brian Hutton, Birmingham

Right: James Griffiths treats
himself to a rolled cigarette. He
was born in Berriew near
Welshpool and was a junior at
Whitchurch Junction, LNWR,
when called up to duties in World
War I. He joined the Cambrian on
demobilization and was posted as
porter-signalman at Boughrood,
he was then posted to Talyllyn
Junction and finally to Brecon
where he retired around 1956.
        Malcolm John, Brecon Museum

Three Cocks *circa* 1900, time 1.53 pm when all four platforms had trains. *Left:* Cambrian Railways to either Moat Lane or Builth, *centre left*, Sharp, Stewart class '61' 4-4-0 No. 68 ex-Moat Lane; the train, *centre right*, heads to Hereford and the one, *far right*, has just come in from Hereford, both then operated by the Midland Railway.   *Brecknock Museum & Art Gallery*

Talybont-on-Usk bridge over the River Usk shored up after damage to the trestles by flood. Date unknown but texture would indicate pre-World War I so this would have been a problem for the Brecon & Merthyr Railway and not for Caersws as this section was added to the Oswestry Division around 1923 by the GWR.   *Brecknock Museum & Art Gallery*

The goods shed at Talgarth dated 1912. The locomotive is an Aston 4-4-0 built by Sharp, Stewart.
Brecknock Museum & Art Gallery

Talyllyn Junction (north) shows train heading to Three Cocks and then either Hereford or Builth Wells/Moat Lane in the mid-1950s. This is the furthest point south for the Cambrian ownership and shows the original Mid-Wales Railway station that closed in 1878.   *Malcolm John, Brecon*

The Moat Lane train is opposite the Cambrian platform at Talyllyn Junction and proceeds to cross the points to stop at the old Brecon & Merthyr platform prior to entering the tunnel on the final section to Brecon. *Malcolm John, Brecon*

Arrival of Ivatt Mogul No. 46519 at Brecon station in 1958 completing the journey from Moat Lane. The signal box can been seen through the steam. *Malcolm John, Brecon*

The Royal Train arrives at Brecon station on 6th August, 1955, either ex-Hereford or Newport. The pilotman was T.E. Power, brother to Bill Power of Builth Wells signal box.

Brecknock Museum & Art Gallery

The turntable at Brecon with a Newport route pannier tank. This is where Astons, Deans and Ivatts would have been turned prior to heading back to Moat Lane.   *Malcolm John, Brecon*

Llanelwedd Quarry

Various products of quarries were marshalled at Moat Lane after arriving or being dispatched west, south or east. One of the larger quarries with rail access was at Llanelwedd just south of Builth Wells. Bramwell Evans started work on leaving school in 1944. His father was general foreman at the quarry for 25 years. 'Bram' left the quarry for National Service for two years and then returned to work until 1956. His first duty was in the quarry as cleaner and he then moved to the fitters' shop. He was to work on various dams after 1956 including being workshop foreman at Clywedog.

There was a long abandoned quarry that supplied masonry and ballast for the 1900s Elan Valley dams. The roadstone quarry was started by Thomas Lant after World War I. The British Quarrying Co. took over around 1940. Ron Jones can recall booking up to 15 Lant's wagons at Moat Lane in 1938, both full and empty returns.

Bram describes the internal and exchange transport system as it was when he was a child and when he joined as a young lad. He can remember three portable steam engines that were redundant. The plant was powered with a 300 hp Blackstone diesel driving a dc generator and a 150 hp National driving the compressor. There were four stone crushers on site, three Broadbents and a Hatfield on standby. A Baxter came in in 1951 with a conveyor belt that carried rough broken stone to a disc crusher to produce the various chippings and screens.

The quarry had two working levels with an incline working up the side. Maybe the incline had been a gravity system but Bram can only recall that the drum of the incline was powered by an electric motor with a tension wagon behind to keep the rope tight.

There was a permanent track in each level and the skips (trams) were horse hauled. A temporary track was laid to the working rock face and to the scree tip. Four men were employed loading and pushing each skip filled with rock from the face. The rock face was harvested by controlled explosion. A sink was placed in the lower quarry to get some valued stone. This required full skip haulage up the slope and a standby water pump. The rock moved down to the crushers. Men then pushed the various grades of road stone through a tunnel tramway under the the the road to space by the loading loop where it was stockpiled in bunkers or value added by being dried and processed through two tarmacadam plants.

The railway siding was a loop that was parallel to the main line. No locomotive was allowed on to the private loop. The wagons were loaded from the bunkers by hand shovel. Coke and bitumen/tar came in from South Wales for the tarmacadam plant. The warm tarmacadam was easy to load but there must have been problems at the receiving siding once the product had cooled. The empty wagons were pushed by the locomotive from Builth Wells, maybe a distance of 800 yards. The points were opened, the wagon next to the engine was unhooked and the driver gave enough of a nudge to deliver up to 10 wagons to the loading wharf headed by a brake van. The brake van then ran on the short distance to join the already-loaded wagons. Bill Burton worked with a pinch bar plus the wagon brakes to assist. He sometimes had to pinch bar an individual wagon to the correct point. Bill would then lever each filled wagon further along the loop so that the first loaded wagon was close to the curve of the points at the south end of the loop. The locomotive usually had three empty wagons behind it. The locomotive would proceed down the short length of main line to the south points. The empty wagons could then couple-up to the full wagons so the total was hauled out on to the through line. There was an experiment with an electric winch to move the wagons but the older system prevailed. The full wagons were then pushed back to Builth where they would be marshalled on to a goods train with guard's van. Most proceeded to Moat Lane Junction and on to North Wales where the material was used for top road surface. This shunt took place daily at 11.00 am and a second took place at 3.00 pm during busy periods.

The company had private wagons with 'BQC' in large letters and with 'Llanelwedd Granite Quarries' on the lowest of the five plank sides. There were other BQC wagons sometimes from Clee Hill (near Ludlow), Criggion (Shropshire & Montgomershire Light Railway) plus other private wagons and GWR wagons. Some had to be brushed out because of the dust of a previous load before loading. Virtually all stone left by rail in the 1940s except for some local stone. The one exception was lorry delivery to make a series of hard core access sites within the Sennybridge firing range on the neighbouring Epynt Mountains immediately before and during the war. An increasing percentage of stone started to leave the quarry in the 1950s by road and one of the main hauliers was Berry Wiggins. Bram returned to a very different quarry in 1969 and worked there until retirement in the mid-1990s. The rock was now loaded by three Ruston 'Bucyrus' tracked shovels (and later by 360° hydraulic swivels) into dumper trucks to be taken to the crushers. The railway and tramway had closed and everything left by lorry. (The private siding agreement with the railway terminated on 31st December, 1962.) The company still operates from an adjacent quarry. The trading name changed several times, it has been Amalgamated Road Stone (ARC), Amey Roadstone, Amey Powell Dyffryn and Hansons.

Cambrian wagons are being loaded with crushed stone at the siding at Llanelwedd Quarry *circa* 1910. The post-1920 quarry area with loading loop described by Bramwell Evans was a new face just to the east of this illustration.

Mrs J.C. Davies, Newbridge on Wye/Radnor Museum

The decline and fall of the Caersws Empire

The railway industry showed a profit for the first few years after state ownership in 1948. Some of the more rural branches such as Kerry had received a life extension because of petroleum-based fuel shortages. The use of indigenous coal for steam power was valued. The whole situation started to alter rapidly in the early 1950s with increased availability of petrol/diesel and a huge increase in the number of private cars, lorries and buses. The railway industry received political support for modernization.

There was a already a smell of decay for rural railways. The proposals for closure were moving from very lightly-loaded branch lines such as Llynclys to Llangynog to some quite extensive systems. The late 1950s witnessed the withdrawal of substantial secondary lines in Lincolnshire and Norfolk. These had an agricultural freight business more suited to the lorry and only had good line occupancy on summer Saturdays.

An article in the local paper in 1957 asked that an experiment should be made with the lightweight railbus to see if this type of unit could cut costs and raise revenue on such lines as Moat Lane to Brecon. A reply came from C.J. Rider, Publicity Officer for British Railways, Western Region. The plans for the diesel units were tentative so it was not possible to give a date. The Mid-Wales line was conditioned by long stretches of single line, curves and gradients. These factors plus speed restrictions and a very limited traffic potential were not within the designed use of the light railcars although some experiment might be necessary if rail services were to continue. (The light railbus services were not judged a success and had all gone within a decade. None operated within Wales.)

The proposal for closure opened in January 1962 when local organizations called for maximum support to oppose the British Transport Commission proposal to the Transport Users' Consultative Committee (TUCC) to close Moat Lane to Brecon, with the exception of freight only from Moat Lane to Llanidloes plus freight depots with lorries at Newtown, Llandrindod and Brecon. The committee agreed to close the three lines in June withdrawing the Newport-Brecon, Brecon-Hereford and Moat Lane-Brecon services. The Moat Lane service needed to attract 800 extra passengers daily and this just was not feasible. The National Union of Railwaymen voted for action with 200 staff employed between Moat Lane and Brecon with a meeting held at Caersws in late September. The men stated that they welcomed modernization but they were given no opportunity to put their views for a viable service before the closure decision was taken.

An article was written for the local paper on 5th January, 1963 headed 'Goodbye to Moat Lane'. A trip was organized by the Midland area of the Stephenson Locomotive Society and carried more than 400 railway enthusiasts. This was the last passenger train to use the line. The trip was manned by Oswestry crew with the lead locomotive driven by William Pritchard and fireman Graham Mansfield and the second locomotive driven by Alfred Swanick and fireman Donald Rogers. The locomotives were modern 2-6-0s from BR stock.

There are various submissions to the TUCC within Powys County Archives from the various district councils. The following is distilled from these very detailed reports:

- Everyone is guilty of thinking within the original framework of a Victorian service.
- No assessment has been made of future potential with the following examples.
- Mid Wales Development Association is working hard to bring in light industry.

Water column and departure point on the west side of Moat Lane station prior to the climb up to Talerddig in March 1967. Every locomotive stopped here for water.	*David Hall, Manafon*

The edge of the main island platform shows the remains of Llanidloes & Newtown Railway track in the foreground with the now single line Newtown & Machynlleth Railway curving in front of the water tower, March 1967. Note Bryn-felin bridge.	*David Hall, Manafon*

- The increase in leisure time will increase tourism.
- The forests planted in previous decades will lead to much traffic from about 1980.
- There remains possibilities of further dam construction.
- Services are very poor with infrequent trains at odd hours that give no encouragement for use. No serious effort has been made to promote traffic. The timetable should be improved with more frequent trains and better connections.
- Any journey to Cardiff takes all day. Cardiff has recently become the capital of Wales and there will be much future potential traffic.
- Mid-Wales has been designated a retreat area for the population for any future conflict/disaster. It should retain a large volume delivery route as an insurance. The line had made a valued contribution in both major wars.
- The councils felt that the Transport Commission was deliberately running down the service to make closure easier.
- The railway should be considered as a public utility with access for everyone. It was accepted that electricty, telephone and postal industry maintains a service to the most rural of communities and that there always would be non-profit areas as well as the more lucrative urban areas. Also urban people like to visit the countryside. No one was considering shutting minor roads that also could not pay.
- Suggestion that diesel units should be introduced. Smaller stations should close and introduce conductor/guards.
- Moat Lane would be obsolete with diesel introduction. Services should be over greater distances such as either Chester to Cardiff or Crewe to Cardiff. The trains would have toilets and beverage/snack facilities. An example would be Chester, Wrexham, Ruabon, Gobowen, Oswestry, Llanymynech, Welshpool, Newtown, Llanidloes, Rhayader, Builth, Talgarth, Brecon, Merthyr, Pontypridd and Cardiff.
- This most attractive route should have weekend and summer scenic tours maybe in partnership with the Coast Line.

Level crossing, signal box and part of Builth Wells station viewed in the late 1950s when her husband, Glyn, was one of the duty signalmen.   *Pat Power, Builth Wells*

All objections came to no avail. It was necessary to operate an alternative bus service with assistance from the Ministry of Transport. Crosville sent a bus from Newtown to Brecon in the morning and this returned from Brecon in the afternoon. Western Welsh sent a morning bus from Brecon with return from Newtown in the afternoon. The bus companies submitted a report that they would close this service in 1964 once the subsidy ceased. Both companies could not see any financial viability (most bus replacements for rural line closures struggled to survive everywhere in the UK). There was a daily coach both ways from Chester to Cardiff timed to meet the Bangor to Cheltenham coach at Newtown in the 1970s. This soon became weekend- and summer-only until being withdrawn. The Brecon to Newtown bus service was reinstated in January 2006 as one of the TrawsCambria Services with funding from the Welsh Assembly.

The situation deteriorated in 1963. The remaining lines transferred from Western Region to London Midland Region (LMR). The Beeching Report recommended the closure of all lines from Welshpool to Whitchurch, Ruabon to Barmouth and Carmarthen to Aberystwyth. The Bridge Department territory was shrinking rapidly and the staff had been reduced from about 80 to 50. The new LMR transferred bridge maintenance to Shrewsbury and then Crewe so only a small team was retained at Caersws. The Beeching Report recommended the closure of nearly all intermediate stations on the main Cambrian line leaving only Welshpool, Newtown, Machynlleth and Aberystwyth. All this went forward in 1965 against major protest that led to a reprieve for Caersws. Many felt that Caersws would become a dormitory village for Newtown and many young people would leave. The whole culture was built around the railway. The station master, Mr Morgan, recalled that his grandfather worked with the contractors when the track was built. Mr D.E. Nicolas had six members of his family, brothers, father and uncles in the industry. He was now approaching retirement after 50 years of service and feared the village would be only for pensioners and the village awaited the future with dread. Fifty-one stations closed over this short period in Shropshire and Montgomeryshire. It is now known that a variety of other work came into the area so the pessimistic future as seen in 1963 did not come about. The railway industry has continued to struggle with closure proposals for both the Central Wales line in 1969 and the Cambrian Coast line several times in the 1970s but both continue. Several say that Moat Lane to Brecon should never have closed but it did. There is little prospect that it would be rebuilt. The line between Cardiff and Bridgend via the Glamorgan coast plus the commuter line to Ebbw Vale have re-opened but these still had freight services in place. It is far easier to close than re-open. Such closed lines as Bangor to Afon-wen and Aberystwyth to Carmarthen linking Bangor to Cardiff/Swansea would be the first priority if huge investment was to take place. So it is little wonder that many younger people in the area have little or no concept of the little cultural economic gem called Moat Lane Junction.

Geraint Goodwin wrote a novel *The Heyday on the Blood* and several short stories centred on the Newtown area of the Upper Severn Valley using fictional names. He was to suffer a premature death with tuberculosis. He would have been thinking of the hills on the northern side of the valley when he wrote as follows:

To the west the land rose up into the sky: to the east it opened up into the valley which gave on to England, field upon field of loamy earth which ran off into a haze. Far away a little plume of steam curled over an engine that was shunting petulantly at the junction set in the fields. But the noise of it travelled right up the valley although it was miles away. First there was a curl of steam and then, much later, the noise of the engine as it travelled through the still air.

There is a further description of the junction set in the fields when a young couple prepare to leave to seek work in London. The lass went into the buffet to buy chocolate and raisins. The up express comes in from Machynlleth. The porter runs along the platform singing 'change for Brecon and South Wales'. The couple move to the through coach to Paddington.

Geraint Goodwin referred to red grouse shooting on the high moorland. He viewed the three gaps cut by the rivers which show the railway routes to Llanidloes, to the Van lead mines, and Talerddig. Caersws and Llandinam shelter below with their Roman and Celtic stories. The route for the drovers could been seen moving to the Penstrowed hills and to the Kerry Ridgeway. Two Norman moats can be seen hidden within trees. The hidden line of the Roman road, the railway, the turnpike and several bridges are all in view. Seventy years ago, Geraint would not have anticipated the Llandinam and Carno windfarms, the placing of mobile phone masts, the heavy volume of traffic on the trunk road, NATO/RAF low flying practice, several caravan parks and the demise of 'the junction in the field'. The nature has also changed with several commercial conifer plantations, several protected areas for the upland sessile oak and the flood plain. There would be more reclaimed grass fields and less rough grazing and heather moor. The now rare red grouse is fully protected so no local men now go beating for the guns. Whatever happens, Moat Lane Junction deserves a full place within the rich local heritage. It is a little place of past mystic magic.

The engine shed still showed the remnants of the outside pit, the water crane, a lamp post plus the extraction vents in the roof in March 1967. The concrete shed was part of the stores, mess room etc. Both buildings were only erected in 1957.   *David Hall, Manafon*

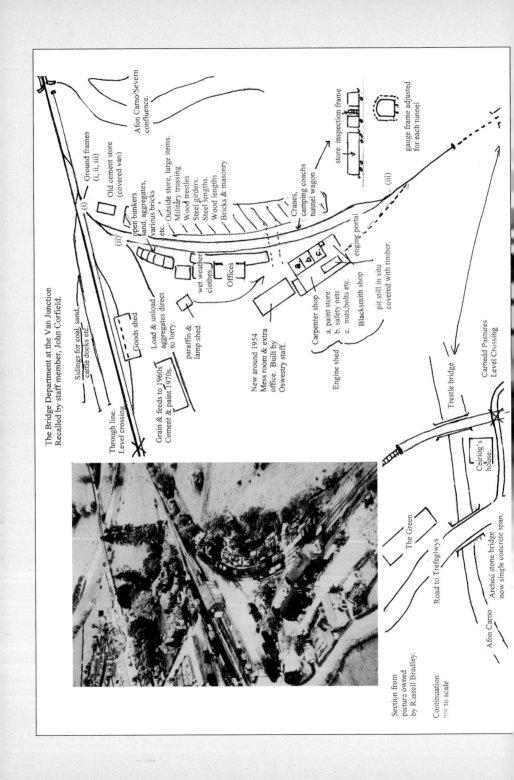

The Bridge Department at the Van Junction.
Recalled by staff member, John Corfield.

Afon Carno/Severn confluence.

Ground frames (i, ii, iii)

Old cement store (covered van)

Sidings for coal, sand, cattle docks etc.

Through line. Level crossing.

open bunkers sand, aggregates, various bricks etc.

Outside store, large items.
Military trussing
Wood trestles
Steel girders.
Steel lengths.
Wood lengths
Bricks & masonry

Cranes, camping coachs tunnel wagon

store inspection frame

gauge frame adjusted for each tunnel

(iii)

engine portal

Goods shed

Load & unload aggregates direct to lorry.

wet weather clothes.

Offices

paraffin & lamp shed.

Grain & feeds to 1960s
Cement & paint 1970s.

New around 1954
Mess room & extra office. Built by Oswestry staff.

Carpenter shop
a. paint store
b. safety nets
c. nuts,bolts etc.

Blacksmith shop

pit still in situ covered with timber.

Engine shed

Trestle bridge

Carnedd Pastures Level Crossing

The Green

Ceiriog's house.

Road to Trefeglwys

Afon Carno

Archeú stone bridge now single concrete span.

Section from picture owned by Russell Bradley.

Continuation not to scale

Chapter Five

The Bridge Department at Van Junction, Caersws

A fairly common occurrence within any development can be change of use. The original plan is rendered obsolete by unforeseen changes often within a relatively short period. The site is then used for another valued purpose within the company or sold on for other use or allowed to blend back into the countryside. The Van Junction was the start of a single standard gauge line built to serve the Van lead mines about 6½ miles south-west from Caersws. The line was the final local contract carried out by David Davies of Llandinam. The Van Railway Co. was registered in 1870 and opened for freight in 1871. It was built within the Railway Facilities Construction Act, 1864, to hasten development of industrial lines to mines, quarries and factories. The mines boomed on a share bubble and it was decided to seek permission for passenger operation. This was allowed with the provision of crossing gatekeepers at Pwllglas, Cerist and Garth Road so there was a passenger service from 1873 to 1879. The excess share price turned into a spectacular crash so the mines plus the railway traffic limped on until complete closure in 1893. The Cambrian took on the line in 1896 with the main purpose of using the substantial spoil tips for use as a weed-killer on ballast. The mines re-opened in 1905 as the world price of lead hardened due to the armaments race. Modern stationary steam engines were used so both coal and other equipment such as lubricants came in and lead, zinc ores and baryites left the mine. Up to 130 men were employed prior to and during World War I. The mine closed immediately after the war when the Board of Trade contract ceased. The GWR took over the line in 1923 and carried out some repairs. Traffic had virtually ceased by the mid-1930s and the line was closed in November 1940 and lifted a few months afterwards.

The lead dust was only used on secondary lines as a weed-killer as higher speed locomotives sucked the dust up into the working gear. Signs of lead toxicity circles, maybe from a spill when unloading the wagon, have been observed by the author near Whitchurch, Llanidloes and Builth when walking to a closed bridge after a period of over 80 years. There are several disused sidings where the toxicity can also be observed in addition to the specialized vegetation that has colonized the dry ballast.

A lead paint works was established at the Van to use the lead waste and operated from around 1915 to 1929. Red lead and bitumen were the two main products used to protect steel and iron work on the bridges so many a drum of these products was delivered to the Bridge Department site.

The *Montgomeryshire Express* published an article on the Van Railway in March 1941. Much of the article was concerned with John 'Ceiriog' Hughes. The paper asked John Spoonley to recall Ceiriog. John Spoonley was a highly regarded elder citizen of Caersws and he had retired as Inspector/Manager of the Bridge Department in 1931 so he would have been in his late 70s. John was apprenticed to John Evans, builder, as a carpenter. This builder maintained the property of the Van Railway including the bridges. John, at some stage, must have transferred his skills to the Cambrian. The name Spoonley also occurs as a station master at Builth Wells and this man may have been the nephew of John.

John Hughes was always known by his bardic name of Ceiriog. Ceiriog was born in Llanarmon Dyffryn Ceiriog in 1832. He left the valley to work in Manchester as a railway clerk. He returned to work in Wales as station master of Llanidloes in 1865 and

Van engine shed on left showing the then sliding doors. The Van station is centre right beside the through line to the junction. The date and personnel are unknown but this view was possibly taken in the late-1950s. Some of the wagons for the department are on extreme right. The coach in the background may be an engineer's coach. There was one in dark military green purchased from the Royal Engineers for a short period. *Powys County Council, Llanidloes Museum*

An opposite view from the junction looking towards the Bridge Department. Note the points set for the through loop. This is dated 1963 as transfer was due to take place from Western Region (Oswestry) to London Midland (Crewe). The huge square wagon is likely to have been the tender of a 'ROD' class 2-8-0 as several came on to GWR books. 'ROD' is the Railway Operating Division of the Royal Engineers from World War I. The tender was used as a reservoir of water for such duties as cement mixing or pressure hosing of stonework, etc., on Sundays out on site. *Elwyn V. Jones, Newtown Library*

Left: Bert Smout, the Bridge Department blacksmith takes a break in the Van shed surrounded by a selection of the tools of the trade. This image dates from the late 1940s. Jack Smout (Bert's brother) was the station master at Llanbrynmair. Their sister was the mother of Elwyn V. Jones and there are several photographs by Elwyn in this research.

Neville Smout (son), Newtown

Below: Peris Evans (uncle) stands on right in front of the Thornycroft BR lorry. The site is at the goods shed. Part of the Mogul locomotive can be seen. Peris would have travelled in the guard's van from Moat Lane Junction for shunting duties at the Bridge Department.
Philip Gethin, Caersws

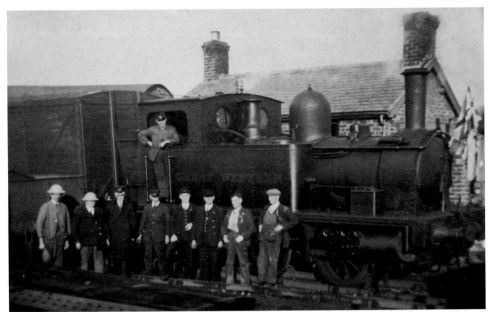

The last train at the Van station in November 1940. Jack Lewis, striker for Bert Smout, is on the viewer's right and Les Bradley, crane driver, stands beside him. Note two men with air raid precautions (ARP) helmets.   *Vivian Bradley, Caersws*

One of the two Caersws cranes with the match truck has been parked at Newtown in the long holding siding between the station and the Dolfor bridge in 1963. Note the railway internal telegraph/telephone poles.   *Elwyn V. Jones, Newtown Library*

Nostalgic view from the signal box dated early 1960s shows part of one of the two local cranes hidden behind the corrugated roof curve at Van Junction. There is a very clear view of the always-attached match truck with chains, hooks, winders, clips and other tools.

John Colin Reed, Caersws

Jack Morgan left the village to train as a fireman at Old Oak Common and stayed until retirement from Paddington including driving HST units. Brother Ted stayed on working within the Bridge Department. Jack took the photograph of the Van station in the late 1980s, several years after the Department closed. The goods shed in the background had become a vehicle repair workshop as Russell Bradley diversified from his father's (Cliff, Moat Lane guard) and grandfather Charlie's railway careers. *Jack Morgan, London*

Arthur Aldridge took this photograph of the Van engine shed in 1989. One chimney has been removed but the forge chimney remains. The roof vents for engine smoke can still be seen. Grandfather, Tom, was the senior engine driver for the independent Van company in the 1870s. There were a number of Aldridges over several generations employed within the region.

Vivian Bradley, The late Arthur Aldridge

The last known use of the Van loop was to hold two diesel locomotives. One of the men looks closely as the units draw over the points in case of weight problems. This is a little different from Charlie Bradley with Cambrian locomotive No. 22. Note the crew-bus between the station and engine shed.

Ken Jones, Llandinam

was then appointed to manage the Van line as it opened for trade. He died in 1887 and is buried in churchyard at Llanwnog. He was and remains a very popular poet, lyric writer and musician. Spoonley could recall Ceiriog from his earliest childhood memories dating from 1875. Ceiriog was an eccentric and would appear one day dressed in best frock coat, etc., and the next day, he would appear looking as if if he was one of the manual labourers. He called various rooms at the junction by names and the two station rooms were Machynlleth and Llanrwst. He could not stop rhyming in either English or Welsh and he once observed one of his men bungling the duty of coupling two trucks and exclaimed 'one of the duffers between the buffers'. The station house was close to the yard between the Carno bridge and the level crossing to Carnedd Pastures. The house was called Carnedd Villa but would also be known still as Tŷ Ceiriog. The Aldridge family took on the tenancy after the death of Ceiriog and the last railwayman to live in the then tied house was Jack Hatton, one of the Moat Lane engine drivers. There is an inscription on the wall of the house recalling Ceiriog. The house still stands within private ownership. The engine shed was cleaned out and decorated for the wedding reception of Delyth, the daughter of Ceiriog. That must be a novel use of a motive power depot even in Victorian times.

It is not certain, within a precise timetable, what happened between 1896 and 1916 as recall blends into memory and the mist of time. The Cambrian took over the two light locomotives. The logical decision to close the engine shed was taken and the engines were serviced at Moat Lane. The line was managed by the Caersws station master. Both the station and the engine shed had lost their designed purpose so the Cambrian started to concentrate bridge maintenance at this very central point for their system. The system is not known prior to 1900 but there is oral evidence and some written evidence that all the bridge staff gradually moved to this central point. Certainly, by 1916, the engine shed had become the workshop and the two rooms of the station had become the office for the Bridge Department. Any traffic for the Van started at Moat Lane with a token to travel from Moat Lane West to Caersws prior to the signalman at Caersws issuing the key to unlock the branch for 'one engine in steam' only. The line was lifted in 1941 leaving a short shunt spur to almost where the bridge had been and the loops were used solely for Bridge Department until 1984. The little Van Railway station served passengers for just over five years and then at least 80 years for the office and stores of the Bridge Department.

This chapter introduces the bridge maintenance staff. Much of railway research and much of the past and current interaction of the general public is with locomotives, carriages, station staff, signal boxes and certain spectacular views with the local example being the Barmouth bridge. The bridge is often used as the place where the photograph is taken rather than the image of the bridge. Local examples are/were Llanidloes, Llanymynech, Machynlleth, Newtown and Welshpool. The permanent way gangs, bridge maintenance gangs and their supervisory staff hidden in their offices are the anonymous heroes of the system. Without them, there would be no railways.

The Bridge Department was a section of Oswestry Engineering Division. Budget control and major design alteration remained at Oswestry while inspection and maintenance was the duty bequeathed to Caersws. A number of anecdotal stories maybe based on truth are always part of local folklore. Someone had written a letter to Oswestry in the 1920s and observed that every time he was in a train, he saw labourers leaning on their shovels doing nothing and wondered if they did any work. The reply from a senior engineer queried whether the complainant would like to shovel ballast or re-point bridge masonry!

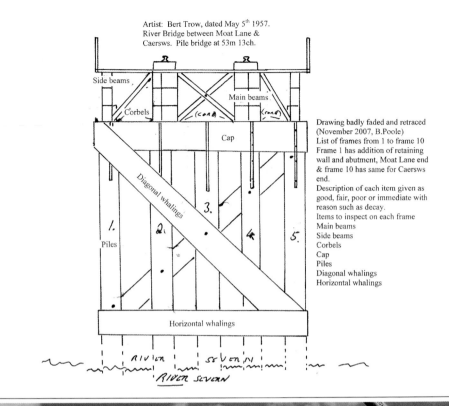

Artist: Bert Trow, dated May 5th 1957.
River Bridge between Moat Lane &
Caersws. Pile bridge at 53m 13ch.

Side beams

Main beams

Corbels (CORB) (corb)

Cap

Diagonal whalings

Piles

3.

1. 2. 4 5

Horizontal whalings

RIVER SEVERN
RIVER SEVERN

Drawing badly faded and retraced
(November 2007, B.Poole)
List of frames from 1 to frame 10
Frame 1 has addition of retaining
wall and abutment, Moat Lane end
& frame 10 has same for Caersws
end.
Description of each item given as
good, fair, poor or immediate with
reason such as decay.
Items to inspect on each frame
Main beams
Side beams
Corbels
Cap
Piles
Diagonal whalings
Horizontal whalings

The placing of new piers for Caersws bridge caused the line to shut for a week with replacement
bus services in March 2004. The contract was carried out by Ainscough Engineering, issued by
recently created Network Rail.   *Author*

The work was to ensure the safety and welfare of all staff. A weekly notice plus any emergency details were issued to all drivers, signalmen and those scheduled to work on the line. Staff on such work as bridge repair knew train times and a flagman gave further protection. They therefore came off a bridge (or went to a refuge on a larger bridge) several minutes before a train was due. They were most welcome to rest on their shovels and chat as the train progressed passing a speed restriction rather than the alternative of being knocked over.

Two men had a transport role in the area in 1940s to 1960s. Dai Brunt was a platelayer between Moat Lane and Tylwch. Ray Brunt was a bus driver for Crosville and he often was the driver for the bridge boys taking them to site on Sundays when maintenance had full line occupation.

Benjamin Brunt was related several generations back. He lived at Argoed, in Trefeglwys by 1875 close to the Van line that had just opened. His very large family was coming of age. The upland areas of Montgomeryshire had over-population so both internal and overseas emigration was common. Both he and most of his family went by horse and wagon to Caersws to travel to Liverpool and then sail to Puerto Madryn in Patagonia. The Welsh colony commenced in the Valley of Chubut in 1865 and the final Welsh speakers group arrived in 1914. Benjamin sailed in 1881 and established a farm within the Welsh-built irrigated section at what is now known as Dolavon.

John Aldridge came to Caersws in 1870 as engine driver for the construction of the Van branch and stayed on. His two sons worked for the local railway. Tom Senior had six sons and three daughters. They lived in Ceiriog's house.

Five of the Aldridge boys joined the railway and Tom (engine driver), Arthur (fireman) and Jack (porter) all worked at Moat Lane, Sidney worked for the Bridge Department while Charlie was relief station master on the Mid-Wales line. Philip Owen recalls his grandfather. William Aldridge was based in Welshpool and was a driver on the Llanfair line and other duties in the 1910s. Uncle Vic Aldridge lived at Oswestry and was a driver in the 1930s. Someone must have said, 'Go east, young man' to the uncle of William (maybe cousin to John from 1870) because Philip has located a photograph of William Charles Aldridge dated around 1890 when he had become a superintendent of the South India Railways.

Memories from Bridge Section Documents

There is virtually no documentation within local families concerned with the bridges during the Cambrian reign. Some of the bridge reports list a date of major reconstruction. Some of the bridges were doubled several years prior to the line doubling taking place in 1912. Many are aware that grandfather or great-grandfather worked within bridge maintenance in the Victorian period but can offer no detailed information.

The *County Times* recorded the death of David Manuel in December 1943. David was 88 years of age and he retired from the railway around 1925 after 40 years working within the Bridge Department. This could date from 1885 and may have been general maintenance work rather than specific to bridges. David was born in Manchester and moved to Llandinam as a young child around 1858. It is likely that his father was a railway contract labourer. David was apprenticed to the carpentry trade and worked with John Evans, builder of Caersws. This was the period when much of Caersws was built to accommodate the rapidly expanding railway labour force. David remains one of the earliest records of staff of the Bridge Department.

The railway in Patagonia was extended west from Trelew to Gaiman in 1909. A letter from Benjamin Brunt to his relatives in Trefeglwys/Caersws praises this extension at Gaiman.

Bibloteca Berwyn, Gaiman

Uncle Vic Aldridge stands second in on the right at Welshpool station. This photograph dating from the 1930s shows 'Dean Goods' class 0-6-0 No. 2455. The service would most likely have been either to Oswestry or Whitchurch but could have taken the route to Shrewsbury from Buttington Junction.

Philip Owen, Bury St Edmunds

Bridge Department Staff in the 1930s

A few records from the GWR between the wars has survived within the area. They were found within a recess when material was moved after the final closure of the Van station/engine shed. Most records are individual GWR memoranda between the Divisional Engineer's Office at Oswestry and the bridge inspector at Caersws.

J. Spoonley was the senior inspector dating from the Cambrian days until retirement in the early 1930s. He can still be recalled by some of the oldest people in Caersws as he continued to contribute to the village life for the decade after retirement. Much correspondence is concerned with staff promotion, retirement etc. Several conferences or meetings took place at Moat Lane station with regard to economy. In 1924, over 24 staff were employed at Welshpool within Spoonley's division. The long term proposal was to centre all staff at Caersws and the other points should see staff transferred to permanent way work, or the post abolished or transferred to Caersws. Certain immediate problems could be done by a local craftsman. One note highlights a problem that could not be solved until the use of road vans. The various bridge inspections were done on an annual visual basis with a detailed inspection every five years. The staff member would travel by train so that the yearly inspection could be done between several stations and return to base or lodgings at the end of the day. The duty would be varied so most lines had a section inspected within a fortnight period to enable staff to also see a bridge that had some unforeseen problem. The real difficulty was an emergency inspection where a staff member would spend several hours travelling, then half an hour at site and then wait for several hours before catching a train back to base as many lines only had three to four services daily.

Bridge inspector Morris took on site management in the 1930s. A letter in 1938 shows the sub-depots, so the staff was as follows:

Caersws: clerk 1, masons 7, painters 2, smith 1, chargemen 3, repairers 10, striker 1, labourers 24
Barmouth: masons 2, labourers 2
Llanymynech: chargeman 1, labourers 5
Welshpool: masons 4, labourers 2
Machynlleth: masons 2, labourers 1.

A total of 68 staff. During World War II this number increased and with post-war reorganization the staff total climbed to more than 80 at Caersws.

There was much correspondence concerned with pensions, ill health, qualification for free travel, etc. Bridge repair was and remains a physically demanding duty. Staff did not qualify for pensions in the 1930s until 65 years of age or over. The instruction was to place older men on light duties. The problem appears to be that there were more on light duties than light work available. One pensioner did eight years service for the Cambrian between 1893 to 1901, then worked elsewhere until 1921 before retiring in 1937. No one could work out within the rubrics whether the man qualified for free travel. Another concerned a Barmouth labourer who had lost sight in one eye and therefore was not considered fit to cross running lines. Mr Morris replied to the Divisional Head Office that he could not fit any more light duties into the system.

A Mr Edwards takes on site management in the 1940s and was likely to be on site during the transfer from GWR to BR. The inspector in the 1950s was W. Lewis. The poor man must have been distracted from bridge repair by staff queries. Many were letters to consider grade promotion. There were one or two letters concerned with

This astonishing photograph shows the contractor's locomotive on the Banwy bridge close to Llanfair on the light railway constructed in 1904/1905. The Caersws staff patched-up this bridge in the late 1940s and early 1950s in order to keep the freight service going. The piers had taken a severe battering by floods. The Royal Engineers helped the new heritage railway to repair this bridge in the early 1960s.   *Powys County Council, Powysland Museum, Welshpool*

Very few photographs prior to 1922 have been located. This very early view of Welshpool station shows the overbridge to Leighton known as Severn Road to the Severn bridge that had replaced a ferry. Early maps show a plan for an accommodation level crossing. The bridge had to be strengthened during World War I because of the weight of traction engines hauling timber to sidings.   *Powys County Council, Powysland Museum, Welshpool*

disciplinary procedures such as an incorrect overtime claim or failure to turn up for duty with no reason such as ill health. A manager rarely faced an easy week. There was one sad example where one man's excuse for failure to turn up to travel early on Monday morning was due to his wife's illness. His wife died before the procedures were complete. The man was so furious that he gave his notice in and would not accept the apologies for the misunderstanding. The widespread ownership of telephones from 1970 onwards would have prevented such a misunderstanding.

Four GWR work records were also within the long lost paperwork and a précis follows. Much is very faded. All are concerned with long-closed routes:

Cattle creep between Llandinam and Dolwen 56miles 45 chains. Planning starts with a new design and indent requisition on 17th January, 1938. It is five precast slabs type 'A' and two type 'B', 44 coping stones and four stops as per design. Confirmation from GWR Taunton works follows. The total costs of the work would be £241 6s. An application for occupation of line both to and reply from permanent way inspector at Welshpool follows. The date chosen was Sunday 1st May and required absolute (not between trains) from 7.00 am to 6.00 pm. A speed limit to follow of 10 mph until 10th May. The engine, workmen's coach and van plus guard's van to leave Moat Lane at 6.30, pick up hand crane No. 451, wagons with materials and men. The train would leave Caersws at 7.00 am for site of work. Work as required during the day and return to Caersws on completion of work setting down men as required. To use the Van engine and this would run from site to fetch and return the Llanidloes permanent way gang. The locomotive to be set on Llandinam side so it can run to Moat Lane at midday for train staff relief.

Llanrhaiadr, Tanat Valley line. Under-bridge at 10miles 63¾ chains. Bridge examination on 5th March, 1940. The recent flood has badly undercut abutment wall by 2 ft and there is a danger that next flood will undermine the total abutment. Immediate authority to build a dry wall on right hand Llangynog side to protect the masonry and to keep the structure under observation

All concrete culverts on Aberayron line to be inspected and report back to Oswestry by 1st March, 1941. Also examine and report on timber beams spanning cattle guards at crossings. The reason was proposal to withdraw engine route restriction for war duties. A full report plus drawings was returned on 7th March stating that culverts were in good condition.

Culvert in lower coal yard, Llanidloes Station, 9th May, 1947. The problem was water from yard was eroding soil off the company's premises with surface run-off. The problem was found to be a collapsed 9 inch drainage pipe. The pipe under the running line was 12 in. feeding into the coal yard pipe of 9 in. Authority given to replace the broken pipe, add another 9 in. pipe, rebuild end wall and then report back. The cost estimate was £102.

Ken Jones has retained a copy of a manual owned by H.M. Pearson, dated 1927. It is Pamphlet No. 5 of 'The Expanded Metal Company Ltd' with their works at West Hartlepool dated 1923. This manual shows use of expanded metal especially of reinforced rods and weld mesh to reinforce concrete. Many of the bridges locally that were built in 1860s have an arch from local masonry with some of brick. Longer spans were wrought iron on masonry abutments and piers or wood trestle bridges. Timber was used for narrow spans for cattle creeps, overbridges on accommodation lanes and footbridges. The Aberayron branch of 1911 had many culverts and bridges of mass shuttered concrete built on site. Forms of ferro-concrete started to be used from the 1920s onwards and these were pre-cast from such sites as GWR works at Taunton. Reinforced concrete was suitable for narrow spans such as cattle creeps but tended to be used for foot and minor road over-bridges. The technical change of pre-stressed concrete from 1950s onwards enabled longer spans that could carry railways. The commonest example are on the new motorways. There is a road example over the River Severn in Newtown.

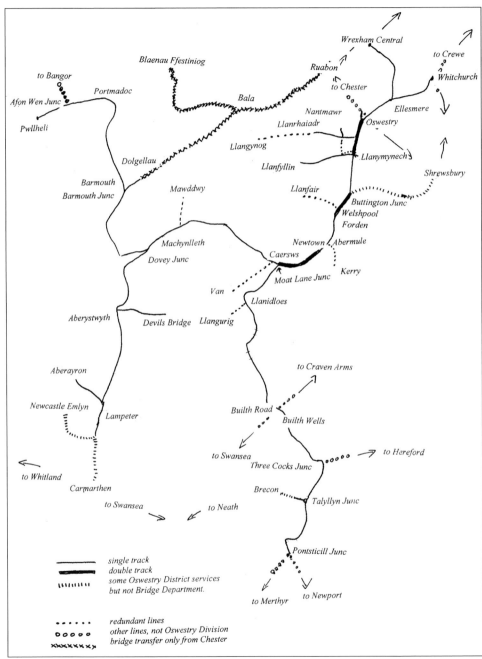

Guide to the zenith of routes for the Caersws Bridge Department. This map has been based on one published in the Working Timetable, Section L, Oswestry District 1957.

Vivian Bradley and his family archives

Vivian is the son of Les Bradley, Les worked at the Bridge Department with the final duty of crane driver. Sadly Les died in 1962 at the age of 57 when Vivian was still a teenager. Les started to work in the department in the late 1920s and gradually worked his way up the various skill grades. His brother, Cliff, was a guard based at Moat Lane and Cliff went on to form Bradley's Garage. The family is one of many with a record of railway employment going back to the 1860s.

Grandfather, Charlie Bradley, was a guard on the Van Railway, then the Cambrian and finally for the GWR. He was the guard on the Royal Train visit to the Van lead mines. He died in 1927 long before Vivian was born. Charlie married Sarah Spoonley. John Spoonley was head of the Bridge Department and his daughter, Connie, lived in the village until the early 1970s when she succumbed to old age.

Brothers of Charlie worked at Llanfyllin (clerical officer), Carno (station master) and Llwyngwril (signalman). John and Marg Lewis were great-grandparents and they lived in the crossing keeper's cottage on the Llanidloes Road junction. Marg looked after the gates while John was on other railway duties involved with line maintenance. Their duties may well go back to the 1870s. A selection of photographs and other artefacts have been chosen dating from before the Great War and post-war with the GWR and BR.

A record of the two cranes held in the Van yard has been handwritten and this now follows allowing for any inaccuracy because of fading:

4 ton crane No. 442
long end   11'2"
short end   8'2
over buffers   1'6"
single chain free on rail
loads*   15'0" to lift 3 tons
                  18'0" to lift 2 tons
                  21'0" to lift 1¼tons

girders out and double chain
loads*   15'0" to lift 6 tons
                  18'0" to lift 5 tons
                  21'0" to lift 4 tons
no rail clips or slewing (hook?)
on this crane

12 ton crane No. 211
long end   14'4"
short end   8'9"
over buffers   1'6"
single chain free on rail
loads*   23'0" to lift 3 tons
                  21'0" to lift 4 tons
                  18'0" to lift 5 tons
                  15'0" to lift 6 tons
balance box screwed back, rail clips
girders out and double chains.
loads*   27'0" to lift 5 tons
                  23'0" to lift 7 tons
                  21'0" to lift 8 tons
                  18'0" to lift 10 tons
                  15'0" to lift 12 tons
gross weight on six wheels was 20 tons

* Load is decreased with jib reach so length is shortened so toppling-over risk is reduced.

This memo aid was enclosed within a brown folded card for crane traffic. Les had written the following details on the inside and one must assume that the interval at Oswestry was for crane lift duties:

Newtown 10.25, Welshpool 11.43 to 11.53, Buttington 12.3, Llanymynech drop off stores, Oswestry 1.30, Oswestry 3.10, Llanymynech 3.23 to 3.30, Welshpool 3.48 to 4.40, Caersws 5.30.

Some of the bridge staff are taking a break. The works train can be seen in upper background. Lester Bowen, a 1930s chargehand at Caersws is sitting on the ground. The lad on the right with a large grin is Albert Evan Bradley(brother of Charlie). He was the signalman at Llwyngwril and he plus his wife Mary have joined their Caersws friends. The line in the background is on the gradient that starts to climb to Friog Rocks. *Neville Smout, Newtown*

Bridge Department gang on sea wall near Aberdovey. Bert, Neville's father, was out on site as steel weld was placed (almost certainly before concrete pour). Uncle Cliff Slee is third man in from our left on rear line and Bert Smout stands with his right elbow on the lad in the foreground. *Neville Smout, Newtown*

Vivian Bradley has retained the diaries of his father. Viv's wife was delighted that this 'codl' stored in the attic for decades is suddenly of value for research. Codl, pronounced coddle, has nothing to do with keeping someone or something warm but is an example of Welsh retained in English dialect in Montgomeryshire. Codl means rubbish or nonsense. Some of the diaries continue through the year while some finish around March when Les must have lost interest and good intentions. Many days were concerned with travel with lifting only taking an hour or less. Sometimes Les shows more concern for his Ulster premium potatoes and his scarlet horn carrots.

He would have travelled to every corner of the Oswestry Division and sometimes beyond. A selection has been taken. It was essential that the crane man was on the train when the crane was travelling to site. The crane could be parked and Les would travel home 'on the cushions' or on the Crosville bus, or the Caersws lorry and several times by taxi.

The month of January 1934 commenced at Afonwen seawall, followed by time in the yard making bedstones for bridges at both Strata Florida and Gobowen. Bridge examination took place between Wrexham and Ellesmere, then Whittington to Whitchurch, followed by Llynclys to Nantmawr Quarry and duty inspection to finish with the Llanfyllin branch. The final days of the month were delivering steelwork to Brecon.

Duties in January 1935 included working from Abermule to Kerry plus an emergency visit to Red House side bridge on the Van line to lift out a car that had parked in the River Cerist during a short period of sub-zero temperatures. Les was now on the crane spending several days at Talybont-on-Usk and then travelling to unload a petrol engine at Barmouth followed by loading and unloading material at Friog Rocks.

Few notes were made in 1938 but they included inspection after heavy floods, work close to Dolwen and most of February on sea walls along the coast section. Les put in a time sheet of 71 hours for one week in February.

Only a few notes from Les have been retained during World War II. Time was spent at both Wrexham and Ellesmere erecting signal frames. A 'Halifax' Heavy Conversion Unit bomber on a training flight crashed at Aberhafesp less than two miles from Moat Lane Junction so staff from the Bridge Department were released for Home Guard duty. A section of a bridge near Doldowlod was replaced. The weighbridge at Llynclys was lifted for inspection. Several Sundays were spent at Maesygrugiau near Pencader Junction involving 14 hour shifts with paraffin floodlight support.

The diaries resume again in 1956 so transfer has occurred to British Railways. Most are now kept for the year. The diaries were 'gratis' from either Levers Farmers or Welcome Veterinary. Levers sold livestock feeds and dairy detergents from an agent based from the concrete shed on stilts close to the Bridge Department and Les was a close friend of Mr Ferguson, one of the local vets. Mechanization of certain duties occurs with plant. Les would often be loading or unloading a Jones crane (four rubber wheels, self-propelled light crane), a Bristol 20 crawler tractor, a Platypus crawler tractor, a Matisa tamping machine, various compressors and generators. Much work was done placing pre-stressed beams on under-bridges within the area of Poolquay and Lampeter and all this work would be abandoned within less than 10 years. The two cranes were taken to Oswestry works for service such as reconditioning gearing and to Wolverhampton for steel rope tests and replacements. There was one occasion where one crane was working at Tregaron and the other north of Barmouth when immediate work was required near Ellesmere so they used the Oswestry breakdown crane. Les would travel with the heavier Shrewsbury and Wolverhampton steam cranes when these were called in for lifting complete bridge sections. The heaviest crane could be called in from Swindon.

Great-grandfather John (ganger) and Marg Lewis (gate crossing keeper) are seated in front of the cottage at the level crossing at the Llanidloes/Caersws turn between Moat Lane and Caersws. The young lad is Tom Price (fostered to family and worked at the signal box in Newtown later), then grandmother, Mary who married the striker, Jack Lewis, at the blacksmith's shop, Dick Lewis, platelayer and Tom Lewis who may not have worked for the railways. Note the bike, the forgotten symbol of rural independence a century ago. *Vivian Bradley, Caersws*

Grandad Charlie, with his beloved shunting pole, stands by a light Cambrian locomotive used on the Van line, probably just prior to World War I. This may be on the loop at the Van Junction. The little boy to the right of Charlie could be Les Bradley. *Vivian Bradley, Caersws*

A selection of duties follows. Most are routine but several are now little treasures of local railway history. An example of the latter took place in January 1956 when crane No. 211 was taken to Cemmaes Road to take out the river bridge over the Twymyn on the Mawddwy branch. Work on Corwen footbridge required a visit to Ruabon to bring back an electric welder. There was an emergency to Aberdovey when a retaining wall had collapsed. Sesswick Halt on the Ellesmere branch had the problem of a cutting through clay and the batter would be lubricated in wet weather and start to slide. The problem was faced by building weld mesh cages and filling these with stone at the base of the cutting. A visit to Bangor-on-Dee took place to renew decking on the wide single-span bridge over the Dee. Several duties took place at Aberystwyth transfer to load or unload material for the Rheidol line. The Shrewsbury steam crane was required to a 14 wagon 150 ton block train for estuary walls near Arthog. Bed-stones were required near Llansantffraid. An example of tunnel inspection took place in November. The tunnel train, floodlights and tool van were prepared in the yard. Occupation of the line was given the following night to inspect Torpantau and Talyllyn tunnels and this was followed the next night by inspection of Rhayader and Marteg tunnels so they arrived back at Moat Lane for breakfast.

Duties continued in 1957. Material and cranes were at the ill-fated Poolquay bridge. Les worked at the Buttington Junction footbridge to dismantle the structure. There are examples of working with other bridge departments and an example was the Neath crane at Lampeter in July.

Work continued all over the system in 1958. A footbridge was unloaded in the yard from Redruth. Footings were placed the following week at Harlech, the first erection day was postponed due to atrocious weather and success was achieved the following Sunday. A Moat Lane engine hauled the crane and tool coach to Llanymynech. A War Department (WD) engine hauled the unit to Kinnerley. Les wrote as follows, 'Dismantled WD boiler to take out for repair and returned to Llanymynech'. About a month afterwards, they were taken to Kinnerley to replace the boiler on the engine. They were taken home to Caersws in a WD car. They returned when an Oswestry fitter assembled and checked the engine. Kinnerley had the workshops for the Shropshire & Montgomery Light Railway taken over by the War Department for a large munitions depot during and after World War II, so the Caersws lads were 'out of territory'. The line was soon to close. The engine may have powered the pulley gantry systems in the workshop as contemporary photographs show a tall water tower with a windmill for the water pump. Les was starting to take sick leave. A visit to Aberystwyth shed was necessary in November to exchange a triple ram pump in the pump house. The grand geographical tour continues in 1959. The cranes were tugged to Afonwen, Tregaron, Llanymynech, Porthmadog, Ellesmere, Penrhyndeudraeth, Dolgellau, Derry Ormond (Lampeter), Torpantau, Builth, Borth, Three Cocks, Bala, etc. The Shrewsbury steam crane was necessary at Afonwen sea wall. The tunnel wall at Torpantau was cleaned down. Tunnels Nos. 1, 2 and 3 were inspected at Aberdovey on one night and Aberdovey No. 4 and Barmouth tunnel were done the following night.

The diaries conclude in February 1960:

Monday, January 18th, crane No. 211 to Llwyngwril to load Jones crane and return with special to Machynlleth. Tuesday 19th, returned with crane ex-Machynlleth to Moat Lane at 9.30 am. Wednesday 20th, travelled with crane 211 Moat Lane to Oswestry on 4.30 am goods. Thursday 21st travelled with crane to Fenns Bank. Friday at depot, Saturday free.

The Caersws hand crane out on site shows both left-hand winder and counter balance weight. Another essential item was a water pump when repairing piers and abutment foundations. The date and location of this view are unknown but it may be estuary work west of Glandyfi.   *(Both) Vivian Bradley, Caersws*

Jack Lewis, striker, at the Van Junction, Caersws.   *Vivian Bradley, Caersws*

Sunday 24th Fenns Bank with reconstruction of canal bridge at 2 m 50¼ ch. Crane 211 lifting and extracting smaller pieces. 45 t steam crane from Shrewsbury came in from Whitchurch end to lift in complete lengths of pre-stressed beams. Wednesday 27th, left Moat Lane at 6.45 am Llani Whitchurch passenger to Fenns Bank. Crane 211 collected and returned to Moat Lane via Oswestry.

Most services started at and returned to Moat Lane Junction. The duty shunter would collect and return the crane unit to the Van bridge section. The Bridge Department coaches and wagons were then held at Moat Lane loop or siding to be attached or unhooked from the appropriate goods service unless a special locomotive and train was used, such as for tunnel inspection.

The other GWR period memories come from Neville Smout. Neville was born in 1936 at Caersws. Grandfather Slee was promoted from Neath (South Wales) to Caersws to be inspector of permanent way gangs. He died around 1933. The youngest children moved to Caresws in 1923 and Cliff joined the Bridge Department and worked throughout the 1930s and 1940s. Grandad Smout was a blacksmith and joined the Cambrian prior to World War I. Neville has no idea of his duties. His son, Bert was to marry Irene May Slee, sister of Cliff. Bert became the blacksmith at the Bridge Department. Bert's brother, Jack, joined the railway and one of his final duties was station master at Llanbrynmair.

The illustrations are from Vivian Bradley and Neville Smout. Neville has a number of pictures of these railway relatives in uniform during World War I, two Smouts in Caersws Football team for 1923, several unknown but likely to be in the Neath area and finally various gold watches and chains for long service.

A ledger in the Bradley family archives from *circa* mid-1930s is titled *Tunnels on the Central Wales Division* and a précis follows:

Aberdovey No. 1. Length 200 yards. Inspection 4th October, 1933. Occupation Dovey Junction to Aberdovey from 9.00 am to 10.20 am and 11.20 to 11.55, engine, guard, tunnel trucks to leave Machynlleth at 8.50 am. Date of previous inspection 16th October, 1928. Absolute occupation for Barmouth Junction to Barmouth the same day from 12.40 to 1.40 pm.
Aberdovey No. 2. Length 219 yards. Same dates for current and previous inspection.
Aberdovey No. 3. Length of tunnel 190 yards, again same dates.
Aberdovey No. 4. Length of tunnel 533 yards, again same dates.
Barmouth. Length of tunnel 70 yards with same date for inspection but later in the day.
Marteg Tunnel. Length of tunnel 372 yards. Inspection 10th October, 1933, previous inspection on 26th October 1928, absolute occupation of the section St Harmons to Doldowlod from 11.00 am to 1.00 pm.
Rhayader Tunnel. Length of tunnel 270 yards with inspection, occupation and previous inspection as for Marteg.
Talyllyn Tunnel. Length of tunnel 674 yards, Inspection 10th October, 1933 with absolute occupation from 2.30 to 3.50 pm. Brake, composite and tunnel truck to be (fully passed at Brecon? Maybe means to store overnight).
Torpantau Tunnel. Length of tunnel 666 yards. Inspection 11th October, 1933, previous inspection 28th October, 1928. Engine, guard, vacuum brake van, tunnel truck and compo. To leave Brecon at 9.30 am for Pentir Rhiw, inspect tunnel and afterwards return as required to Moat Lane. Absolute occupation required of the Pentir Rhiw to Torpantau section to be granted from 10.40 am to 11.25 am.
Bryn Teify Tunnel. Nearest station Bryn Teify, length 100 yards with 125 sleepers.
Tynygraig Tunnel. Nearest station Strata Florida, length 86 yards 106 sleepers.

Right: Crossing a salt marsh, site unknown. It could be the closed line on the Mawddach estuary. There are two straight runs either side of Penmaenpool.

Vivian Bradley, Caersws

Below: Site unknown but many of the Bridge Department staff of the 1930s are shown including a then young Noel Manuel and Maldwyn 'King' Jones, Cliff Slee, Percy Smout and Jack Lewis.

Vivian Bradley, Caersws

Chapter Six

Memories from the Oswestry Division

Clem Mumford

Clem was a Llanwnog lad who left school in 1943 to work on local farms. He opted to join the army in 1947 and served for five years. He joined the Bridge Department as a painter in April 1953. Dic Brunt was the chargehand. The first duty was the Dysynni bridge near Tywyn. The gang worked methodically along the line to Pwllheli painting tar (bitumen) on to the prepared surfaces. The Caersws camping coach was the lodgings; it was stabled at Barmouth, Penrhyndeudraeth, Porthmadog, Criccieth and Pwllheli as the work progressed. The next duty was identical except the work was from Moat Lane Junction to Pontsticill Junction. The gang travelled daily to Newbridge and then the camping coach was used from Builth Wells and Talybont-on-Usk. They would travel out daily on the platelayers trolley. Extra work took place for two weeks replacing and building a new culvert near Pontsticill. Men would be boys as the ganger would speed the trolley so the vehicle would gain some speed from Torpantau down to Talybont.

Clem transferred to the carpenters' section with Bill Myatt as chargehand. Bill's correct name was William Watcyn or Watkin and he had acquired the Myatt from his older sister who had brought him up 50 years previously when he was a child. Duties included general repair between Aberystwyth and Pencader Junction. Major renewal took place between Whitchurch and Buttington Junction especially with a number of cattle creeps where the steel or wood was replaced with concrete. Work included bridge No. 1 just from the curve at Whitchurch. This was done on a very hot day and the rails would not fit back so several men had to walk further along the line loosening the joint (fish) plates so the bridge rails would fit in. The men lodged in Ellesmere for these duties. Bridge repair was carried out on a bridge at Marchwiel.

A new bridge was placed near Wnion Halt with the staff lodged in Dolgellau. The redundant branch lines were inspected by others so Clem never worked on the Kerry or Mawddwy line but did repair a boundary fence on the Van. Some work was done on several bridges between Llanyblodwel and Llanrhaiadr when that section was still open to goods traffic. The Wern bridge was being painted near Criccieth with scaffolding in place. Clem's boots must have just been on the overhang when the Crosville bus caught them. Clem looked down an hour later when the bus was on the return journey and he could see his hobnails had scratched through the Crosville Green to the undercoat leaving a wavy line. The so called Black bridge (every bridge with wood was black because of bitumen paint) was the final bridge to cross the Severn at Morfodion just east of Llanidloes. The bridge had started to dip on one pile when a locomotive passed over. They were packing the top of the pile when the fault was obviously at the base in the river. Pryce George, one of the Llanidloes lengthmen remarked: 'What is the point of giving a man a hair cut when the heel of his boot is worn down'.

Clem is still known as 'Clem the crane'. He was deputy to Les Bradley and took on an increasing role when Les was ill and then took on the duty full time when Les retired about 1960. The crane was on six wheels (three axles) with a rigid frame. It was hand-operated with four men, two on each side. The jib and the stabilisers had to be firmly secured before travel. The jib was held by the match wagon. The crane was No. 211 with a lift capacity maximum of 12 tons. The duty was always assessed and the heavier steam cranes from Shrewsbury etc. would be called in when

Reconstruction of bridge between Llandderfel and Llandrillo near Bala. Staff, *left to right*: Walter Lloyd, Caersws bricklayer, Ewart Williams and Iori Jehu both from Carno, William Watkins, chargehand and Tom Green, both from Caersws, and Dennis Stephens of Llandinam. The railway spelling of Llanderfel is another example of incorrect Welsh. *Clem Mumford*

Reconstruction of bridge No. 176 west of Pontdolgoch. Pre-stressed longitudinal beams were placed on Sunday and the upper parapet and fettling were finished the following week. Noel Manuel stands closest to the camera. Fettle is a now rarely used dialect word both in English and Welsh in the area and means to tidy up. An alternative name for road and rail lengthman is fettler. The author recalls older people saying 'mae rhaid i fi ffettlo cyn mynd i'r gwely' meaning 'I must tidy up before going to bed'. *Clem Mumford*

Military trestles in place during reconstruction of the Dwyfor bridge. This gives rigidity and the space prior to lowering the replacement or repaired girder back on to the bed-stone. Clem sits (or perches) on the viewer's left, Ray Trow is on the masonry and Ewart Williams is on the right.   *Clem Mumford*

Working on the Dee bridge near Llandderfel when the camping coach was parked in the siding at Llandrillo. Drinking water was delivered by churn for bridge and platelayers staff but also to many isolated signal boxes. The staff from viewer's, *left to right* are: *lower*: Bob ?, Bala ganger and flagman duty; Clem; Ewart Williams and Gyp (Gerald Smith Jones); *upper*: Ray Trow; Maldwyn 'King' Jones (bridge inspector); Ernie Jones and Wil Watkins (chargehand).   *Clem Mumford*

necessary. The relayers had a small Jones crane with a six ton lift. The rubber wheels were set to straddle the standard gauge. It was used for lifting sleepers and rail lengths. It was transported to site on a Friday for Sunday work and collected on the Monday. It was loaded and unloaded from a flat truck by crane No. 211.

Clem enjoyed his railway career. Men would curse the weather but outdoor work was always interesting. He left after Moat Lane had closed so he worked for the final few months within the BR Oswestry Division. He worked in a local factory and then worked for the district council on house repairs until retirement.

Gerald Smith Jones

Gerald Smith Jones is the last of the few local men interviewed who worked for the Bridge Department in the 1950s. He is always known as 'Gyp' and this nickname goes back to his primary school days in the 1930s. Gerald was from a local railway family. Dad was the cook, storeman, clerk for the 25 relayers who renewed rail, ballast and sleepers from the depot at Newtown. The train of four carriages plus wagons was towed around the system. There was another relayers gang at Oswestry. Joseph Smith Jones would have worked at the Abermule crash site in January 1921 and Gerald has retained the postcards of this sad event. Grandad Leonard Jones was a guard at Moat Lane. Gerald only has a childhood memory of grandad who joined the Cambrian in the late Victorian period. Mum's family were also railwaymen. Gerald joined the Bridge Department in 1950 after working on local farms for six years.

His duty was labourer to bricklayers and masons. This was a gang of around six men. The work was the care of masonry and bricks on abutments, arches and parapets. It would include re-pointing and also to take out bricks or stone to reset or replace with new. Many older girders were being replaced with pre-stressed concrete. The duty was to check abutments and bed-stones for the new span. An example would be the numerous flood reliefs between Poolquay and Buttington Junction. Gerald worked every section over the 13 years including sea walls and detailed work within the Torpantau tunnel. A sad event took place near Borth where the B-road goes under the rail. They were replacing the iron girders with pre-cast pre-stressed beams on a Sunday. The crane driver was lifting one of the beams when the chain slipped a short distance on the beam causing a tilt. Sadly poor Tom Turner was knocked off the bridge and died after impact on the road.

The team worked on bridges from Monday to Friday either placing material for Sunday full occupation or repairing parapets, floors and abutments. There was always a flagman on duty and a speed restriction of 10 mph or less enforced. There was much opportunity for Sunday overtime when spans were taken out and replaced. Gyp has slept in the camping coach in many sidings, the coldest was Pontsticill/Dolygaer and they were also parked in Aberayron station after closure to passengers. Although duties were planned ahead, staff would always be moved to an emergency. An example would be a clay slip after prolonged rain at either of several cuttings between Ellesmere and Wrexham or the Harlech sea cliff. Glutinous clay was shovelled into the wagons until the line was cleared and checked. Gerald opted to leave in 1963 to take on duties at Clywedog dam. He worked as maintenance man, greaser on the blondin or cableway. He was the relief driver taking over at lunch breaks and holiday so he switched from rail to monorail (or wire). He worked in local factories from 1967 until retirement so bridge work now seems, and is, many years ago.

Emrys Davies

Emrys Davies started with the Bridge Department after completing National Service in 1954 as a bridge repairer on general duties. He opted to leave in 1965. It was with some relief as he had tired of always being away from home and only spending time with his family on Saturdays. He worked for a local agricultural merchant and then for British Telecom for the remainder of his working life.

He was within the team that would often move for immediate repair. The depot had a Thornycroft lorry with Cyril Marchant as driver. Emrys listed some of the repairs done at every point of the system.

The Van. To inspect and repair side occupation bridges over the Cerist for internal farm access. Line closed in 1941

The Kerry. To repair the abutments of a bridge in the Mule Gorge. To place new hand rails on the bridge between the Goetre and Hodley as several sheep had fallen off. Line closed in 1956.

The Mawddwy. A continuous 10 day duty to remove the bridge over the Dyfi. Emrys worked to cut the trestle piles at river bed surface. It was a cold and wet job. The stumps can still be seen at low water-flow. Line closed in 1951.

Welshpool to Llanfair Line. Work on the Lledan Brook pile bridge through centre of Welshpool. Shafts of light penetrated through the wood plank walkway. The Banwy Bridge was patched just to keep it safe. The ganger called Cochrane assisted the staff. The line closed in 1956 and was purchased by the heritage railway company.

The Llanfyllin Branch. There was a bridge over the River Vyrnwy that was patched. It was close to the only aqueduct and this was a problem for the canal company which was ex-LMS so Caersws inspected it. Llanfyllin branch closed in 1965.

Much time was spent from Buttington Junction to Whitchurch replacing wooden and iron spans with concrete. All substantial investment which would be abandoned between 1962 and 1965. The rail bridge over the canal near Pant was removed and the bed filled with Oswestry engine shed ash (this will have to be dug out if the plan to open the canal proceeds). Time was spent on a long single-span bridge over the Dee at Bangor-on-Dee and this was followed by work on two viaducts on the outskirts of Wrexham at a place called Kingsmill.

The contrast was the work between Llanidloes and Talyllyn where the Mid-Wales Railway had iron girder bridges of standard parts. There were some substantial bridges over the Wye and the Ithon. Three steam engines came up from Merthyr to test measure the Boughrood bridge for any deviation. The really tough section was on the old Brecon & Merthyr line between Talyllyn Junction and Pontsticill Junction. There were two long inclines either side of Torpantau tunnel. There were numerous side streams with culverts designed for flash floods with wings and sometimes stepped stone floors to reduce flood erosion. These could be bone dry during summer. Goods traffic was in decline by the late 1950s but the older local lengthmen said that double-headed trains such as the Llynclys-Dowlais dolomite bulk wagons took a toll on the track. All this would close in late 1962.

Emrys thought he must have had a jinx on his attempts at bridge repair as closure soon followed. The journey for work on the Aberystwyth to Pencader Junction section was usually on the Crosville bus. A bridge near Tregaron had to have all timbers replaced. The Trefechan road underbridge on the then outskirts of Aberytwyth had major timber renewal. Many of the bridges over the Teifi had underslung lattice girders and 90 years of vibration had taken their toll with rust

Grandfather Charles Davies was the ganger between Tylwch and Rhayader. He poses with his large family at Cwm-bach crossing on his patch. The rails can be seen in background. Uncle Reg became a lengthman. Emrys' father was the youngest and is sitting on Dad's knee. One of the young boys survived an impact with a engine and this was reported in the local paper when he was taken to the recently-opened Llandrindod Hospital.   *Emrys Davies, Caersws*

Right: Men working near Marchwiel on the Ellesmere to Wrexham branch. They are sitting on the longitudinal timbers for the Forge Mill viaduct. Longitudinal and cross girder timbers were replaced when showing signs of rot. Some may have been the originals dating back to the 1890s.
Top row: Bob Martin, ganger/unknown/unknown/Evan Jones (Llandinam), Edfryn Jones (Caersws). *Front row*: Sid Williams (Carno), Sid Barclay, ganger, Emrys Davies. The two gangers/lengthmen were from the Overton-on-Dee gang.
Emrys Davies, Caersws

extension around the rivets. The bridge at Lampeter was renewed with concrete and others would have followed except the line closed in 1965.

The Aberdovey harbour branch was still owned by BR. A coaster brought in local sand. This was loaded and dispatched to various engine sheds including Moat Lane. Dried blown sand was ideal for engine sanders. The short branch was a failed concept to have a package route from Aberdovey to Waterford dating back to the 19th century.

Emrys was within the Caersws St John's ambulance team. Montgomeryshire was one of the final counties in the UK to have a volunteer ambulance service so Emrys was also one of the ambulance drivers until the full time service took over in the 1960s.

Much work was done on the coast route and Emrys has worked on every tidal bridge except Traeth Mawr at Porthmadog. Sadly his magic touch of failure also applies as he worked on sea walls and bridges between Arthog and Dolgellau and this also closed in 1965. Many coast bridges were trestle, the Dysinni was a steel girder exception. This was trestle until around 1912. The longtitudinal beams of the bridge were repaired in a continuous winter wind and Emrys started to wonder if his ear lobes were still attached to his head. The Blewitts bridge at Penrhyndeudraeth had the road toll section closed for two weeks to store timber as both the road and rail section underwent major renovation. The Afon Wen sea defence was another major duty. Access to Afon Wen station was over a weight limited restriction bridge owned by British Railways. Tom Higgs of Llanidloes had taken the Crosville bus and told the crew that gross weight was more than the restriction so everyone got out at 6.00 am in heavy rain with their work tools, etc. Tom, full of laughter, brought the bus over the bridge to turn round, and headed back to Llanidloes.

The childhood home of Emrys was at Bridge End on the Moat Lane side of the Caersws rail bridge. The cottages were knocked down in the 1960s as they had taken a battering from floods. Emrys learnt to be a strong swimmer in the pools of the River Severn when he was a child. He always took his trunks with him for a sea or estuary swim when on summer duties. There were safe warm pools under the Barmouth bridge when the tide was out. Emrys would have had no idea that the teredo worm also found the warm pools ideal. One of the bomb craters of 1941 was several hundred yards from the cottages. Emrys gave his son a fragment of the tail fin of the bomb. The Home Guard built a fire trench beside the cottage. This was usually full of water and was rapidly colonized by tadpoles and small fish.

Emrys was from several generations of railwaymen. His father-in-law was a lengthman between Moat Lane and Tylwch. Harry Lewis was finally in charge of a fencing gang based at Newtown with five men who worked anywhere within the division. Emrys and Ann (née Lewis) married in April 1960. They had the traditional send off from Llanidloes station on their way to their honeymoon in London. The locomotive crew played a tune on the engine whistle and then the train moved forward over the points to run over detonators. The train would soon cross Morfodion bridge that Emrys had just helped to repair. The work had been on the horizontal waling inspection. Heavy rain caused the Severn to cover the walings so the staff stood by for a day until the water receded. Senior railway staff read the riot act concerning poaching salmon. The bridge on the Wnion near Dolgellau was floodlit for repairs and this seemed to trap the salmon into a trance in a deep pool near the bridge. The poachers traps could be observed along the Wye from Marteg to Boughrood. The traps were carefully hidden from the fields and roads. The poachers must not have been aware that they could be observed by staff on bridge

A photograph prior to the Great War of the ill-fated Buttington Junction footbridge; Thomas Leighton (Ann Morgan's grandfather) was one of the signalmen there. The right-hand tracks heads to the single line to Shrewsbury and the left side heads to Poolquay and Oswestry.   *Ann Morgan, Welshpool*

Men work by floodlight with the steam crane in background after the sad accident to John Roberts. The line to Oswestry was closed for 30 hours but the line to Shrewsbury was soon opened. The bridge was not replaced and Buttington plus all other stations to Shrewsbury such as Westbury closed in 1960.   *Geof Charles Collection (C10762)/National Library of Wales*

repair. The water bailiffs would have observed such folly if they had chosen to walk, with caution, along the track.

Bobby Lumsden was a close friend at Caersws school during the war. Mr Lumsden worked at Pontdolgoch until the family moved, maybe around 1944. Emrys met Mr Lumsden again in the late 1950s. The family lived in the Glandyfi station house and Mr Lumsden looked after Dovey Junction. BR had decided to put a modern rectangular building with electricity, etc. at the exchange station but Mr Lumsden thought such an investment with few passengers boarding and only a few exchanging trains in the middle of a bog was not wise use of money.

Emrys was awarded the 'Order of Industrial Heroism' (sponsored by the trade unions and the *Daily Herald*). An accident took place over the River Vrnwy at Llanymynech in April 1957. Llewelyn Jones from Caersws fell from a girder. Emrys dived in from the top girder and managed to hold Llew for a short period. Other lads were running along the bank throwing a rope towards them to see if Emrys could catch the rope. It was bitterly cold so all efforts failed and poor Llew was swept down stream and his body was recovered the following day. He may already have received a head blow.

Sadly this accident happened three weeks after Gwynant Williams was killed at Poolquay. This may have been a girder burst when he was trapped as tension was released. Poor Jack Roberts from Shrewsbury then lost his life when the Shrewsbury steam crane hit the footbridge at Buttington Junction when on the rescue mission.

The close knit railway community of Caersws suffered a spate of accidents during a short period. Tom Turner was killed at Borth and Ewart Jehu lost his life at Llanaber sea wall. These sad events enter the culture of the community in the same way as a pit or quarry disaster.

An inquiry was held at Llanymynech behind closed doors. Two railwaymen died on 10th March, 1957. Gwynant Williams of Machynlleth died under a bridge girder at Poolquay on Sunday at noon. The rail bridge over the Severn tilted out of position. Williams was one of four men placing new bedstones for a new bridge when the girder moved 18 inches pinning Williams between a cross timber and an abutment. The three others received slight injury only. The 12 ton crane (Caersws crane) was stationary on the bridge but was not dislodged even though the track was twisted. The men sawed through the cross timber but they knew poor Gwynant was dead.

The breakdown crane with 30 ton lift was sent from Shrewsbury and worked through the day and afterwards in floodlight to clear the debris. The crane worked back to Buttington Junction so that the Caersws crane could be moved off the bridge. The jib of the Shrewsbury crane struck the steel footbridge causing partial collapse. It was decided to dismantle the bridge and, about midnight, a steel part of the lattice struck crane foreman John Roberts. He was rushed to hospital but sadly died the next day.

This 'Black Sunday' closed the line for 30 hours. The inquest concluded that the Poolquay accident occurred because of main girder failure and not due to the extensions girders, the wood blocks and jacks underneath the preparation.

The Buttington station footbridge incident may have been a crew mistake or pure accident. Death by misadventure was recorded for foreman Roberts. Sadly, the third fatality followed within the month at the bridge at Llanymynech.

View across the Llanymynech bridge over the Vyrnwy showing the fresh girder, abutment and trackwork, taken after the fatal accident. A powered trolley is parked. The new line (1896) to Llanfyllin curves on the left and the footbridge towards Llanymynech station can be seen in the background. A film of this bridge had been made by the British Transport Commission several weeks before. In the the local paper (20th April, 1957), several councillors suggested that the Caersws area was suitable for a nuclear generating plant. The Welsh one was finally awarded to Trawsfynydd. *Geof Charles Collection (C10990C)/National Library of Wales*

Another view of the bridge. The double caissons were placed (and still stand) but the double track was built between Oswestry and Llanymynech stations only. This looks so tranquil that it is difficult to imagine that Emrys dived off the girder to grab poor Llewelyn Jones. Llew may have lost his footing and his cry attracted attention. Emrys battled in the river while Percy Smout, Walter Lloyd and Edward Meredith, all from the Caersws area, waded in further down stream to try and help without success. *Geof Charles Collection (C10990)/National Library of Wales*

Ted Morgan

Ted Morgan worked at both Caersws sites. Ted's father worked in the Bridge Department after returning from the Navy in 1945. Ted left school in 1954 to work on the farm of Major Kinsey at Maesmawr. A vacancy became available as a cleaner at the Junction so Ted worked at Moat Lane for about 12 months prior to National Service between 1957 and 1958.

Ted was demobbed on a Thursday and joined the Bridge Department on the following Monday. His first duty was to help Tom Turner with bridge inspection in the Talybont-on-Usk area. He carried the ladder over and under the canal, road bridges, streams and the river. He was then allocated to the painters' section of bridge maintenance and, over the next seven years, he must have visited every line that was still in operation. A period of over a month was spent at Wrexham where they carried out major work on viaducts and bridges between Wrexham Central and Bangor-on-Dee. A number of bridges were rebuilt using pre-stressed concrete around both Poolquay and Lampeter. Staff left Caersws in the Crosville bus or with the depot lorry driven by Cyril Marchant. The only time they went out on a train was when their section of the engineering train was hauled out to site. The local gangers took them to and from the necessary bridge from the siding where the camping coach was parked.

Some work was done on the tunnels at Aberdovey. The inspection wagon was a converted horse box with both a measure gauge and a central area of the side and roof cut out with an arch frame inside so that men could work within reach of the internal tunnel face. A new technique of roof pointing, using a powered gun to force the extrusion into the gap, was used. The team also helped at Llanaber sea walls to lift granite stones into position. The work was physically demanding, whether in summer heat or a winter storm. Ted finished as the Midland Region took over and Caersws became a sub-depot with only a handful of men. He found work with the textile company of Laura Ashley that had started to rapidly expand from a small base at Carno station.

The only other member of the family to join the railway was older brother, Jack. Jack started as cleaner at Llanidloes under the watchful eye of Peter Poole's father. The training for fireman grade involved a move to Old Oak Common. Jack stayed in London and remained with the railway for about 45 years until retirement. He was promoted to driver. He would have been one of the crew on the footplate that brought the 'Cambrian Coast Express' from Paddington to Shrewsbury where the heavy engines changed to 'Manors' and the crew changed to lads from Shrewsbury, Machynlleth or Aberystwyth. The Paddington, Snow Hill, Shrewsbury, Chester work was hived off to the Midland Region at the same time as the reduction of the Caersws Bridge Department. Jack remained at Paddington driving the diesel-hydraulics, the diesel-electrics and then the high speed trains through Reading to either Bristol or Cardiff. Jack would usually spend a week each year at Caersws. Both brothers have retained an interest in the local railway and have several documents and photographs plus a wealth of local recall.

Right: Ted Morgan apologises for the poor focus of an unusual bridge. The semi-private footbridge was at Acrefair/Trevor only a short distance from the junction at Ruabon. The footbridge linked the two sites of Monsanto Chemical Works either side of a deep valley where the train headed to Llangollen and Barmouth at the base. Four Caersws men lean on the parapet. They are, *left to right:* Two old hands, Doug Tanner and chargehand, George Davies; plus the then two younger men, John Corfield and Ted Morgan.

Ted Morgan, Caersws

Left: The pier and the span gives some idea of how this footbridge, with only a section shown, soared across the valley. The safety nets are placed underneath the section being inspected and painted. These nets were hung in the Van engine shed when not in use.

Ted Morgan, Caersws

Right: Ted took this picture with John Corfield on the viewer's right of the group while the three older men were the lengthmen at their base at Talyllyn Junction, Brecon.

Ted Morgan, Caersws

Chapter Seven

Caersws Section Staff 1964-1984, and later

John Corfield

John Corfield has bridge knowledge that spans between the two periods of control from Oswestry and Shrewsbury, and Crewe. John attended the parish primary school at Llanwnog and then Penygloddfa secondary school at Newtown. He left school at 15 years of age and worked for several years in local rural jobs prior to joining the Bridge Department in 1954. The older men had all worked for the GWR and there were still several who had started with the Cambrian. The basis of training was that of the older men passing on their skills from different decades and this was inherited from those who started work way back into the 1870s. The territory expanded from the original Cambrian as the GWR added Talyllyn Junction to Ponsticill Junction plus Aberystwyth to Pencader. BR added Dolgellau to Ruabon plus Bala to Blaenau Ffestiniog around 1954. The gang could be moved out of territory, if necessary, so John has worked on sections from Shrewsbury to Ludlow.

There was an inspector and sub-inspector plus Evan Jones, the clerk. There was then a chargeman (foreman) for each gang and each gang had around six men. There were three brick and stonemason gangs and Con Jones and Maldwyn Jones nicknamed 'King' were two foreman. There was one steel gang, with Norman Gethin as chargehand. There were two painting gangs. John was assigned to one of these but the then youngsters could be moved round to broaden their training base. There were three carpenters' gangs or bridge repairers and some would be at the Van site within the carpenters' shop as needed. Two men operated the cranes. The final two on site were the blacksmith and his mate known as the striker.

The normal shift was Monday to Friday on site. The gang either stopped in lodgings or the five to six men stopped in the small camping coach. Return to home daily was only possible on the main line where there was a suitable train service. Routine painting was done in sections such as Aberdyfi to Tywyn and then Tywyn to Morfa Mawddach. Barmouth bridge was a single item and the whole length could take up to four months. The paint was tar (also known as pitch or bitumen) for the steel surface and red lead for the undercoat. Rust on steel/iron was a constant problem. It would crust and blister and had to be scraped off. There was always an opportunity for Sunday overtime when there was full line possession. Staff were taken out and returned from site using a Crosville bus from the Llanidloes depot. An example was the major relaying of track on sections between Brecon and Moat Lane.

Various trestles, ladders and ropes came to the painting site for overhang work from the Van store. The camping coach was a rare experience in the winter. There was a central stove for heat and cooking. The pillows would stick to the carriage side with condensation and frost. A brick would be heated and then placed in the bed to try to remove the dampness. Drinking and washing water was carried in churns. The oil lamps gave a very poor light so it was difficult to read after evening food.

John left in 1962 to work at the Llanbrynmair sewerage scheme, then on to the Clywedog dam, then to the Welsh Office trunk road bridge over the railway at Penstrowed and later to a factory in Newtown. He returned to the railway in 1972 to be based at the Van Junction until 1984 and then at Machynlleth. The large workforce of both Moat Lane and the Bridge Department was now history. About 14

Bridge No. 210 is situated between Llanbrynmair and Cemmaes Road. It is the first of four bridges that cross the Afon Twymyn as the river descends through a heavily wooded gorge. The masonry was cut from the Talerddig cutting during construction in the early 1860s. The men are mixing concrete and placing the material in sandbags. *John Corfield, Caersws*

Scaffolding necessary for the work. The filled and hardening sandbags can be seen placed at the arch base. Their purpose is to prevent base erosion. Note gas bottles for welding and steel cutting. These arches are large with a top width to carry the additional earth embankment. River cut back and erosion is continuous on fast flowing mountain streams so bridges need extra wing walls and solid floors immediately upstream and downstream of the bridge. *John Corfield, Caersws*

staff were retained after 1984, all based at Machynlleth and this continued until privatization around 1996. Duties now included both fencing and level crossing maintenance as well as bridges.

John worked on until retirement in October 2000 within GEC Tarmac Railway Maintenance (GTRM) on contract to Railtrack. The Shrewsbury Bridge Section had shut so Machynlleth men could find themselves travelling to work within the Birmingham conurbation. The final years were not easy. The ratio of travel time to work did not make economic sense to John. Forms were like a flood, every asset was measured but somewhere along the line it was necessary to maintain the bridge with craft skill and not office measures on a computer. Some of the duties during both periods within Western Region and London Midland are recalled.

No one realized that the some of the piers of Barmouth bridge were being undermined by a marine worm. Some nightshift work with floodlights was necessary because of tides limiting access to the lower section of the piers. A swing scaffold was used on the steel sections and a solid scaffold was clamped for access to the wooden sections. John helped to operate the swing bridge on about three dates. Certain work required a huge spanner nicknamed 'Big Bertha' and this required three men. Maybe an immunity to rain, wind and cold developed at such places as Barmouth bridge and Torpantau in the Brecon Beacons. John has worked on all the branch lines except Llangynog Light Railway. A culvert was rebuilt on the Van line. The bridges were enhanced from Trawsfynydd to Blaenau Ffestiniog when the nuclear power station opened so that the wagons with the flasks could take the material to Sellafield in Cumbria. John helped to take out the two river bridges over the Twymyn and the Dyfi on the Mawddwy branch line. Several of the other accommodation bridges were also removed. Conversely repairs were done on about four bridges on the Kerry line within the Abermule gorge. A walk near Trawsfynydd involved visual inspection and crossing over the Prysor viaduct and this was the only very large masonry multi-arch viaduct within the system. The Rheidol line was inspected every winter when there were no trains operating. One of the final duties was to walk from Welshpool to Bow Street painting every ¼ mile post with a yellow background and then walk back putting black paint on the figures.

John was one of the staff on extra weekend duties at both Poolquay and Llanymynech fatalities. These were truly sad events that go right to the soul of everyone within the gangs and within the village. John is one of a number of men who recalled observation of wildlife and he retains this interest although now within the comfort of his Caersws home. Birds and mammals seemed to ignore the maintenance men high on the bridges or walking along the line. Some bridges within the gorges looked down on the oak canopy, others close to fast running streams hid wagtails and dippers. The view from estuary bridges would have gulls, ducks and various waders harvesting their tidal diet. Others have recalled seeing otters, polecats, etc. inland, and the sudden switch from red squirrels in the early 1950s to greys by the mid-1960s. Dolphins and seals have been observed on occasions from the estuary bridge or sea walls. John recalled a raven which was full of carrion from a dead carcase such as a fox or a badger by the track. The raven was sitting on the signal within view of the box so the signalman let the arm down suddenly and the poor bird only just recovered before hitting the ground.

Maybe such bonuses were deserved as compensation for sleeping in a camping coach in the winter. The three camping coaches held at Caersws were for working staff only, they must not be confused with the summer holiday camping coaches along the coastal section stations. These were very popular over several decades.

Bridge No. 217 crosses the Afon Twymyn within a gorge just up from Cemmaes Road. There are two smaller spans butting on to the embankments and the large central span over the river. The masonry stone was cut from Talerddig cutting in 1862 but there was only enough left for the base. The arches and parapets are brick from Ruabon. The scaffolding was hired. One section of scaffold was taken by flood and several planks were swept as far down as Dyfi Junction. Howard Latham is both re-pointing and resetting bricks on the segmental bridge arch. His size gives some idea of this very large bridge hidden from view within the heavily wooded gorge.   *Ken Jones, Llandinam*

Bridge No. 226 crosses the Afon Dulas west of Machynlleth station. The bridge is being battered by flood and the potential problem of debris pressure can be seen. The pole on the centre section between two girders acts as a measure and the bridge has to close when water arises over a marker. The right-hand near bank shows some willows that are planted to reduce bank erosion. Local railwaymen and farmers often call these trees sallies and this comes from the Latin name of 'salix'. *Ken Jones, Llandinam*

Ken Jones

Ken Jones was born in March 1941 and he was a Llandinam lad. The earliest of his railway memories were the freight trains with military equipment working to or from Moat Lane towards the end of World War II. Ken left school in 1956 and joined Evans & Owen as a carpenter apprentice. This was one of the larger of Montgomeryshire's building companies and was based at Caersws and the Evans was descended from the Evans that maintained the independent Van line until the 1890s. Ken completed his apprenticeship and continued working in the building industry. He joined the railway in 1972. Staff employment at the Bridge Department had been run down after 1964. Lack of maintenance had caused deterioration and there were four men at Barmouth, two at Machynlleth and eight at Caersws and this expanded to around 44 staff by the mid-1980s. Maybe the hidden agenda was to close the lines but this became politically unacceptable in the 1970s with continual pressure to improve track for more reliable services.

Ken started as a carpenter, he was promoted to chargehand, then junior supervisor and finally the senior supervisor. Caersws Area Works Supervisor (AWS) had responsibility from Forden (39 milepost) to Aberystwyth, the Rheidol line and the coast line to Pwllheli, plus responsibility for disused bridges. The line further south from the junction just south of Llanidloes had become the duty of the Neath Division. The Bridge Department closed at Caersws in 1984 and moved to the more central point of Machynlleth. The work included any bridge from a culvert over a small stream to the largest structure of the well known Pont-y-Bermo or Barmouth bridge. There was every possible combination of masonry, brick, wood, concrete, iron and steel with arches and spans. There was a division of responsibility between the county council highways and British Railways. The main trunk roads with bridges crossing over the track were highway bridges with examples at Commins Coch and the replacement concrete bridge at Penstrowed. Bridges over the railway on minor roads and farm access were under the control of the railway. Weight restriction was an increasing problem with heavier farm traffic. (The author had responsibilities at the Vaynor Farm. In 1960 milk would have been taken by 10 gallon churns to a platform at the end of the lane. In 1975, the bulk tank lorry would cross the Vaynor bridge with a combined weight of lorry and milk of up to 20 tons over a bridge with weight design of around 8 tons. The problem was solved by the farm being sold for a housing estate so the bridge is now a pedestrian/cycle route only.) All highway bridges with railway underneath had also to receive rail inspection and this necessary paperwork was forwarded to the highways divisions. All underbridges where the rail crossed over the road were rail responsibility. A vehicle collision with a bridge, known as a 'bridge bash', would necessitate the highways and police informing the railway for Bridge Department call-out.

The change of organization was bewildering. Ken was part of a skills tradition from older long past craftsmen going back to the 1860s. The difference was mechanization with new plant and new technology. Control in 1972 was from Shrewsbury. It then transferred to Crewe and finally, just before privatization, control transferred to Birmingham. Ken received a redundancy notice when Railtrack took over in 1995. A request was received from the private contractor (GTRM) in 1997 asking if he would return. The problem was obvious. The rail industry had not only lost the older local craftsmen but also the skill to transfer to younger workers. Bridge maintenance needs someone to leave their office, their computers etc. and delegate duty to someone who can paint and point across open areas in all weathers. Ken worked a further five years

In 1960 most bridge material was delivered to site by railway with some by lorry. There were sidings to take refuge every three to four miles and the light rail draw off for the powered trolley was even more frequent. There were only a few single refuge sidings by 1990. Most material was delivered by road. This remains difficult to impossible on sea wall/cliffs, peat bogs, estuaries and gorges. The 'tram' (as it was known locally) stabled at Machynlleth delivered new material and returned with scrap rail and timber.   *Ken Jones, Llandinam*

Demolition of the relatively new concrete footbridge at Borth. This replaced a lattice girder bridge erected around 1900 in 1954. The hired road crane is demolishing the reconstructed bridge around 1990. The road crane has close access by road and has the hard surface of the lifted loop to work from. There were no light or heavy rail cranes available by 1985.

Ken Jones, Llandinam

with a far larger territory moving as far north as Crewe and south including the Cardiff area and out to Fishguard. He worked with two other staff on bridge examination. The contract switched to Owen Williams of Swindon. All GTRM equipment such as the van, safety clothing, tools and paper systems were collected and given in on a Friday. The replacement material was acquired from the new contractors over a period of several weeks. Ken is entitled to his opinion but is emphatic that small local gangs with local pride on routine inspection from a regional base were both cheaper and more efficient. It also had an important cultural impact in maintaining a skilled secure work force in small towns such as Caersws and Machynlleth and this should be more important than shareholder speculation on assets.

A 'bridge bash' could result in a call-out at any time. Trains would be stopped until initial inspection was made. The trains could then run over at slow speed until further detailed inspection. Ken was called out to a 'bridge bash' at around 01.00 hours to a bridge east of Telford. It was sheeting with rain and Ken had never even seen the bridge before. His assessment was such that he authorized movement so the line was cleared. The commuters to Woverhampton and Birmingham moved the following morning albeit with a speed restriction. He doubted that anyone would have known that a Llandinam man had travelled 50 miles as he was the nearest available that night with the necessary skills to inspect. Every article on such items in the local press say a railway bridge is involved which is correct, but these are road accidents and problems.

Ken had fully retired by 2001. Chris, his wife, shares both car and free rail travel with him. Ken proudly looks up or under or across 'his bridges' and proudly states: 'That is bridge 203 and we worked on that one with scaffolding around 1978'.

Glenys and Bill Gratton

Bill Gratton came to succeed Maldwyn Jones (King) as the bridge examiner initially based at Caersws. Bill was a trained foreman-bricklayer working for Patent Shaft at Wednesbury near Wolverhampton. He and his wife visited Borth for their honeymoon in 1954, travelling from Wolverhampton via Whitchurch/Oswestry on the mail/newspaper train. They must have liked Borth for a caravan was acquired. The children and Glenys would spend the summer by the sea. Glenys became very friendly with Mrs Phillips, the crossing keeper and her husband, Merfyn, who was one of the local platelayers. Mrs Phillips suggested that Glenys should apply for the duty of gate keeper once she retired. Glenys did this and was successful. Bill was offered work as bricklayer/general shopman at Caersws. The wage was low compared with the West Midlands but the two wages made the risk worthwhile. Soon British Rail offered the duty of bridge examiner and this needed attendance at a series of courses at Watford. This was done and Bill inherited Maldwyn's duties. Bill had an office within the Van engine shed by the blacksmith's shop in 1979. He never had the chance to receive transfer of the encyclopediac knowledge of Maldwyn 'King' who had retired before Bill's promotion. Both the craft skill and the technical knowledge of 'King' dated back to the GWR prior to World War II. There was only a handful of Caersws men left within a small team so it was a logical decision to move to Machynlleth in 1984 to be with the other tradesmen. Closure of the Brecon and Oswestry lines had also moved the geographical centre several decades earlier.

The view of the Dysinni bridge looks north toward Tonfanau. The original trestle bridge was a constant problem as the rolling gravel with tide flow started to cause flood problems. The central walings were skewed but the problem continued. The current bridge was placed prior to World War I with the off-set girders placed on four steel caissons. There was much pressure to place a footbridge but funding between the Cambrian, the then Towyn Urban District and Merioneth County was not resolved. Tonfanau generated much railway traffic with the military camp. Tonfanau Quarry was set within the hill on the right with a half-mile-long siding serving crushing plants and internal tramways, inclines similar to Penstrowed Quarry.   *Bill Gratton, Borth*

Three bridge numbers on one site at Machynlleth. No. 228 is the main structure over the main road with masonry abutments, steel main girders and steel trough floor. No. 229 was the standard gauge underbridge for the Corris Tramway on the route to Derwenlas estuary port. The semi-circular arch has been blocked both sides. The railway killed the port trade within a few years so the tramway ceased and exchange took place at Machynlleth from the steam narrow gauge Corris Railway. No. 230 is the hidden bridge for the down side platform widening. It has an outer steel girder with steel joists holding concrete slabs. It is said that Nos. 228 and 229 were the first bridges built by Savin after the split from Davies. *Bill Gratton, Borth*

Glenys became crossing keeper at Borth in 1977 and remained on this duty until about 1990 when the gates were automated. The original purpose of the road was to serve a farm but the district council developed their refuse depot here. The gates were normally shut to road use but opened for every road vehicle. This could be busy as men came in and left shifts in private cars and the lorries rolled in and out. Later the more common system of gates normally open to road traffic and closing across the road for trains took place. Glenys went on to be a guard for a few years working from Aberystwyth to Pwllheli and Shrewsbury. She had to honour a most unusual request. A retired platelayer had requested that his ashes were placed between Welshpool and Newtown. The urn, the vicar and some friends got on the train and Glenys had to unlock the rear driving cab for an opening window as the new dmu had double-glazing and air conditioning, but no slide-down opening window in the public section.

Many of the duties have already been described by John Corfield and Ken Jones. Bill's duty was to give each bridge a detailed comprehensive inspection. Ken's duty was the annual visual inspection. Both would report to Crewe if further action was required. Time was allocated for emergencies such as river flood, tidal storm, bridge bash, etc. One of the staff had to attend when other bodies had access to cross sections of the bridge. This would be mainly public utilities such as gas, water, electricity, telephones or the highway departments of the then Powys, Dyfed and Gwynedd county councils. Bill retired in 1999 due to ill health. His final years were with GTRM.

Certain side bridges were taken out on the redundant lines. A redundant arch bridge would suffer from water ingress that could start to move either stone or brick. A bridge needed the weight of passing trains to keep the keystone and other stones or bricks firm within the arch. It was said that the bridge started to flatten so it was easier to knock the moving stones out and collapse the bridge. Another duty was to work down from Pwllheli to Machynlleth knocking down most of the former signal boxes once radio control and automated crossings were installed. The timber work was burnt and the bricks buried on site. Another gang worked from Buttington Junction to Aberystwyth. Trough girder bridges were the most difficult. The drainage tubes could corrode and the hidden inside sections posed problems of examination. BR understood the time needed but it was one of the sources of conflict with the sub-contract as inspection of such bridges was time consuming compared with other bridge designs.

Bill was the only BR examiner with a narrow gauge steam line (the Vale of Rheidol). Staff were proud of this unusual duty and regretted the transfer to a heritage company in the mid-1980s. The first bridge* was a trestle bridge over the Rheidol near Llanbadarn. There were several culverts over side streams including a large culvert plus embankment near Aber Ffrwd. The final bridge was a steel trough occupation bridge just before the terminus. The abutments were the natural cut in the rock face cutting.

Bill Gratton and Ken Jones would have been the final men of many who were based at Caersws. Their then young colleague, Barry Morgan, continues in the

---

* Bridge No. 1 was the closed M&M bridge heading to Pencader Junction with the extra single line, under the standard gauge, installed for the Rheidol train. This must be the only example where the Cambrian owned both the under- and over-bridge. The GWR also moved the terminus closer to the main station in Aberystwyth in the late 1920s so there was a further bridge (1a) funded by Aberystwyth Corporation. Both had gone by the time of Bill's inspection so the trestle bridge was the first for him.

This redundant three-arch brick bridge with the road over heading to Crickett is hidden in a cutting 300 yards west of Frankton station in 2008. The station is hidden in the jungle. It is 13 m. 6¾ ch. from Whitchurch Junction. Len Hamer recalls a view on the evening train from Whitchurch to Llanidloes. The bridge at Frankton station has vertical abutments and a single steel/iron span. This bridge would act like a picture frame to show the three arches in the cutting highlighted in the summer evening dusk. The author was puzzled by the redundant code on the Crickett parapet (*inset*). The explanation was given by Barry Morgan. GNQ4 is a section centred around the code of Gobowen/Nantmawr Quarry. *Author*

Barry Morgan's new territory in 2008 extended to Nantwich, Wrexham and Llandrindod. He therefore has several multiple-arch viaducts at Chirk and Knucklas for inspection. The south end of Whitchurch had the junction and start of the old Caersws Bridge Department. The north end has an public suspension footbridge dating from the 1870s connecting the town to a foundry complex. Railtrack wished to close this but the local civic societies have secured the future of this unique rail bridge. It once spanned the exchange loops for the Cambrian and LNWR plus the branch to Malpas/Chester. The train is a Cardiff to Manchester service. *David Hughes, Pontrobert & Shrewsbury*

industry but his base is Machynlleth. There is now no one employed in the rail industry living in the parishes of Caersws or Llandinam, just pensioners. The photographs selected from a large source show some aspects of bridges west of Machynlleth.

Machynlleth depot post-1984

Barry Morgan would be the last man still involved with railway bridge maintenance who worked at Caersws. Barry was a graduate in economics and he joined the Bridge Department in 1982. His wife was from Llanidloes and they wished to return to the area. He started as a general labourer under the wing of Ken Jones. He quickly transferred to general clerical duties working in the Van station office. This was 110 years after the same space was used by 'Ceiriog'. In 1984 Barry moved to Machynlleth. He was office bound during the week but would work out on site during the weekend.

A vacancy occurred for a bridge examiner so Barry applied and was accepted. The railway school at Watford had closed recently so he was trained by consultant engineers at Stoke. British Rail ceased in the mid-1990s and transfer took place to GTRM on contract to Railtrack. There was also a closed line contract for Mid & South Wales plus the Forest of Dean. The Cambrian line reverted to Railtrack's Western Region around 2001 and the contract transferred to Owen Williams at Swindon. The area again altered merging with the Shrewsbury area. The territory extends to Wrexham, Nantwich and down to Llandrindod and Ludlow. Amey purchased Owen Williams within 18 months and Railtrack was replaced by Network Rail in 2002. This was the situation as at 2008. Barry does much of the management work from his own home and visits sites to ensure contract is to specification. Soon Barry will reach retirement and a young assistant examiner is being trained. Barry lives at Talybont, Ceredigion between Aberystwyth and Machynlleth.

One of his neighbours is Maurice Jones. Maurice's father, the late Maurice John Jones, was the projectionist at the Coliseum cinema at Aberystwyth. This site is now the Ceredigion Museum and has some fine transport displays. Maurice senior became a keen photographer. A number of long-forgotten railway negatives were found in the attic during the sad task of house content dispersal. Barry and Maurice junior have developed some of these. Dad must have travelled to the points of major railway activity from the 1940s to the 1970s because most photographs are centred on Aberystwyth, Machynlleth, Barmouth, Welshpool, Oswestry and Shrewsbury.

The January 1883 landslip from road above to the rail has thrown No. 29 *Pegasus* on to the beach. The footbridge, just visible, was for miners to cross the line to sections of the Anna Maria copper mine. Note the early masonry sea wall with portal that may have been part of the mine. There are various adits and shafts that increased the maintenance problems.   *C.C. Green/Peter Compton, Llandinam*

Framework temporary structure at Friog ready to move for shuttering roof, walls and encasing steel arches. The men are the Caersws team and they pose in a fan-like shape in an almost art form in the horizontal frame.   *Vivian Bradley, Caersws*

Chapter Eight

Friog Rocks and the Barmouth Bridge

The coast line between Dyfi Junction and Pwllheli must qualify as one of most scenic routes within Europe as most of the line is never far from the coast with shoreline, estuary and mountain views continually unfolding.

The line climbs from Llwyngwril from the south. The slope between sea and land gradually changes until both road and rail have to transverse along a ledge cut into a steep hill. The hill is known as Gallt Ffynnon-yr-hŷdd usually shortened to Yr Allt.

The routes clear round the headland and then moves down to sea level again at Y Friog or Fairbourne. The hill is part of the lower range that peaks at Cadair Idris. The problem is to try to defy nature. The first reason is that the steep slope is unstable due to downward erosion caused by frost, rain, water seepage and occasional slight tectonic movement. The second reason is both road and track are running over 100 ft above a rock strewn beach where a combination of high tide and storm again contributes to erode the base, adding to instability. The lower slope has been mined for copper with a honeycomb of shafts and adits that adds to the complications. A tunnel was not considered due to the cost of what was always known to be a likely secondary rail route. The route was built and was subject to frequent inspection. A cottage was built in 1871 for the 'Friog Watchman'.

Slips and rock falls were dealt with. The first disaster took place on the first day of January, 1883 when one train had cleared to the loop (Llwyngwril or Fairbourne) but soil, walling and rocks crashed down on the line in the intermediate period causing the locomotive coming up from Llwyngwril to crash down to the beach. Both driver and fireman were killed but passengers survived. Maintenance work was continuous with constant inspection. An almost identical accident took place at the same section of line in March 1933. It was decided to build an avalanche shelter. Arch steel ribs were delivered to be part of the reinforced concrete now seen. Men of Caersws Bridge Department helped prepare the site, erect the shelter and so acquired another item to maintain. It is listed as DJP33, Friog Rock Shield, with a length of 182 ft and a span of 19 ft 6 in. Its concrete piers carry reinforced concrete arches and slab roof.

Barmouth Bridge maintenance and problems

Some internal memoranda have come to light from the GWR days in the 1930s between the bridge inspector at Caersws and the divisional engineers at Oswestry. Some were concerned with the authority that could involve capital expenditure. Ken Jones had received a trade apprenticeship within the building trade. Both he and others received additional training within British Railways systems. This includes the retaining of many technical manuals. The author asked Ken, 'Some of your bridge reports need further authority before action'? He gave me the address of the senior officer at Crewe.

Roger Woodward is a retired chartered railway engineer and commenced work as a technical officer with BR in 1956. He was soon responsible for minor works schemes including bridges. He was one of many involved in the electrification of the West Coast main line and this involved numerous bridge alterations, including height increase of most overbridges. He worked through various building and

A sequence of images of avalanche shelter construction at Friog in 1934. *1*. The jib of the crane prepares to lift the steel framework for shuttering to move to the site that can be seen 200 yards further down the track. *2*. The foundation concrete base of the piers have been built with reinforced vertical tie bars. *3*. The crane swings support structure into postion as the pre-fabricated arches are placed in position. (A tool shed has been placed between piers. Did someone cycle to site?) *4*. Work progression of arch placement. The steel ribs were fabricated and delivered from a shipyard with sections to be bolted numbered almost like a Meccano kit. *5*. The first steel sections have been placed. The framework has been placed so that the first six arches have been encased in concrete with both roof and wall shuttered with use of steel bars or weld mesh and the shuttering frames have been moved back ready for the next steel arches. *Vivian Bradley, Caersws*

Photograph on the Llwyngwril side as track comes down from the summit to the avalanche shelter showing some of the mammoth work to maintain both road and rail routes around the steepest part of the headland. *Roger Woodward, Crewe*

Rock bolting to install permanent anchorages was done in 1986/1988 with specialist contractors. Men are shown working on the Alco-track boring rig. The drill would penetrate up to 20 metres of fissured rock. A specialist grout would be placed in the hole and a steel anchorage bolt would be placed to stitch the fissured rock into a solid mass. *Roger Woodward, Crewe*

utility structures through the 1960s and 1970s. He became the bridge engineer at Crewe from 1980 until 1992 so AWS Caersws became one of his management responsibilities. He had already been involved in the alterations of the Britannia bridge over the Menai Straits from Bangor to Anglesey. In 1980, he was one of several faced with the problem of the Barmouth bridge. Much of the following information is drawn from details from both Roger and the late George Cutting. George took responsibility for the monitoring of the repairs on site. Both men, and also Chris Preston, would spend considerable time on site. Roger had many other bridge duties and would often visit Caersws to meet the staff in the local office that was the old Van station. Roger was also a member of the National Panel for the Revision of Handbook 6, *Examination of Structures*. He was unaware that Ceiriog, the bard, had thought out some of his poems a century before, so Roger's revision could be the second classical work mused within the Van station office! Roger also had the littoral duties of sea wall maintenance. These duties not only included the inherited Cambrian but also much along the North Wales coast, especially at Penmaenmawr, plus an avalanche shelter and another Tywyn that was badly flooded in the 1990s. There was a vicious tidal flow under the rail bridge on the Stanley Embankment shared between road and rail joining Holyhead Island to Anglesey. Roger was promoted to structures engineer for the North-West and retired from British Railways in 1995. The same early retirement took place for several Caersws staff at a far humbler level. Soon certain senior staff were back with Railtrack as consultants to cover the huge skills gap that was soon apparent. Roger could almost certainly have risen to an even more exulted position with the BR hierarchy in other sectors. He just loved bridges, their structure, the aesthetics of their setting and the challenge of maintenance. The Cambrian was rich in every combination of stone, brick, iron/steel, wood and concrete. He joins the local lads of Caersws in that he can look back and feel a sense of pride.

Barmouth bridge must be one of the most frequently photographed railway structures in Wales. There are superb views from every point of the estuary. The bridge was ordered by the Aberystwyth & Welsh Coast Railway (A&WCR) in 1861. Both design and contract was awarded to Thomas Savin. The A&WCR entered into the Cambrian Railways in July 1865. Savin was declared bankrupt in February 1866. The Cambrian therefore took on completion and retained Savin as a consultant but both parties soon fell out. The bridge was ready by June 1867 and started with a horse-drawn cab as the line further north was not completed until October 1867. The opening of the bridge had an immediate adverse effect on the local ferry services.

The bridge was over 800 yards in length. It had and still has 113 timber spans on 500 piles. The original drawbridge on an eight-span wrought-iron section was changed when much work was done around 1900. The drawbridge was replaced by a central pivot swing bridge during this period and the eight spans became five. The railways caused a severe decline in small sailing coasters needing to sail to the upper parts of all the estuaries. The drawbridge and the following swing bridge were not frequently used. The Board of Trade required an annual test and supervised opening. It was opened for the local regatta until 1984. Any sailing ship was requested to lower the mast and use the auxiliary engine from then onwards.

A routine maintenance schedule built up over the years. No exact dates can be ascertained but it is likely that the bridge engineer at Caersws had responsibility by World War I with a small team held at Barmouth until the 1930s. Caersws men stopped in lodgings or within one of their camping coaches. The bridge was used for the filming of *The Ghost Train* with Jack Hulbert and Cicely Courtneidge in 1931.

Timber repair team at Barmouth, *circa* 1954. *Back row*: Bert Reynolds, Emrys, Edfryn Jones, Cyril Marchant, the very tall lorry driver (all from Caersws) and Ron Edwards (Barmouth). *Front row*: Percy Smout, chargehand, one of the Berridge brothers of Barmouth and Bill Gethin. Ron was one of the Barmouth lengthmen allocated to help. The Berridge brothers had a fishing boat called *Welsh Girl*. They made their living with off shore fishing and summer tourism. They knew the estuary flow and sand banks and they were most skilled with access to the bridge when hired by the Bridge Department. *Emrys Davies, Caersws*

Above: left: Frances Lewis' late husband, Maldwyn, holds the Caersws Bridge Dept ladder *circa* 1950. The men are preparing to help the diver go overboard at Barmouth for base inspection. The bell helmet will be screwed on. There was a hand air pump with a flexible tube to push fresh air down to the diver's helmet and an exhaust tube so that the breathed air could escape.

Mrs Frances Lewis, Caersws

Above: The greasing of the gearings is taking place prior to opening the swing bridge for the annual inspection *circa* 1960. All are Caersws lads: Jack Thomas and Sid Williams are on the side of the track, Ted is sitting on the cross beam by the spanner and Ernie Jones, with protective glasses, is working in the well.

Ted Morgan, Caersws

Right: Ted stands beside the girder of Barmouth bridge on a temporary platform for access to steel work painting on the seaward side *circa* 1960.

Ted Morgan

August bank holiday 1984 may have been the last time that the bridge was opened for the yacht regatta. Ken Jones was in charge with eight other men. The mechanism was manual with men on both sides with huge handles. The area manager and other staff came down from Crewe (a good excuse for a day out). Ken recalls the staff as follows: Barry Morgan, Jim Roberts and Howard Latham (Machynlleth), Bill Robertson (Barmouth), Brian Williams and Arwel Roberts (Llanbedr), and John Corfield and Norman Evans (Caersws). *Ken Jones, Llandinam*

This *circa* 1955 plate shows the division between the fixed section and the swing bridge. A large brass key was held at Barmouth signal box. The removal of this locked all tokens and permission to travel between Morfa Mawddach and Barmouth. The second key needed was held in the safe at Caersws. Permission from Oswestry and later from Stoke Traffic HQ was needed to operate the mechanism. *National Library of Wales*

Piles and other woodwork were painted or replaced as needed. There are few situations more hostile than crossing an estuary close to the sea mouth. Metals are subjected to corrosion. Timber marine structures suffer from decay, drying out and splitting, bolt corrosion and tidal erosion all built on a shifting floor of sand, mud and gravel with the creation of scour pools. The portions immersed or within the tidal range suffer attack from marine creatures. The main attack along the Cambrian bridges is a small crustacean commonly called the sea louse or gribble. They attack the timber surface. This attack is destructive but can easily be seen and appropriate remedial action taken.

Work was proceeding in 1980 on this normal routine which would include the renewal of seven piles due to gribble attack. Work commenced in April 1980 with both in-house staff and specialist contractors. Two piles were to be replaced at frame 87. The pontoon or boat to carry plant and materials bumped against the frame and the impact crumbled two inner piles that looked healthy. The fractures were immediately examined, research followed and the Marine Biology Department at Bangor University quickly confirmed that 'teredo navalis' attack had taken place. The extent of the damage was not known so locomotive crossing was immediately prohibited and dmus were restricted to 10 mph.

The teredo is called the shipworm. It is common in the warmer Atlantic especially in the Caribbean area. It caused Columbus to abandon two ships, it caused Cortez to tell his men that the ships were too rotten to sail back to Spain and it became a major problem to the imperial navies of Spain, Portugal, France and Britain. Pepys wrote of the worm in his diaries. The problem had some resolution with copper-plated ships' bottoms but copper reacted with the iron bolts. Zinc bolts were used from the late 1700s. In England, the worm caused Bournemouth pier to collapse in 1876. The intermediate or larval stage of the mollusc were carried both by the Gulf Stream and by boats into British waters but conditions were too cold for species establishment. The creature is not a worm but a marine bivalve mollusc and is an elongated clam. The two shells are the head area only and they function as a cutting tool. The burrow is lined behind with a calcareous coating. This was observed by Marc Brunel (Isambard's father) and used as the design basis for the Rotherhithe tunnel shield. It remains the basis of cutting a modern tunnel through sedimentary rock. At Barmouth the outer wood always looked satisfactory with no external evidence, yet the damage could be extensive. No satisfactory method of non-destructive techniques could be devised as both X-ray and ultrasonic testing gave poor results. Boring only worked if the bit penetrated into a worm tunnel. Notching could only give a guide if the notch cut across a worm bore. So the summer was spent without any real guide to the extent of the damage. A political maelstrom swirled as strong as the tides. Some of this was justified as the community was still suspicious in the post-Beeching era, because attempts had been made to close both the Shrewsbury to Swansea and the Cambrian coast line in the late 1960s. The role of the engineer was to report, within the then current technology, on the extent of the problem and to recommend a solution. It is then a political and economic decision. Examples of some of the most extreme views was that there was nothing wrong with the bridge, and this was a ruse for closure, or that the entire bridge had to be replaced at prohibitive cost that would again lead to line closure.

The engineers requested closure from October 1980 into 1981. The method was to cut out a section and replace with greenheart timber using a special fabricated saddle plate. The attack was very random but a pattern could be discerned. There was no attack above high water level. There was no or little damage on the piles closest to

Right: The fibre glass concrete weave shields in position with a specialist grout fill between the shield and the new wood pile. The idea of the shield is to prevent any further penetration of the larval stage of the teredo worm.

Roger Woodward, Crewe

Below: The teredo found a most northerly niche in the warmth of the higher saline scour pools caused by tidal flow around the trestle base. The pools were scraped by a back hoe, the level floor was then filled with gravel held by a wire frame with further strength given by the base waling. The piles have already been encased.

Roger Woodward, Crewe

The *Caernarfon Barmouth Viking* was hired to transport materials to and from the pontoons and as a tug. It is anchored on the north shore with a panoramic view of the bridge looking into the estuary.   *Roger Woodward, Crewe*

The bridge re-opened for dmu traffic only with a speed limit in the spring of 1981. Both the train and much of the plant can be observed.   *Roger Woodward, Crewe*

Storm conditions as high tide starts to ebb. Work had to continue in all weather conditions and gale force wind would jeopardize safety but a day spent in the mess shelters was rare. The high tide-only island on the right is Cerrig-y-gorllwyn. Ken witnessed a tragic event. Sheep had walked out from the saltings and became stranded on the rock so the incoming tide swept them away. *Ken Jones, Llandinam*

The bridge re-opened for locomotive-hauled services with several special excursions. The return trip slows to hand in the Talerddig-Caersws token and to collect Caersws-Newtown token in 1986. The headboard on the locomotive front had a picture of the girder section of the bridge and re-opening of the bridge in Welsh and English. The bridge re-opened but the Bridge Department AWS Caersws had closed in 1984. *Sam Compton, Llandinam*

Barmouth approaching the iron section because of the higher percentage volume of river water lowering the salinity. All other trestle bridges were examined but they were all clear due to their placement further back in the various estuaries so the surrounding water had lower salinity. The major zone of damage was that below normal beach level especially where scour pools formed leaving the lower pile in a low tide, high saline, warmer pool.

Enough information was available to give a report to a meeting in mid-February and the bridge opened to dmu traffic only on 22nd May, 1981. The recommendations of immediate work were carried out by Construction Specialist Services and Diving International Engineers. Certain piles were replaced between the report and the May re-opening. Other piles were identified to be strengthened against both gribble and teredo attack. These reports were completed by July 1981. There was then an hiatus until funding became available in mid-1982. Diving International Engineers continued but construction switched to Lehane Mackenzie & Shand. Work was done on stone pitching to reduce pool scour. Trials took place on placing the pitching stone within a steel mattress. The casing of piles then commenced to prevent ingress of the work larvae. The casing was a fibre glass concrete weave from the BR works at Taunton and a resinous grout was then used to fill the gaps. The final contract was placed with E. Nuttall Ltd for cover casing the remainder of the piles and this was completed by December 1985. The first diesel locomotive-hauled train crossed in April 1986. Class '158' dmus operate the current service. There are now rare diesel-hauled excursions and the steam summer service is suspended. Currently, no heritage diesel units are used so the network diesel locomotives held at Shrewsbury equipped with ERTMS (in-cab signalling) haul the rare excursion but all ballast trains. Diesel-hauled excursions are popular so the technical problem may be solved later.

The local conclusion must be that the investment in the bridge during those uncertain days in the early 1980s has been worthwhile and the line has a secure future, unless there is a period when the anti-railway lobby gains political clout to give the rural communities another touch of the 'Beechings'.

There must be a huge number of photographs of Barmouth bridge. The Hogan family would hire a camping coach at Arthog when they lived at Chester. This picture has been enlarged, framed and hung within their various dwellings including company housing at Singapore and Curaçao oil refineries. Bob was the plant electrical engineer at Stanlow Oil Refinery in the early 1960s. The train crosses the trestle section as dusk rapidly turns to night, with the brooding heights of Cadair Idris in the background. *Bob Hogan, Petersfield*

Postscript

This postscript is from one of the final men nurtured within the local railway culture. Alan Jones is the son of the late Evan Ianto Jones. Alan left school to work on a local farm in 1970 and was a student of the author in the local college. Alan joined the railway at Newtown in 1975 on track maintenance with Jack Phillips as ganger. Alan was placed in the Caersws signal box in 1977 as emergency cover. British Rail then asked him to be relief signalman so he worked at the loops at Westbury, Welshpool, Newtown, Caersws and Talerddig and sometimes further west. Many of the older men were starting to find change a challenge but Alan enjoyed the new electronics so he was involved with the installation of the radio signal systems soon to be centred at Machynlleth around 1988. Alan's railway career now took off. He was appointed signal inspector for the Cambrian until 1991. He moved to Shrewsbury to manage all inspection from Chester/Wrexham/Shrewsbury, Crewe to Shrewsbury and Shrewbury to Wolverhampton with main boxes at Wrexham, Oxley at Wolverhampton and Gresty Lane at Crewe. The new Railtrack moved Alan to a Midland senior safety auditor post based at Stanier House in Birmingham. This would include special duty for paths for Royal Trains including Princess Diana's funeral to Long Buckby and the Government Heads Summit from Birmingham Snow Hill to Aylesbury. He was to spend some time with the independent Rail Safety Board and then returned to Network Rail to work on signal standards for the total system (from Penzance to Thurso) and anywhere between. Work was on major signal projects. He was due to retire when he called to see the author in Newtown in February 2009, but he will return to the independent Rail Safety Board at their head office in London. This is not a bad record for a school leaver at the age of 15 from the Carno/Caersws railway families going back to the Victorian Cambrian company.

Alan's grandfather would have been in a team of lengthmen of about eight allocated to 10 miles of through line plus sidings in the 1920s. One of their duties was weeding. The weedkiller train is at Porthmadog in 1987. The use of a herbicide prevented the track looking like an abandoned allotment. The problem of weed free track and the chemical control has not been resolved within total environmental audits. *Alan ap Ianto ap Tomas*

Conclusion

My aim was set to record the railway story of Caersws using material collected within the Cambrian operational area only. The amount collected far exceeds that necessary for any volume so quite severe editing and choice has taken place. There must be much further information available at such places as the National Railway Museum at York, the Welsh Maritime & Industrial Museum at Swansea and the National Archives, Kew. Several families had cuttings from the GWR house magazine and most of these are held at the GWR Museum at Kidderminster. Certain local archives were not searched in detail and these would include Gwynedd Archives at Dolgellau and Shropshire Archives at both Shrewsbury and Oswestry.

It is hoped that someone will progress the story of the bridges over the next 40 years. The author has visited much of the total area of the Bridge Department. Photographs have been taken and many have been included to illustrate an historical point. Some bridges deserve close monitoring as they may well be subject to alteration or demolition. Such a wide range of design and construction materials may need conservation for future generations.

It has been and remains difficult to choose the form of Welsh spelling so both have been used. The first would be the anglicized version chosen within early Ordnance Survey maps and the railways. Should it be Pantydwr or Pant-y-dŵr? Should there be a 't' in Llansan(t)ffraid? Several Caersws records of the 1930s spell Dolgellau and not their own paymaster's form of Dolgelley.

It has sometimes been difficult to think in imperial measurements after three decades of working in metric. What was a bushel or a firkin or a furlong? The author had long forgotten the mass of imperial measurements on the back of the exercise book within the primary school in the 1940s. So he asked a friend of the same vintage how many chains were there to a mile. The answer of 80 could not be recalled.

The Cambrian Railways continues to provide an wonderfully attractive rail journey along the entire Aberystwyth & Welsh Coast line and the main route incorporating a section of the Oswestry & Newtown Railway and the Newtown & Machynlleth Railway, plus the joint LNWR/GWR from Buttington to Shrewsbury. There is much left to explore on all the closed through routes and branches. The heritage lines are a bonus. The year 2009 was the 150th anniversary of the Llanidloes & Newtown Railway. Many of the original bridges still stand after this long period. It reflects well on Davies, Savin, Piercy and Williams plus the legion of local staff that maintained this infrastructure.

And that is it! Some remain, some have gone and the station at Moat Lane Junction with over 60 staff is no more. Only a handful of staff of the Caersws or Caer-sŵs Bridge Department remain. The interest in the collection of material for this work has been immense. It is therefore essential to record my thanks to everyone for their time and support. This is a team effort

Diolch yn fawr iawn am y cymorth. Diolch yn fawr iawn am y croeso. Mae'r ymdrech wedi bod yn eiddo i bawb.

Bibliography

There are a large number of books about both the Cambrian Railways inheritance and the other railways of rural Wales. No doubt, there are more to come. The list included below is those that have been valued in support of this research.

The County Library at Newtown has a local history resource centre, this includes a microfiche of every copy of the Montgomeryshire local newspapers from the late 1860s. Both the *County Times* and the *Montgomeryshire Express* have much detail of staff changes, promotions, annual Directors reports, etc. A walk on a wet morning to the library for study would always produce a further detail. The library has most of the related books. This is of value as many are out of print.

The history can be found in the following:

The Story of the Cambrian, A Biography of a Railway, C.P. Gasquoine, 1922
The Cambrian Railways, Vols. I & II: Christiansen & Miller (David & Charles)
A Regional History of Railways of Great Britain, Volume 11, Mid & North Wales, Peter Baughan (David & Charles)
The Cambrian Railways, R.W. Kidner (Oakwood Press)
The Mid-Wales Railway, R.W. Kidner (Oakwood Press)
The Elan Valley Railway, C.W. Judge (Oakwood Press)
The Lampeter, Aberayron & New Quay Light Railway, M.R.C. Price (Oakwood Press)
The Manchester & Milford Railway, J.S. Holden (Oakwood Press)
The Wrexham & Ellesmere Railway, S.C. Jenkins & J.M. Strange (Oakwood Press)
The Mawddwy, Van & Kerry Branches, Cozens, Kidner & Poole (Oakwood Press)
Atlas of the GWR (Revd Ed.) by R.A. Cooke (Wild Swan Publishing)

All books researched by C.C. Green contain many period photographs of bridges. *Cambrian Railways Album* Vol. 1 (Cambrian) and Vol. 2 (GWR) are excellent visual records. He set out to record the 'Coast Lines of the Cambrian Railways'. Volume One is Aberystwyth to Machynlleth and Volume Two is Dovey Junction to Morfa Mawddach. He died before the third volume from the Barmouth Bridge to Pwllheli had started. These books are a rich resource of track details, including bridges.

Gwyn Briwnant Jones has written volumes on Welsh railways in both languages. *Llinellau Coll (Lost lines)* looks at the closed lines in Mid- and North Wales. *The Newtown & Machynlleth Railway* is detailed in two volumes. *Railway through Talerddig* covers the total history and *Talerddig in Great Western Days* supplements this with more information from 1923, including BR days.

There are many volumes with photography exploring the system. Most are excellent but would be poor on bridge images. Two examples with good bridge images are *Steam on The Cambrian*, Rex Kennedy (Ian Allan) and *Steam in Mid Wales*, Michael Hale (Welsh Railway Research Circle).

There are a number of Videos/DVDs on the market. The 8mm film and camera came on to the market in the late 1950s. The increase in skill and use of this coincided with the closure of many lines and the final use of the steam locomotive so material is not too common. B&R Videos in Shropshire have several on the Cambrian routes. *Four Ways to Brecon* contains film from Moat Lane Junction to Pontsticill Junction. Cab Rides from Kingfisher Productions was filmed from a '150' 'Sprinter' cab just before the manual tokens changed to radio control in the late 1980s. *No. 17 Shrewsbury to Aberystwyt*h and *No. 18, Machynlleth to Pwllheli* gives views, sometimes fleeting, of the bridges as seen from the cab and by track and bridge maintenance staff.